IF HONORS STUDENTS WERE PEOPLE

Holistic Honors Education

IF HONORS STUDENTS WERE PEOPLE

Holistic Honors Education

by Samuel Schuman

Series Editor | Jeffrey A. Portnoy

National Collegiate Honors Council
Monograph Series

Manufactured in the United States

National Collegiate Honors Council
100 Neihardt Residence Center
University of Nebraska-Lincoln
540 N. 16th Street
Lincoln, NE 68588-0627
www.ncnchonors.org

Production Editors | Cliff Jefferson and Mitch Pruitt
Wake Up Graphics LLC

Cover and Text Design | 47 Journals LLC

Cover Photo Courtesy of Georgia Perimeter College

International Standard Book Number
978-0-9835457-8-1

TABLE OF CONTENTS

ACKNOWLEDGMENTS

Scores of my teachers, colleagues, and friends, as well as thousands of my students, have enabled and inspired me to write this book. I have tried to repay some part of that debt by writing it with gratitude and affection for them all. Three institutions—the University of Minnesota Morris, the University of North Carolina Asheville, and the University of New Mexico—have supported my work generously. In particular, those with and for whom I worked at all three merit my thanks: Mark Yudof and Bob Bruininks in Minnesota, Rosalie Otero in New Mexico, and Anne Ponder in North Carolina. The National Collegiate Honors Council and its Publications Board have supported my thinking and writing about American higher education for over four decades. Elizabeth Isaacs at Cornell College first threw me into the bracing waters of honors.

I am especially grateful to those whose words and comments I have cited in the text. They have responded to my queries patiently, promptly, and thoughtfully. Especially gratifying to me, and I suspect engaging to my readers, are the remarks of the students included here.

A group of colleagues have made suggestions, responded to my questions, and offered important assistance as this project has developed. Among them are Sandra Olson-Loy, Amanda Cuevas, Gary McGrath, Shannon Hodges, Aron Reppman, Jeffrey Portnoy, Ada Long, John Korstad, Jack Rhodes, and Rick Chess.

My family has taught, and teaches me every day, what it means to be a whole person. My joyful gratitude to Dan, Angela, Leah, Scott, Hannah, Rachel, and Abby is quite simply inexpressible. My most profound thanks belong today, as they have for more than half a century, to Nancy.

IF HONORS STUDENTS WERE PEOPLE

Holistic Honors Education

CHAPTER 1

Introduction

A CLASSROOM

The first day of classes is always an exciting time at any college or university. Picture such a day: an energetic Assistant Professor strides into an honors seminar room and takes her place at the head of the table. Facing her are ten honors students, eager to begin their first-year honors seminar. The young women and men are bright, eager, and ready to go. Their pens are new, their notebooks are crisp, and their tablet computers are fully charged. They are ready to learn. The instructor clears her throat, takes a deep breath, and prepares to launch into the introduction to the seminar.

It is worth pausing for a few moments to ask what is known about these students beyond the fact that they are eager to learn. After all, the more teachers know about their students, the more effectively they can communicate with them, the more efficient their instruction will be. It turns out that much information about these students exists.

According to Alexander W. Astin, Helen S. Astin, and Jennifer A. Lindholm, one fact is known: regardless of the type of college, public or private, large or small, where this hypothetical class is meeting, most students consider themselves to be religious and spiritual persons (*Cultivating, passim*).[1] Eight of these ten students believe that finding life's purpose is an important reason to go to college, eight attended religious services in the year before they came to college, and about the same number say they believe in God and pray. Of the ten students, one or two regularly meditate. Six of the students will discover that, in spite of their interest in exploring life's big questions during their college years, their professors will never raise or discuss those issues in their work together.

Seven or eight of these students describe themselves as searching for meaning and purpose in life.[2] That search for spiritual understanding and sustenance, in many cases, has not necessarily left them more at peace and contented. Sometimes it has left their spirits troubled. Three of the ten report that they have been diagnosed with at least one mental health condition during their young lifetimes, and about half of those or 13%, according to a 2010 survey of some 35,000 students at seventeen institutions by the Boynton Health Service at the University of Minnesota, have had such a diagnosis in the past year (7–12). At least one of them has been diagnosed with anxiety and two of the seats around the table (19.5%) could be filled with students who have been diagnosed with depression. More than three of the students report that they have engaged in high-risk or binge drinking. Two self-report that they have performed poorly on a test or important project because of their use of alcohol or drugs, and two of them have missed at least one class for that reason (Boynton 7–12).

Although on this first day of class these students look suitably scrubbed and energetic, in fact they are not in good shape physically. Three of them are overweight; one is clinically obese.[3] These students are at risk for metabolic syndrome, a group of five risk factors that are predictive of future medical problems such as diabetes and heart disease. How did this happen? In addition to poor eating habits, these young women and men, Cynthia M. Ferrara argues, are physically inactive. Only four of the ten students exercise regularly, and although this hypothetical college, like most, has a fitness center, three of them never exercise at all. Half the class does not meet the minimum goal suggested by the Centers for Disease Control of 150 minutes of moderate physical activity every week.[4] Yet in the last decade, scientific research has demonstrated conclusively that regular exercise stimulates brain activity. That means that about half of the students in the introductory honors seminar are making choices that weaken their collegiate learning experiences.

Although these honors students are highly motivated and intellectually promising, they are not empty cognitive vessels ready to be filled with professorial knowledge. They are, instead, complex, multifaceted young people, sometimes troubled, often delighted and delightful. While at college they are learning how to live their lives not just as intellectual creatures, but as whole, integrated human beings, with minds, spirits, and bodies.

Unfortunately, college and university teachers, administrators, and staff in today's institutions and in honors programs and honors colleges may be less likely than in the past to view students as complex, many-sided individuals. Because many professors may find that compartmentalizing their function in the institution is inviting, they interact with students not as whole people but as disembodied intellects. A century ago virtually every college and university in America had a physical education requirement, and most, even the public institutions, also required chapel. By the middle of the twentieth century, required gym and chapel (sometimes called convocation) were increasingly obsolete, and they became objects of student and faculty dissatisfaction in the 1960s. With a few exceptions, mostly at specialized institutions such as faith-based private colleges and military institutions, these requirements have been eliminated, going the way of the freshman beanie and the housemother. This evolution in postsecondary education seems natural and proper; few lament their passing and most applaud it. Attention to the bodies and spirits of students has moved to the optional periphery of colleges and universities. Emulating the Germanic model of the research university, American colleges redefined their role away from the earlier cultivation of the whole individual in favor of an entirely intellectual core mission. Honors programs have often embraced this mission with even more zeal than the rest of the institutions of which they are a part. But when universities did away with required gym and chapel, by and large they forgot to ask what genuine human needs those mostly outdated elements of collegiate culture had been serving and what, if anything, should take their place. The pages that follow seek to demonstrate why and how contemporary American postsecondary honors education might restore some balance in the cultivation of minds, bodies, and spirits.[5]

Because of the austerity plaguing American postsecondary institutions during the early decades of the twenty-first century, they cannot easily afford the time, personnel, energy, and money to attend to their students' spirits and bodies as well as their minds. In a period when educators struggle to find the resources to perform their primary functions of teaching and learning, why should they assume more responsibilities for students' lives? In the chapters below, some answers to this question emerge:

- College-age women and men, including those in honors, are at a crucial time in their development, and for some four years of that important period, they are living their lives at schools. This observation is especially, but not exclusively, true at residential colleges. Students do not cease to exist after class; they do not think that their college experience is limited to cognitive cultivation. They are actively seeking answers to core questions about the meaning of their lives and their pathways for their futures. They are developing the physical habits, good and bad, that will determine their health and wellness for the remainder of their days. If educators are to serve as responsible guides and mentors, they have a responsibility to attend to the development of their students as whole persons.

- A somewhat more crass reason colleges and universities need to attend to these issues is that they will boost student recruitment. Prospective honors students and their parents often look for and at campus fitness centers. It is a rare college viewbook that does not affirm attention to the whole person.

- Most importantly by far, treating students as complete, complex persons strengthens powerfully the first and primary honors job of cultivating their intellects. Because physical activity has a demonstrable positive effect on learning and memory, honors programs can help students become better learners by stimulating them to develop regular patterns of exercise. In addition, because spiritual issues are central to students' understanding their own and other cultures, especially in grappling with the great works and the biggest questions that are usually the focus of honors curricula, professors will do a better job of teaching if they include those issues in their courses, or at least if they do not exclude them entirely from their syllabi.

A more integrative approach to college learning often involves doing some things differently, not just adding more things or making radical changes. Thus, I suggest below that one way to stimulate increased physical activity for students might be to modify the daily/weekly class schedule so as to create some periods each week that invite students, faculty, and staff to exercise by not scheduling other activities. This costs nothing (except, perhaps, a mild headache for the Registrar's office).

Today, most colleges and universities, from public two-year schools to Research I universities, from the wealthiest private institutions to the least affluent, offer students some options to improve wellness and probe spiritual matters. At wealthier institutions and at larger universities, the range of opportunities for students to improve wellness and probe spiritual issues is inevitably greater. Almost always these institutions house a fitness facility as well as some faith-based clubs or organizations. Those extracurricular options, however, are too often like the healthy food choices available at restaurants: rarely is any effort made to educate students about why they might want to take advantage of these possibilities. Indeed, in an honors culture that measures success and failure largely by classroom performance, students who work to develop themselves as whole persons risk being penalized. An hour at the fitness center is an hour away from the library; an evening's discussion of one of life's big questions is an evening not spent studying chemistry. Colleges and universities need to find a middle ground between the *in loco parentis* requirements of a century ago and the peripheral options of today. This monograph suggests both *why* that balance is important to create and *how* to create it.

I will be focusing primarily upon spiritual and physical growth because I believe that cultivation of the intellect is what most contemporary American honors programs and colleges are already doing and doing well.[6] That focus does not mean that I advocate, in any way, the lessening of emphasis and weight upon intellectual development in honors work. Indeed, I would argue vigorously that of the triad of mind, body, and spirit, honors programs at colleges and universities must heed the first of these human attributes more than any other. This discussion does not seek to substitute spiritual growth and physical wellness for cerebration; however, it does suggest that the brain is best served by simultaneously cultivating the body and the spirit. The cultivation of physical vigor and spiritual depth enriches intellectual development.

PREVIEW

The next chapter of this book scans the history of American higher education, focusing on the integrative and holistic aspects of colleges and universities and how these have been defined and developed over nearly four centuries. I give some attention to developments over the past fifty years that have deflected many institutions away from their traditional holistic orientation. The remainder of *If Honors Students Were People* is divided into two sections, the first focusing upon theory, the second on practice.

First, I examine the area of physical fitness and wellness, athletics, and sports: the cultivation of the body. I discuss some of the most recent discoveries of neuroscience regarding the link between vigorous physical activity and cognitive development. I also look at intercollegiate sports from both the positive and negative perspectives. I briefly survey a few of the ways the bodily activities, sometimes called integrative disciplines, like yoga and tai chi, have found a place in today's colleges and universities. Finally, I turn to the subject of physical work, first looking at some psychosocial rethinking of physical work and then at an illustrative example of a particular institution in the work college category.

A second theoretical chapter examines the broad area of spirituality at college. The groundbreaking studies done at UCLA through the Higher Education Research Institute project on "Spirituality in Higher Education" reveal the spiritual lives of contemporary college students and, to a lesser extent, their teachers. I then look at contemplative practices such as meditation and mindfulness. Two profiles focus on national programs, both originating at Wellesley College but now widely disseminated throughout the nation's schools. Finally, I examine in some depth the issue of moral education and the interesting debate surrounding it.

Part Two looks in depth at some practices that specific colleges and universities have instituted to integrate the physical and spiritual cultivation of students into their undergraduate programs. This section includes material about honors and also features some information about several institutions that have tried intriguing holistic programs unconnected to honors. Although this survey is by no means comprehensive, it exemplifies some of the newer or more interesting ways that a broad range of institutions and programs have addressed students' physical and spiritual needs by integrating physical and spiritual enrichment into their current institutional profile. These institutions and their programs are described, not as ideal models to be imitated but as cases that merit thoughtful study: they are stimulating examples of what has and has not succeeded for real colleges and universities.

This second section of the book reflects a concern that contemporary American higher education has a lamentable tendency to grow somewhat insular in a way that is unnecessary and counterproductive. Within institutions, offices and individuals in one area may not be aware of what is happening across campus; thus they lose opportunities for effective positive reinforcement of each other's activities. Too often, for example, little communication transpires between the honors program and the fitness center, not to mention the intercollegiate athletics program. Those working in student affairs may not be aware of recent developments in the curriculum. Even more dysfunctionally, the various institutional segments of the postsecondary community often ignore each other or view each other with hostility or through the lens of institutional competition. Honors programs at public secular institutions could learn much from the largely ignored but generally thriving honors constituency at religious colleges. Private liberal arts colleges might benefit from paying heed to what is happening in honors at public liberal arts colleges. Large research universities and small liberal arts colleges might well learn something about the possibilities for holistic higher education by looking at each other with appreciation and open-mindedness. If all students should be educated as whole persons, asking what a range of universities and colleges are doing to achieve a rounded and integrated undergraduate experience is worthwhile.

Throughout *If Honors Students Were People*, interviews with a variety of individuals provide a personal perspective to the larger issues being described. These conversations appear between and within chapters and include honors students, a faculty member holding a named professorship in honors, a campus chaplain, and a national higher education leader. Because honors students are people, they have voices, and interspersed among the pages that follow, some of their voices and the voices of those who work with them each collegiate day are heard. In particular, I have encouraged the students to develop their ideas fully and have frequently incorporated their thoughts and words. They speak and write in the style of fine college students having a thoughtful conversation, not, mercifully, as scholars or academic writers. For me, and I know for most people in this vocation, attending to the words of imaginative, reflective, bright, and growing women and men is a constant delight. Transmitting the meditations of these outstanding young adults is an honor.

HONORS, PHYSICAL WELLNESS, AND SPIRITUAL CULTIVATION: A RATIONALE

Why should honors programs and colleges (that is to say, honors directors, deans, faculty, and students and those who supervise honors programs such as provosts or academic vice presidents) be particularly concerned about this constellation of seemingly non-intellectual issues?

1. An impressive range of contemporary scientific studies has confirmed the anecdotal and intuitive belief that a fit body enhances a keen mind. (See Chapter 3.) The adage asserting the relationship of a sound mind in a sound body is not simply an abstract humane ideal but a functional prescription for intellectual development.
2. Honors students are, after all, students, and substantial and incontrovertible evidence suggests that spiritual matters are important to a wide range of college students across the spectrum of American higher education. Honors students are, like all humans, physical, fleshly beings. Bodily fitness and wellness are universally understood to promote longevity, personal effectiveness, and a sense of individual well-being.
3. Honors programs and colleges include in their curricula works of substance and challenge, often classics. Those works often embrace a spiritual dimension at their cores.
4. Honors programs and colleges offer an outstanding undergraduate learning experience to their participants; substantial evidence suggests that practices that cultivate students' spirits also enrich their intellectual development. (See Chapter 4.)

Fitness and Learning

"When I get some exercise, I can think better." This truism is often uttered and heard. Chapter 3 will discuss significant research in the field of brain science that has established physiological justification for this linkage. In the past few years, scientists have come to an increased understanding of the biological and chemical processes that link bodily exercise with heightened intellectual capacities. Laboratory experiments have demonstrated that physical activity stimulates neurogenesis, the creation of new brain cells. Out of the lab and in the classroom, programs such as the one at the Naperville, IL, high school, which is described in Chapter 3, have demonstrated concrete, practical boosts in learning activity directly attributable to fitness activities.

Given the increasing evidence for this link between exercise and learning, educators dedicated to undergraduate honors learning should pay serious attention to physical as well as intellectual cultivation. If they know that certain activities promote learning, memory, and thinking, they must not fail to promote those activities for themselves and their honors students. This need is particularly acute because of the image that honors students all too often have, both across campus and to themselves: they are frequently seen, and sometimes see themselves, as one-sided bookworms, pale from spending all their days in the library or lab, focused solely on their studies.[7]

The Spiritual Quest of College Students

For a long time, the higher education community made a set of assumptions about the spiritual condition and development of college students that were largely untested in any sort of rigorous way. Until about a century ago, most college students were white, male, and Protestant. In the first half of the twentieth century, the academy became less white, less male, and less Christian. After the turmoil in collegiate culture in the 1960s, however, an opposite assumption increasingly dominated public consciousness and often academics' own sense of self. American media and popular public opinion often focused on countercultural aspects of college life. One common perception became that colleges, especially public ones but also private, non-sectarian schools, were places where students were weaned from faith, religion, and spirituality by largely secular, indeed atheistic and anti-religion professors. Naomi Schaefer Riley maintains in *God on the Quad*, a popular 2005 book, that students who bring a faith, particularly a Christian faith, to most colleges and universities in America today are "a beleaguered minority, both in the classroom where their beliefs are derided and in their extracurricular lives" (1).[8] She asserts that most colleges and universities are characterized by the "intellectual relativism of professors and the moral relativism" of students (5). Other writers, such as James Tunstead Burtchaell, George Marsden, and Julie Reuben, share this view that mainstream American post-secondary education is peopled with the enemies of religious faith. They make these claims without supporting evidence, and, it turns out, their assertions are not true.

Ironically, within mainstream American post-secondary education, a similarly slanted and unproven set of assumptions exist about faith-based schools: religious colleges exist to promulgate unexamined religious doctrine; they discourage critical thinking, especially about matters of faith; they eschew modern science; and their goal is to turn out robotically faithful, politically reactionary, humorless, uptight drones. These claims too lack supporting evidence and are also not true. Happily, Alexander Astin, one of the nation's most respected scholars of higher education, turned his attention and focused his considerable resources on the first misconception and the actual overall spiritual condition of today's American college students and professors, including, of course, honors students.[9] Astin and his colleagues at UCLA's Higher Education Research Institute (HERI), including his wife Helen Astin, launched in 2003 the Spirituality in Higher Education project. They surveyed 112,000 first-year undergraduates in 2004, and a subset of 15,000 completed a follow-up study at the end of their junior year in 2007 (Astin, Astin, and Lindholm, *Cultivating)*.[10] These students attended 136 colleges, of every size and sort, selected to be proportionally representative of the range of contemporary collegiate cultures. The project also surveyed 65,000 faculty members to ascertain the levels of their self-described spirituality and their related pedagogical principles and practices. The project defined "spirituality" as the "inner" aspect of students' lives and identified the big questions: "*Who am I? What are my most deeply felt values? Do I have a mission or purpose in life? Why am I in college? What kind of person do I want to become?*" (1). I discuss the HERI study in some detail in Chapter 4, but here is a preview of just a few of the most important findings.

Students come to college with significant expectations in matters of the spirit. Over 80% report that "to find purpose in life" is an important reason for attending college (3). On a whole range of questions, an overwhelming majority of the entire range of first-year students described themselves as spiritual seekers, looking for their reasons for existing, seeking meaning and purpose in life. Students' self-reported spirituality increases between the start of the first year and the end of the third. On the other hand, modest but real declines over the same period occurred in college students' participation in institutionalized religious practices. Measures of what the research team sees as religious conservatism also decline. In sum, college students, including honors students, come to the whole spectrum of American higher education with a strong spiritual self-definition and seeking growth in their understanding of the meaning and purpose in life.[11]

Spirituality and the Honors Curriculum

Honors programs and colleges teach great works and important questions; the curricula feature courses with titles like "Masterpieces of the European Renaissance" or "Nature and Human Nature." One of the defining characteristics of honors is that faculty and students work with the biggest of issues and the biggest of books. An example is the case of William Shakespeare's *Hamlet*, often a key part of a British or world literature course. Studying the play, instructors and students can talk about the imagery and metrics of its brilliant language or its links to the political history of late Elizabethan and early Jacobean Britain. While these topics are interesting and important subjects for classroom consideration, readers distort the play and diminish Shakespeare if they fail to see this work as having at its core questions of the human spirit. Pondering these big questions and examining great works must include focusing on matters of the spirit. After all, what Hamlet discovers in the course of the play is that "there's a divinity that shapes our ends, / Rough-hew them how we will" (5.2.10–11). As Hamlet goes to his death, he alludes to scripture (Matt. 10:29): "There is special providence in the fall of a sparrow. If it be now, 'tis not to come; if it be not to come, it will be now; if it be not now, yet it will come. The readiness is all" (5.2.221–24). What happens in *Hamlet*, what frees the melancholy Dane from his paralysis, is that he finds God. Or perhaps, on the boat trip to England, God finds him.

For most of the other giants in the literary canon, making a similar case is easy; indeed, what is difficult is eluding making a similar case. The central image of Geoffrey Chaucer's *The Canterbury Tales* is that of the pilgrimage from tavern to shrine, from the secular to the sacred, from the Knight's sweet paganism and the Miller's lustful physicality to the Parson's sermon and Chaucer's holy retraction. John Milton and Edmund Spenser write, respectively, of Paradise lost and the Knight of the Red Cross. T. S. Eliot depicts the pointless horror of a spiritual wasteland. Leland de la Durantaye writes: "A point on which all readers can agree is that great literature . . . urges us to see our own fates as connected to those of others and to link the starry sky we see above us with whatever moral laws we might sense within" (6).

Certainly, the teaching and reading of great literature engage people deeply in matters of the spirit. Obviously, the teaching of philosophy or political science or sociology does as well. Many teachers of physics and mathematics make the same cases for their disciplines. They speak of sharing with students the wonder of discovering and exploring a world of pattern and design. A key goal of honors curricula and pedagogy is to go far beyond the transfer of techniques and superficial knowledge to the cultivation of understanding and the seeking of wisdom. That means grappling with life's biggest issues, including the nature of learning and spirituality.

Spirituality and Learning

One of the findings of the HERI Spirituality in Higher Education project that is particularly interesting to those working in honors is its examination of the factors that strengthened students' perceptions of themselves as spiritual persons. Among the key collegiate programs that enhanced student spiritual development are interdisciplinary courses, service learning, and study abroad. Those spiritually enriching endeavors, the HERI projects' findings argue, simultaneously produce positive academic results: "educational experiences and practices that promote spiritual development—especially service learning, interdisciplinary courses, study abroad, self-reflection, and meditation—have uniformly positive effects on traditional college outcomes" (Higher Education).

Similarly, the National Survey of Student Engagement also found that "students who frequently engage in spirituality-enhancing practices also participate more in a broad cross-section of collegiate activities," and such broad participation, in turn, correlates highly with student success measures, such as persistence to graduation and GPA (Kuh and Gonyea).[12] These experiences and practices that promote spiritual development and enhance academic achievement are common, often defining, features of honors programs and colleges.

Honors is at the forefront of promoting interdisciplinary work. While not all honors programs and colleges feature interdisciplinary seminars or classes, this characteristic is probably the most common distinction that sets honors apart from other offerings at universities and colleges. Often, honors is the primary, and not infrequently the only, venue in which interdisciplinary course work is a feature, especially in fiscally challenged times. It is often the primary or only venue in which such interdisciplinary work is regularly taught by a team of teachers rather than an individual. So, for example, the honors program at the College of New Rochelle in New York, a small, Roman Catholic women's institution, offers a series of interdisciplinary seminars each year. Enrollment is limited to a maximum of ten students. The courses are interdisciplinary in content and methodology. They include offerings such as Discourses of Slavery in America and Women and the Law.

Over the past decade, service learning and international education have increasingly become core aspects of the honors endeavors of many honors programs and colleges. It is a rare honors program today that does not offer opportunities for service learning, and many now require it. The Irvin R. Reid Honors College of Wayne State University in Detroit, for example, has three specific requirements for students seeking to graduate with University Honors: an introductory seminar, a culminating thesis, and a service-learning opportunity within the honors college.

Increasingly, honors programs and colleges are stressing the values of international education.[13] A few illustrative examples: the Sally McDonnell Barkley Honors College at the University of Mississippi affirms that "studying abroad is an important emphasis of the program" (University of Mississippi). It supports that emphasis by offering fellowships for a semester or year abroad for honors students. The honors program at Keene State University has a two-week May term study abroad program for honors students at the end of their second year.[14]

What many honors programs practice curricularly and pedagogically is consistent with the findings of research on student success by Kuh and Gonyea; Kuh, Kenzie, Buckley, Bridges, and Hayek; and Astin in *Cultivating*. That research has demonstrated empirically a set of practices that strengthen students' sense of themselves as spiritual persons. These practices, which are common in honors programs and colleges, strengthen their academic achievements. In other words, the educational practices that strengthen student spirituality simultaneously strengthen student academic performance. In chart form:

Honors Practices

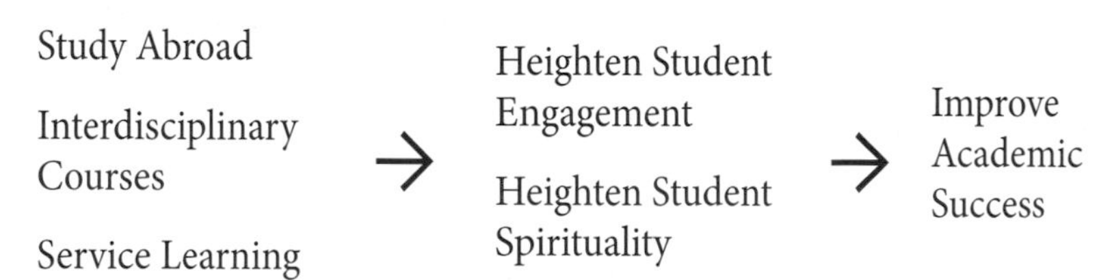

Honors administrators, students, and teachers will want to heed the issues of spiritual and physical cultivation highlighted in the following chapters. Having these concepts pervade all of America's colleges and universities would be ideal. Honors and non-honors students alike come to college with spiritual needs and aspirations, and all would benefit from physical exercise. But, given the current constraints, mostly budgetary, under which so many institutions of higher learning are operating today, that universality is impossible. Honors has often been in the past, and continues to be today, an important venue for experimenting with new and different pedagogies and curricula, serving as a stalking horse for the larger collegiate world. Honors educators were pioneers in areas such as experiential learning, baccalaureate-level research, and interdisciplinary undergraduate seminars. If honors educators can rethink their attentiveness to the spiritual and physical development of their honors cohort, perhaps they can again be leaders at colleges and universities in reinvigorating a holistic vision of postsecondary education.

DEFINITION OF TERMS

This study makes use of words and concepts that have been used for centuries by philosophers, theologians, educators, biologists, authors, and countless others. Different individuals and fields have evolved slightly differing understandings of what these words mean. Defining, albeit somewhat loosely, what I mean by these terms, is necessary and useful.

Spiritual/Spirituality

In his work at the "Spirituality in Higher Education" project, Alexander Astin defines "spirituality" in terms of seeking "the meaning and purpose of life" ("Why Spirituality, 34). Half a world away, the Dalai Lama has written:

> Spirituality I take to be concerned with those qualities of the human spirit—such as love and compassion, patience,

> tolerance, forgiveness, contentment, a sense of responsibility, a sense of harmony—which bring happiness to both self and others. . . . I sometimes say that religion is something we can perhaps do without. What we cannot do without are these basic spiritual qualities. (22)

Stephen Keeva defines "spirituality" as "that inner part of us where we are sensitive to the deepest, most nuanced levels of meaning in our own lives" (175).

For me, spiritual development means *a quest to find the meaning behind the external facts of the world and the internal life of the individual.* Perhaps primary among such questions are those of one's own existence: Why am I here? What is the purpose of my life? Imagining a mature contemporary human being who has not wrestled in some form or another with these core existential questions is difficult. Study after study has indicated that contemporary college students come to higher education seeking to clarify these issues for themselves.[15]

Religion is an important component of the spiritual for some people, but many young women and men perceive themselves to be spiritual beings, deeply interested in spiritual development and spiritual issues, but not in a conventional, sectarian sense, religious people. Speaking of this "spiritual but not religious" self-identification, Diana Chapman Walsh finds that college students are "contrasting the formality, bureaucracy, and behavioral restrictions of organized religion with the emotionality, individuality, and personal freedom of the spiritual quest" ("Search" 117). She defines that spiritual quest as the search for meaningfulness. Some educators, especially but not exclusively in religious colleges and universities, are irritated by these students who proclaim themselves spiritual but not religious. But many young college men and women, in fact, take this stance.[16] The bifurcation of the concepts of religion and spirituality is largely a quite recent development: prior to the middle of the twentieth century, different language that reflected a somewhat different understanding, such as "public religion" and "private religion," would more likely have been used both by college students and in the culture at large.

Not just college students declare themselves interested in life's spiritual dimension but eschew formal religion. A 2011 study by Mark Chaves of Duke University finds that many fewer Americans today affiliate with a religious organization than at an earlier time. Now, about 20% remain unaffiliated, but 92% still profess their belief in God. Thus, more than one in ten contemporary Americans believes in God but is without a religious affiliation. Chaves also notes that religious *affiliation* was increasingly linked to political conservatism, but religious *belief* was not so linked (81–93).

Ethics, values, and morals are also included in the area of spiritual development. Of course, discussing ethics and morality without recourse to matters of the spirit is possible. The Ethical Culture movement, for example, affirms that morality is independent of theology.

Contemporary honors programs, within the curriculum and the extra-curriculum, are increasingly devoting attention to ethical issues such as ecological sustainability. (For example, an honors course at Ohio State University is entitled "Global Climate and Environmental Change.") This is just one example of the many topics that have an intellectual, physical, and spiritual dimension.[17] The intellectual aspect of ecological studies might be studying the scientific research that describes climate change. The physical aspect involves making choices of what to eat or how to transport oneself from place to place, or physically working on some effort such as the collection of recyclables. For example, one honors course at the University of Vermont, "An Ecological Approach to Living Well in Place," includes a service-learning component. But the spiritual side of sustainability addresses the moral questions: Is it ethically better to use electricity generated by renewable sources such as wind or water power? Why? At what point does America's dependence upon the automobile become globally irresponsible? What should colleges and universities do to lessen their impact upon the environment, and what trade-offs are justifiable in doing so? (University of Vermont). In Chapter 4, I discuss briefly the debate surrounding the possibilities and desirability of moral education within the missions of today's post-secondary schools.

As part of their intellectual growth, students can, do, and should study the economics and biological mechanics of food production in the developing world, but asking if they have a personal duty to do something when they learn of a devastating famine on the other side of the world falls within the realm of the spiritual. Astin describes the intellectual cultivation of college students as an external process and the cultivation of the spiritual as an internal process (Astin, *Cultivating, passim).* I understand this to mean that in an external intellectual exercise students might learn the comparative production of nutritional products per acre in, say, Haiti and Italy. The spiritual, internal focus might be "What is my own responsibility to starving Haitians?"

Physical

Physical development refers to *activities that promote the soundness of the body, including sports, the avoidance of behaviors that have a negative effect on bodily health, and a variety of corporeal disciplines that promote the bodily well-being of the individual.* As with the category of spiritual development of college students, the concept of physical education is actually quite broad. Most obviously, this concept subsumes what is now commonly called wellness: activities and choices that encourage good bodily health, and, conversely, the avoidance of activities that corrode good bodily health. The avoidance of smoking or binge drinking is a wellness decision or action. Eating a diet that does not lead to obesity and does provide balanced nutrition is wellness. Jogging, biking, playing basketball, and going to the fitness center certainly are wellness activities. From their beginnings in the colonial era, American institutions of higher education have, in one form or another, encouraged physical activities for their students.[18]

In addition to physical fitness, good health habits, and the avoidance of activities damaging to the body, collegiate competitive sports fall into this category. Obviously, huge differences characterize personal wellness activities and intramural competitive sports from intercollegiate competitions. Indeed, a considerable gap exists even in the latter category between an NCAA Division III women's cross country meet and a superpower Division I football championship such as the Rose Bowl. To many observers, competitive intercollegiate athletics at the highest level are not wellness activities at all: the risk of serious injury, for example, to a starting varsity football player might outweigh the muscular or cardiovascular fitness that player develops in order to participate competitively. Sports have long been an important part—indeed, for some, the definitive and most important part—of American colleges. Student athletes, of course, have been important participants in many honors programs. In Chapter 3, I will look at the role competitive athletics, both relatively informal intramural sports and higher-profile intercollegiate games, play in the development of college students.

Finally, some disciplines, such as yoga or tai chi, while primarily physical exercises, explicitly include a spiritual dimension. A significant minority of college students are attracted to these practices.

Intellectual

Cognitive understanding is certainly the primary goal of honors work within a college or university education. In college, students learn the facts of things: what they are, how they got that way, how they relate to other things. They learn the bones of the human body; the plot, character, and structure of *Hamlet*; Vermeer's use of perspective; modern psychology's theories of human personality. Perhaps more importantly in honors studies, they learn how to reason, to move towards mastery of those skills collected under the rubric of critical thinking: learning how to define a problem, envision a range of solutions, test and weigh them, and determine which seems best. Honors learning should impart a sense of which methodologies from the scientific method to textual analysis work best in various subject matter areas.

Intellectual development in college consists of cognitive experiences that broaden knowledge and deepen understanding. Such growth and development can take place in one or more of four venues: curricular, co-curricular, extracurricular, and a-curricular.

The curriculum at most contemporary colleges and universities is supplemented by co-curricular activities: non-credit-bearing offerings that directly and clearly relate to curricular offerings. Thus, the drama major may act in theater productions, the science student may join the biology club, and the pre-med major may serve in a college-sponsored volunteer internship in the local hospital. Often, honors programs host or offer travel to co-curricular events such as artistic performances, exhibits, or lectures. Extracurricular activities, for example when the chemistry major at a small liberal arts college plays in a campus string quartet, are those with a less clear connection to in-class activities. Some extracurricular activities, such as a Halloween party or prom, are not intellectual, but many are, and most have at least some cognitive component.

Finally, college is a place where an enormous amount of intellectual activity often takes place totally unconnected to any official offering of the institution. This is what happens when a group of students sit on a bench at 1:00 a.m. on a late spring evening, discussing anything and everything under the sun (or, in this case, moon). It happens when a pair of students is studying for an exam together, he in sociology, she in philosophy, and they fall to talking and realize that there are connections between what they are each trying to learn and spend the next two hours exploring those connections rather than preparing for the test. It is what often goes on at all hours in an honors lounge. College-age people are at a time of life when they are curious, receptive, and social, and they learn much about themselves and the world around them from each other. Sometimes, all the university has to do is provide the venue or opportunity that will bring them together.

Holistic

Not infrequently in these pages I use the word *holistic*. By this, I mean a perspective that takes into account persons as unified and whole entities. Unfortunately, this term has sometimes come to refer to practices of a mystical or unscientific nature. While I am not necessarily discomfited by such practices, they are not the subject of this study. I have tried to avoid mysticism, exoticism, and unproven hypotheses or those that are impossible to prove.

WHOLENESS

This chapter has addressed the odd question, "What If Honors Students Were People?" I know, of course, that indeed they are. Honors students, like all other students and like all people, are multidimensional, complex, unique, and infinitely varied. In countless different ways, they are a blend, as are all human beings, of mind, body, and spirit. If the ultimate goal in contemporary honors programs and colleges is to help students learn to be, in every way, the best people they are capable of being, remembering that they are not disembodied intellects is necessary. They think, they feel, they search for meaning, they sweat, they love, they read; they are, in short, whole people, and they are best served if educators never forget their wholeness.

My hope is that the pages that follow will be helpful and of interest to all who work in honors and to a more general higher education audience as well: to college and university professors; to administrators; to collegiate professionals in health, wellness, and fitness; to those who work in student counseling or in religious and spiritual roles; to students of higher education; and, perhaps, even to honors students themselves who, after all, finally have the greatest stake in holistic undergraduate education. A half-century after the abolition of compulsory chapel and gym at most schools, contemporary American colleges and universities need to find new ways to enhance cognitive learning by attending to the spiritual and physical needs of college students.

At the very dawn of the sixteenth century, Michelangelo di Lodovico Buonarroti Simoni liberated from a large chunk of discarded marble the most famous statue in the history of Western art. After a few centuries standing outside the Palazzo Vecchio in Florence, today his *David* resides in the Galleria dell' Accademia, where he contemplates his victory over Goliath, and hundreds of tourists and art lovers contemplate him daily. *David* stands as an emblem of the pinnacle of human aspirations in the Renaissance as well as a symbol of the most lofty vision for honors. Michelangelo's figure is a model of reason, piety, and athleticism. I have become convinced that honors education in particular and American higher education in general, in their eagerness to cultivate the first of these three admirable virtues, thoughtful rationality, have ignored spiritual depth and physical vigor, to the detriment of the institutions themselves, society at large, and certainly students.

CHAPTER 2

History

To have a nuanced and balanced understanding of the successes, failures, development, and strategies for integrated, holistic learning in honors programs at today's colleges and universities requires some historical context. Of particular importance to this history are the creation and evolution of the early colonial colleges, such as Harvard; key groups of institutions, like the land grant state universities; and some general trends within the entire higher education community as a whole, such as the movement from a universal required curriculum to the elective system. Although Francis Oakley, a thoughtful student of America's postsecondary education, has remarked that understanding the ethos of contemporary institutions requires grasping "the dense particularities of their specific individual histories," having an overview of the larger movements of American collegiate culture and practice is also vital (145).

COLONIAL COLLEGES: 1636–1776

Prior to the Revolutionary War, nine collegiate institutions were founded in America. Although their founding dates span more than a century and a quarter (1636–1769), these institutions have much in common. Their stories offer important insights into the subsequent developments of colleges and universities, even as they have evolved far beyond the models–indeed, beyond the wildest visions–of the colonial institutions and their founders.

As William C. Ringenberg correctly observes of higher education, "to be a college in America before the Civil War was to be a Christian college" (77). Very few American college students prior to the end of the Second World War proclaimed themselves spiritual but not religious. Nor, until less than a century ago, would any significant number of Americans understand religion in colleges and universities to be anything other than Christianity. This is not to say that all college students for the first three centuries of higher learning in American were Christians or saw themselves as religious, although historians of American colleges and university suggest that most did see themselves that way.[19] Clearly, the overwhelming majority of America's collegians, for most of the country's history, were white males of Christian descent. Certainly colleges and universities, including public institutions, once they evolved, so identified themselves. Of course, some students from the earliest days of the nation did not wholly subscribe to the tenets and practices of established Protestant or Catholic churches.[20] Some of those students would have been keenly interested in questions, issues, practices, and investigations that today's students would call spiritual; however, prior to about 1960, such students would have described themselves as interested in religious matters but not affiliated with a particular denomination. Arthur W. Chickering, Jon C. Dalton, and Liesa Stamm describe this evolution clearly: they note that "religion" used to be both private and public, but now "spirituality" is used for private matters, "religion" for public ones, and this characteristic dates from the 1960s (5ff). They note a "general shift in religious orientation that has occurred in the US since the 1960s, from the more public expression of religion to the more private and personal" (8). And they observe that a not-insignificant group of college students and faculty recoil from language that "carries baggage from the worlds of established religions and churches with which they do not identify" (6). Until quite recently, the ways in which colleges and universities have cultivated in students a grasp of issues of meaning and purpose in life and a willingness to grapple with the "big questions," to ask questions that go beyond the external and material, were identified by American colleges and collegians generally as "religion" or "religious."[21]

Here are the American colonial institutions, their founding date, and their initial religious affiliation:

Harvard	1636	Puritan
William and Mary	1693	Episcopal (Anglican)
Yale	1701	Congregational
Princeton	1746	Presbyterian
Columbia	1754	Episcopal
Univ. of Pennsylvania	1755	Episcopal
Brown	1765	Baptist
Rutgers	1766	Dutch Reformed
Dartmouth	1769	Protestant General/Congregational[22]

At the conclusion of this period, the combined student population of these institutions was just under one thousand souls, and the approximate number of faculty altogether at all nine universities was 135. Students and faculty were, together, about the size of one contemporary small college. Although today these institutions share a close geographical proximity, that seemed much less the case in earlier eras. All have become relatively large graduate institutions: they range in size from Dartmouth with around 5000 students to Pennsylvania with roughly 22,500. None is a small liberal arts college; none approaches the size of the largest state universities. All the institutions retain strong, prestigious, selective undergraduate programs in the liberal arts. That none of the Colonial colleges, all of which began under some sort of sectarian sponsorship, proclaim a current religious affiliation is significant. All of them offer students diverse opportunities for religious activities, but in no case are these activities part of the institutions' formal instructional program.

These first American colleges are well described by scholars such as Arthur M. Cohen, Sheldon S. Cohen, Douglas Sloan, John D. Pulliam, and John Thelin. The colonial colleges assumed that their task was a holistic one; Christopher J. Lucas writes:

> The antebellum college was organized on the assumption that higher learning constituted a single unified culture. . . . It was the task of moral philosophy . . . not only to integrate the various fields of learning . . . but even more importantly to draw out the implications for living the good life individually and socially. (282)

A part, albeit not too important a part, of this holistic vision included physical well-being. The colleges encouraged students to engage in wholesome activities, such as walking or riding, but in their earliest days, these institutions offered neither formal nor even informal recreational programs. No competitive sports, no instruction in physical culture, and no facilities for exercise existed.

Colonial college curricula were universal and mandated: everyone studied the same subjects at the same point in the college career, rather like today's St. John's colleges or Thomas Aquinas College and some contemporary collegiate honors programs. Studies, notes A. Cohen, "centered on classical texts and the foundations of Christian doctrine" (17). Electives did not enter the American college curriculum until after the Civil War. Thus, John D. Pulliam's description of the early Harvard curriculum can represent, with slight variants, that of all the pre-Revolutionary institutions:

> Aristotelian logic and physics, arithmetic, geometry, astronomy, grammar, rhetoric, dialectic, etymology, syntax and prosodia were taught for the purpose of disciplining the mind. Upperclassmen studied Greek and Hebrew grammar and there were occasional lectures in history and natural science. Students were expected to declaim once a month and great stress was placed on study of the Bible. For a degree the student had to present evidence of his ability to read the Scriptures in Latin. (36)

The colonial colleges had a mixed sectarian/public nature. In this characteristic, according to Douglas Sloan, they embodied the perspective of their era: "the idea that education and religion were inseparable was deeply ingrained in Calvinism" (12). The colleges were chartered as public institutions and educated lay persons for secular vocations such as medicine and the law, but they also all had religious ties and trained clergymen. As Arthur M. Cohen argues in *The Shaping of American Higher Education*, one of the defining characteristics of the American colonies was their "religious spirit . . . Protestantism and Anglicanism newly separated from Catholicism and continually reforming, yielding variations in patterns of observance from deism . . . to fervent sects devoted to emotional worship" (9). In a sense, these institutions were the seeds of several strands of American higher learning that, during the post-colonial history, separated and became distinct.

With its 1,000 students and 135 faculty members at the end of the Colonial period, American higher education was certainly not a major new-world force prior to the Revolutionary War, but it had established a pattern in which religious concerns and secular ones were mixed. Early American colleges included some with strict denominational ties and others that served a variety of Protestant Christian sects. "Each of the colleges," writes A. Cohen, "had a church connection . . . [but] church influence was never absolute, and a tradition of lay governance was established early on" (19). Over the years from 1636 to 1776, secular purposes, populations, and curricula gained in relation to religious missions, but even by the end of the period, imagining an American collegiate institution without a significant religious, Christian character would still not have been possible.

Clearly, physical activity, planned and unplanned, played a part in the lives of colonial collegians, but, as John R. Thelin points out, "The elaborate extracurriculum of athletics teams . . . later associated with the 'collegiate way' were not part of the colonial colleges" (*History* 22). These early institutions adopted, without much introspection, the ancient understanding that the balance between mental and physical activity was a key to proper human development, what some historians of physical education call the Athenian goal of harmony between sound mind and healthy body.[23]

FROM THE REVOLUTIONARY WAR TO THE CIVIL WAR: 1776–1865

The first 130 years of American collegiate history produced nine colleges. In less than a century after the War of Independence, hundreds of colleges appeared in the young land. Not surprisingly, hundreds failed as well. While most of the institutions created during this period, as was the case in the colonial era, had both religious and secular missions, during this time the clear division between these influences also took shape. During this period most American colleges and universities formally incorporated physical education into their curricula and launched the tentative efforts at intercollegiate athletics competition. In her seminal study of collegiate student culture, *Campus Life,* Helen Lefkowitz Horowitz determines that "college life" in the United States was created in "the late eighteenth and early nineteenth centuries" (23). As in the colonial era, but with more variation, the colleges of this period understood their task to be holistic.

Some important developments and collegiate characteristics in this time period include: religious foundation patterns and the "Great Awakenings"; westward expansion; consolidation patterns; the Dartmouth College case; the opening of collegiate instruction to women and African-Americans; the Morrill Act and the launching of state universities; the creation of normal schools; continued broad curricular development; the beginnings of classes in physical education as well as professional groups that focused upon physical education; and the institutionalization of intramural and intercollegiate athletic competition.

All of the colonial colleges have followed the same pattern of religious evolution: all initially served both religious and secular purposes, and all have evolved into religiously unaffiliated institutions today. In contrast, the 170 colleges that were founded in the 1776–1865 era and that still exist today have far more diverse religious histories and are far more religiously varied. This group of institutions includes:

- Some smaller liberal arts colleges that initially had a strong religious affiliation but that today would be considered thoroughly non-sectarian.
- Some that began as small, church-affiliated colleges but have evolved into largely non-sectarian universities.
- Colleges that today retain a strong religious identity and are members of the Council for Christian Colleges and Universities (CCCU).
- America's first Roman Catholic institutions, beginning with Georgetown (1815).
- State universities: well before the passage of the Morrill Act at the end of this period, the first of the wholly non-religious, state-sponsored universities were being created.[24]
- Some of the pre-Civil war colleges that were or became affiliated with municipalities.

The majority of these institutions were Protestant. Of those which survive, 49 began as Presbyterian schools; 34 as Methodist, mostly founded towards the latter end of this time, when the Methodist church changed rather dramatically from its prior distrust of higher learning; 25 Baptist; 21 Congregational; and 11 Episcopal. Other denominations founding colleges included Lutherans, Christian Church (Disciples of Christ), the German Reformed, Quakers, Universalists, the Dutch Reformed, Unitarians, and other small denominations. There were 14 Roman Catholic institutions by the end of this period, according to Donald G. Tewksbury. Twenty-one state-sponsored institutions existed before the Civil War. These state institutions were, technically, non-sectarian, but in practice that meant primarily non-denominational Protestant and that often required chapel attendance, church membership, and course work in Christian dogma; Bradley Longfield explains: "At least until the turn of the [twentieth] century, state schools still functioned, in various ways, as propagators of Christian faith and ideals" (46–47). As late as 1877, President James Angel of the University of Michigan could proclaim: "Michigan is a Christian state and her University can be true to her only by cherishing a broad unsectarian but earnest Christian spirit" (qtd. in Longfield 46). Indeed, well into the twentieth century, strong remnants of an assumed monolithic Christianity lingered in public higher education; George Marsden and Longfield write: "In 1927 chapel attendance was still required for undergraduates at . . . the University of North Carolina in Chapel Hill, as it was at Yale and Princeton. . . . [I]n 1937 nearly one-fourth of *state* universities and colleges still held at least voluntary chapel services" (3).

The earliest experiments in coeducation were taking place during the first half of the nineteenth century. In 1837, Oberlin College, founded by the Congregationalists in 1834, admitted four women into the regular collegiate course, and in 1841 three of them became the first females in the United States to receive the baccalaureate degree. By the Civil War, Oberlin was joined in coeducation by two other Ohio private colleges, Antioch and Hillsdale (which moved to Michigan), and by the public universities of Iowa and Utah. Simultaneously, educational reformers, male and female, founded female academies and seminaries, many of which were the precursors to women's colleges. These include Salem Academy in North Carolina and Mount Holyoke Female Seminary, which was founded by the idiosyncratic and powerful Mary Lyon. The first college-level institutions specifically for women were founded in the mid-Nineteenth Century (Horowitz, *Alma Mater).* Wesleyan College in Georgia was chartered in 1836 as "Georgia Female College," Mary Sharp College (now closed) began in 1851, and Elmira was established in New York in 1855. The first of the prestigious seven sisters was Vassar College, founded in 1865 by Matthew Vassar. Vassar was originally affiliated with the Baptists. These female institutions paid considerable attention to physical cultivation, health, and hygiene although in a less aggressive and competitive mode than at the male schools. The early proponents of gymnastic exercise were committed to the fitness of both men and women.[25]

Middlebury College, founded in 1800 by the Congregationalists, probably granted, according to *Encyclopedia Africana*, the first traditional baccalaureate degree to an African American, Alexander Lucius Twilight, in 1823 ("Middlebury"). Twilight went on to become a teacher in Vermont and a Presbyterian preacher. He was later elected to the state legislature, and today a building is named for him at the University of Vermont. In 1825, two more African Americans were awarded A. B. degrees: John Brown Russwurm from Bowdoin and Edward Jones from Amherst. The first African American PhD recipient apparently was Alexander Boucher, who finished his graduate work at Yale in 1876. Beginning in 1835 Oberlin College, again a leader, began "regularly admitting African American Students" (Oberlin College). The nation's first historically black institutions were created during this period. They were Cheney College, Lincoln University, Wilberforce College, and Howard University. Cheney and Lincoln vie for the title of the nation's first African American college: Cheney was founded earlier, but Lincoln was the first to offer college-level instruction.

One moment of profound significance in the history of American colleges and universities occurred in 1816, when the legislature of the state of New Hampshire attempted to assert its control over Dartmouth College. The case was initiated by a conflict between President John Wheelock, the son of Dartmouth's founder, and the college's trustees (Pulliam 68). The state's position was that New Hampshire had chartered a private corporation to oversee the college for the good of the public. The public, in the shape of the state, should therefore have ultimate governance of the institution. According to A. Cohen, Dartmouth's case, argued by Daniel Webster, affirmed that once a private entity had been chartered, that charter was inviolable (60). Thus, once any group, including any church, has legitimately and legally been chartered to operate a college, that group was legally self-governing and autonomous, in perpetuity. In 1819, the Supreme Court sided with Dartmouth, heeding Webster's famous peroration: "It is, Sir, as I have said a small college. And yet there are those who love it."[26]

In effect, the Dartmouth College case marks the point at which the colonial system of higher education that had been a kind of shared enterprise of the church and state bifurcates. Henceforth, there were public colleges and universities and private ones, including religious ones, but they were not to be the same institutions. Imagining the changed landscape of American higher education had this key judicial decision gone the other way is almost impossible.

As noted earlier, North Carolina and Georgia created America's first state universities just after the Revolution at the start of this time period. The end of the era witnessed the most important step in the growth of public higher education: the Morrill Land Grant Act finally passed in 1862. It had been vetoed earlier by then-President Buchanan. This Act granted to the states land—30,000 acres to each state (thus, "land grant" university)—to fund public collegiate instruction (Pulliam 60). This step or some variant of it had been proposed for a long time, but it finally became law just as the nation was entering into the trauma of civil war. The Act (available in the Library of Congress electronic archive) made these land grants to each state for

> the endowment, support and maintenance of at least one college where the leading object shall be, without excluding other scientific and classical studies . . . to teach such branches of learning as are related to agriculture and the mechanic arts . . . in order to promote the liberal and practical education of the industrial classes in the several pursuits and professions of life. (Library of Congress, 503–505)

The Morrill Act is of crucial importance in the development of America's colleges because it set in motion a vast secular and populist trend. For better or worse (or both), contemporary higher education in our nation today is dominated by large, comprehensive public institutions. Moreover, the Morrill Act required universal military drill for male students at land grant colleges and universities. In some ways, this requirement could be seen as the first broadscale PE requirement in American higher education.

In addition to the creation of the flagship, land-grant state universities, the period between the Revolution and the Civil War also saw the beginnings of American normal schools. Initially, observe L. Dean Webb, Arlene Metha, and K. Fordis Jordan, these teacher-training institutions were quite modest: "Admission to the normal school required only an elementary education. The course of study lasted one or two years. . . . Overriding the curriculum was a concern for the development of moral character" (135). Many of these institutions developed into teachers' colleges, then state colleges, and not infrequently into regional comprehensive state universities. For example, the Illinois State University website reports that in February 1857, Governor William Bissell signed a bill to create a teacher-training school in Illinois. The attorney for the fledgling normal school was Abraham Lincoln. Illinois State Normal University evolved into today's Illinois State University, with 34 academic departments offering 66 majors, 34 master's degree programs, and doctoral work in eight areas to a student population of 20,265 (Illinois).

The years between 1776 and 1865 saw the introduction and institutionalization of regular programs of physical exercise for college students. By 1825, write H. Spencer Turner and Janet L. Hurley, Harvard had "introduced methods of mass physical education," and just before the Civil War, "gymnasiums filled with exercise equipment were common in most colleges and universities" (2). The most popular form of physical exercise during this period, according to Lee, was what was called "gymnastics": mass rhythmic movement, assisted sometimes by apparatus such as clubs and balls (25ff). At the same time in the mid-nineteenth century, Christine G. Zimmer notes, some classes on health and hygiene were being introduced in addition to the gymnastics that today would be called "activity" classes (313).

Intramural and intercollegiate athletics contests began and flourished in the early to mid-nineteenth century. Games that were precursors to baseball were, writes Lee, "being played in most of the colleges by the 1830's" (29). The University of Pennsylvania had cricket in 1843; football (or, more accurately, a football-like predecessor game) was played intramurally at Yale as early as 1807; intercollegiate rowing contests were held in the 1840s; the first collegiate swimming meet was in 1848.

Collegiate leaders moved far beyond the tentative Puritan endorsement of wholesome exercise for college men. So, for example, William A. Stearns, the President of Amherst College (which was an early leader in intramural sports and exercise classes), proclaimed: "students of our colleges have bodies which need care and culture as well as the intellectual and moral powers" (qtd. in Turner 2).

To summarize, in the period between the Revolutionary and Civil Wars, a number of lasting and many transitory small colleges were founded, often in the frontier West; new student populations, especially women and African-Americans, were beginning to be admitted; the programs of colleges included exercise and courses in health and hygiene; sporting contests, both intramural and interscholastic developed, flourished, and won the enthusiasm of student participants and spectators; and the seeds of state-supported public higher education were planted and began to grow rapidly.

FROM THE CIVIL WAR TO WORLD WAR II: 1865–1944

The second half of the nineteenth century and the first half of the twentieth, as depicted in Jon H. Roberts and James Turner's *The Sacred and Secular University*, was a time of significant development in American higher education with important consequences for public and private institutions. Many colleges were founded, and many failed; previously un- or under-served populations developed colleges uniquely designed for their needs; earlier types of colleges such as normal schools and land-grant universities changed dramatically and new types such as the junior college were invented; graduate education began; the American honors movement began; and curriculum patterns changed. At the beginning of this period, American colleges and universities were closely related to their colonial and European roots. During this time, the extracurriculum flourished; college life came to define the college experience for many; and big-time collegiate athletics was created and flourished. By the 1940s a distinctly American pattern had emerged, one that seems rather familiar today. This was a period of almost explosive collegiate expansion, both in number of institutions and in volume of students and teachers at those institutions. At the time of the Civil War, most colleges were smaller than 200 students, and as for the largest, Burton R. Clark writes, "Harvard, Yale, Virginia and Michigan were the giants of the day with five and six hundred students" (172). In 1870 there were 250 institutions in the nation, with 5,553 professors serving 63,000 students. By 1945, there were 1,768 colleges and universities with over 1,675,000 students and some 150,000 faculty members (A. Cohen, 125–156). In just two decades, from 1920 to 1940, Lawrence A. Cremin reports that the population of college students nearly tripled (248). Many of the new institutions created in this period began as small, sectarian private colleges, often at the initiative of one energetic and ambitious frontier churchman or a small band of likeminded pioneer founders. To these founders, and at most institutions, the vision of the collegiate cultivation of what Thelin calls "muscular Christianity" (that is, physically and mentally vigorous and self-confident) was of critical importance (*History* 188). Some of these new institutions survived and continue today as strong, viable institutions, in some cases little changed but usually unrecognizable. Many more did not live much longer than their creators.

Among the new institutions created were colleges designed specifically for populations other than the white males who dominated higher education in the previous century and were the only college students of the colonial era. An example is today's Morehouse College serving African-American men. A number of public separate and unequal agricultural and mechanical colleges for students of color were created in the south. Provision was made for these historically black universities by a second Morrill Act of 1890, which stipulated federal support for "any state in which there has been one college established in pursuance of the act of July second, eighteen hundred and sixty-two, and also in which an educational institution of like character has been established, or may be hereafter established, and is now aided by such state from its own revenue, for the education for colored students in agriculture and mechanic arts" (United States. Dept. of Agriculture).

Colleges for women as well as coeducation showed strong growth during this period. Many new women's schools were created, but by 1880 nearly half of all U. S. colleges admitted women, led by the public institutions. (It is worth remembering that the country's women were not admitted nationally to the polling place for another forty years.) Mechikoff observes that physical education and sports for women made significant strides during this century, with particular emphasis on fitness and health at the women's institutions (200ff.). Late in the nineteenth century, several of the women's colleges, especially the newer ones, added competitive intramural athletic opportunities to earlier offerings in health and fitness (Thelin 98). Nevertheless a widespread and strong distaste for intercollegiate athletics for females during this time remained: a reflection of the Victorian belief that women were too delicate and fragile for vigorous, competitive physical activity.

This period also saw the first systematic attempts to provide more than rudimentary elementary education to American Indians, including the creation of several institutions that began as Native American schools and are today colleges and universities, such as Fort Lewis in Colorado and the University of Minnesota Morris. These institutions now serve a broad and diverse student population including, but not limited to, Native Americans.

Another new development was the creation of the junior college, beginning, some students of higher education like George A. Baker suggest, with the recommendation by the president of Baylor University in 1894 that his institution and some of the smaller Baptist institutions in Texas enter a formal compact whereby the small colleges would provide the first two years of instruction and Baylor would accept their graduates to complete the final half of their baccalaureate education (7–10). In the first decade of the twenty-first century, two-year colleges, including community colleges, technical and/or vocational, and junior colleges granting associate's degree added up to more institutions than BA-, MA-, and PhD-granting institutions . . . combined (Carnegie). Now they have become a major segment of the honors community, and Cindy Hill, the Executive Director of NCHC, estimates that they comprise 20–25% of NCHC's institutional members (Hill).

Also during the time between the Civil War and World War II, the normal schools that were created earlier began to move to state college status. Today Carnegie reports that there are more institutions that offer the master's degree as their highest option (611) than there are either baccalaureate (606) or doctoral (261) institutions (Carnegie).

Another significant development occurred with the foundation of Cornell University in 1869 and even more dramatically Johns Hopkins in 1876. The first institution to elevate graduate education to a position of primacy, Hopkins was, famously, founded on the model of the German research university. A. Cohen notes that at the end of the Civil War, there were about 200 graduate students in the nation, for the most part in various professional programs. By 1930, nearly fifty thousand were enrolled (105). The American nativity of the research university led to several important developments that shape contemporary colleges and universities. The first is the concept of the academic department. Christopher Jencks and David Riesman see the 1880s and 1890s as the decades in which "knowledge was broken up into its present departmental categories ('physics,' 'biology,' 'history,' 'philosophy,' and so forth), with the department emerging as the basic unit of academic administration" (13). Simultaneously, the professionalization of the faculty advanced sharply. Formerly called "tutors," college and university teachers were universally referred to as "professors" by the end of this period. Not coincidentally, the American Association of University Professors (AAUP) was founded in 1915 and issued its "Statement of Principles" in 1940. A professionalized faculty, combined with a heightened departmentalism, did much to move the core focus of American higher education away from the earlier model of small, closely knit academic communities, in which the core goal was not so much professional competence but a holistic inculcation of wisdom, maturity, and virtue. The creation of the research university led directly to today's programs in undergraduate research and to honors research and thesis options.

During this period, argues Reuben, many "educational reformers believed that universities could offer their students a modern form of religious education by promoting the scientific study of religion" (34). Thus, "religious education" came to mean learning about religions in departments focusing upon religious studies, not learning to be faithful in chapel and in prayer. In a related development, Mechikoff observes, the teaching of physical education was also professionalized in this era (224). Although quite often, even to the present, the teaching of health and fitness and the coaching of intercollegiate athletics squads fell to the same, often ill-trained individual. Gradually, health education, physical fitness, and athletics, notes Zimmer, grew apart during this period (699).

A crucial instructional development in the years immediately after the Civil War was the introduction of the elective system into the college curriculum. As noted above, the earliest American colleges had a universal and wholly prescribed curriculum in which every student took the same courses in the same order. A few colleges, including some religious schools such as Thomas Aquinas College, have revived this model in the contemporary period. A significant number of honors programs and honors colleges also advocate a unified and universal curricular path.

Largely under the leadership of President Charles William Eliot of Harvard, who assumed that post in 1869, the elective system became firmly entrenched at American institutions. Not for the first, nor for the last time, Harvard and Yale disagreed: the chief opponent of the elective system was the President of Yale, Noah Porter, who opined in 1871, "The [elective] plan involves the certain evil of breaking into the common life of the class and the college as well as of unprofitable expenditure and insuperable complexity" (qtd. in Hofstadter and Smith 699). It is amusing to ponder what President Porter might think upon examining Yale's current course bulletin with what the college's website describes as a "massive" selection of classes. With the introduction of curricular choice, it is not surprising, asserts Arthur Levine, that the creation of the academic "major" followed closely, in 1877 (28–53). Two other important curricular developments, familiar to almost any living college graduate or contemporary student were the creation of distribution requirements, first introduced in 1909 at Harvard as a mechanism for allowing students choice, but within a prescribed framework, and the invention of the survey course.

Fitness activities remained a part of the weekly programs of most college students throughout this era. In the first decades after the Civil War, gymnastics continued to be popular. Historians of higher education such as A. Cohen, Mechikoff, and Lee observe that these activities waned in importance and prominence in the new century when sports, intramurals, and other fitness activities such as swimming and the bicycling craze of the late 1800s gained wider acceptance. Track and rowing remained popular. Several universities, including Harvard, Bowdoin, and Yale, built their first gymnasium buildings in the late 1800s. By 1887, 77 colleges had purpose-constructed gyms. In 1910, Thomas Wood, a leading educator at the time, proclaimed "through physical education the child should acquire mental, moral, and social as well as physical benefits" (qtd. in Lee 169). It was to that end, presumably, that colleges such as the University of Pennsylvania required four years of physical education of all students.

In spite of these new institutions and new populations, small, traditional, sectarian liberal arts baccalaureate colleges remained at the center of the American higher education system from the Civil War to World War II. David Breneman estimates that at the turn of the twentieth century fully two-thirds of all American college students were enrolled in such institutions; by 1987, he calculates, that figure had declined radically to 4.4% (20).

Another crucial development was the movement of mainstream institutions that were founded with a religious mission away from that historic Christian mission and towards what many see as secularism. This movement might well be seen to span the entire sweep of America's history, from the colonial era to the present, but it could arguably be said that it reached its peak acceleration in the century between the Civil War and the Second World War. A number of students of higher education and religion lament this development; others have taken issue with their grim interpretations. (See esp. Burtchaell, Marsden and Longfield, Gleason, and Sloan.) While some contend that most American colleges and universities have lost their religious underpinnings, others assert that those core principles have merely evolved in a fashion that keeps pace with the rest of the world or that as some colleges and universities have become less religious, they have opened new and more pluralistic pathways to spiritual experiences and understandings. Regardless of how one interprets the data, however, clearly a great many institutions that saw themselves as overtly sectarian in the 1860s had redefined themselves in terms of student population, faculty characteristics, curriculum, and governance by the mid-twentieth century. Simultaneously, the extracurriculum, especially sports, grew almost in direct obverse proportion to the shrinking of sectarian religiosity during the second half of the nineteenth and first half of the twentieth centuries. Some students of the period directly link these two mirrored developments: Mechikoff, for example, ties the growth of physical education to the loss of "faith in the ability of religion to solve social and moral problems" (200).

The honors movement in America began early in the twentieth century. An unsuccessful program of honors courses began at Columbia in 1909, but a decade later, write V. N. Bhatia and Kathleen M. Painter, that university launched a program stressing "interdepartmentalism, direct study of original works and classroom discussions" (2–3). In 1922, President Frank Aydelotte began an honors program at Swarthmore College, basing it on small seminars and independent work. He also stressed study abroad. Late in the '20s Professor Joseph Cohen, according to William C. Baurecht, began honors work at the University of Colorado that led, in the 1950s, to the creation of the Inter-University Committee on the Superior student (1–6). This organization lasted until the mid-1960s, when it was replaced by the National Collegiate Honors Council.

Taken together, the evolutionary developments within American higher education from 1865 to 1944 can be seen as a key transition from earlier European and colonial models to colleges and universities structured in a way that is recognizable from a contemporary vantage point and that serves most of today's college-going constituencies. But both the colleges and their populations were in significantly different proportions then than in the twenty-first century. At the beginning of the era, sectarian small colleges were ubiquitous. At its end they still constituted the core of American higher education, but they were becoming less sectarian and less small, and a rival set of collegiate options, mostly in the public sector, were taking hold, growing rapidly, and in the process of becoming dominant.

FROM WORLD WAR II (1945) TO THE PRESENT

The development of American higher education in the second half of the twentieth century and the first years of the twenty-first has been as erratic as at any time in the past. As A. Cohen notes, "The thirty years of the mass Higher Education Era [1945–75] were higher education's golden era. Enrollments, finances, institutions—all aspects of the system expanded" (175). Few would describe today's higher learning as existing in a golden, or even silver, era.

During this three-decade period of what A. Cohen refers to as higher education's golden era, about 600 new public institutions were created, most of them two-year colleges. In many cases, these public community and vocational/technical colleges replaced the older, private two-year junior colleges, some of which ceased to exist and some of which became baccalaureate institutions. At least in their early days, the public community and technical colleges, according to Thelin, tended to be "devoid of the extracurricular learning and living experiences that were so crucial in enhancing cognitive skills and changes in attitudes and values" (*History* 103). About 650 private institutions were opened, but only about half of them survived (A. Cohen 187). During this same period, the regional comprehensive state colleges and universities grew and evolved very rapidly—by 1975 a third of all the nation's bachelor's degrees were awarded by this sector. Some of that ebullience continues to the present day. The final quarter of the twentieth century and the first decade of the twenty-first, however, have seen strains and reversals as colleges and universities that seemed to behave after WWII as if there were no tomorrow have had to come to the realization that in fact there is a tomorrow, and it arrived yesterday.

As large public universities, both research and comprehensive, and community two-year colleges flourished, higher education grew increasingly fragmented. Even where spiritual and physical aspects of college students' development were recognized by institutions, Mechikoff argues, they were often treated as distinct, segregated, program elements: "By the mid-1900s . . . religion was relegated to the spiritual aspects of a person; sport was related to the physical" (277). Later, suggests Lucas, "toward the end of the twentieth century, there was little to indicate there was much consensus on how to achieve that venerable goal of holistic development" (297).

The ratio between enrollments in public and private colleges tipped just after the war. In each of the three post-war decades, the percentage of enrollments at public institutions grew by 10%: in 1945 it was 49%; by 1975 it was 79%. At the same time, small liberal arts colleges declined in number. The Carnegie Foundation considered 719 colleges in this category in 1970, and a decade later the number had dropped to 583. Breneman's study concluded that the number of colleges with a claim to liberal learning fell dramatically (11–15). Some of the smaller liberal arts colleges disappeared; more evolved into larger, more comprehensive institutions. Sloan notes that in the two decades after the war, one major trend was the "nearly complete triumph of the research university in determining the primary ethos and goals of American Higher Education" (72). Still, as late as "the mid 1960s about one-third of all colleges and universities in the country were private, and more than half of these . . . were affiliated with religious bodies, 57 percent of these Protestant" (Sloan 203–204).

With the return of war veterans, whose schooling was supported by the generosity of the 1944 GI Bill, most institutions in the country experienced a rapidly expanding student population, which was particularly welcome and noticeable after the shortages of the war years. Temporary housing and classroom space were thrown together to accommodate those vets. Some of those temporary structures lasted a half century. To the dismay of deans of students across the nation, returning veterans, many of whom had marched across ravaged Europe or fought from one jungle-covered Pacific island to the next, were not willing to revert to a passive and subservient adolescent style of life when they came back to campus. From the vantage point of the twenty-first century, it seems likely that the days of *in loco parentis* were numbered at most American campuses on the morning the first GI Bill returnee arrived back on campus. Behavior codes that had been universal early in the twentieth century were and are maintained at a few colleges, but they largely came to be perceived by the educational establishment and by most students as outmoded and idiosyncratic. The vestiges of those codes took another beating from the countercultural activism of students in the 1960s. The differences between student behavioral codes and expectations at today's military and Christian colleges on the one hand and their civilian secular counterparts on the other are a marked feature of post-war collegiate history.

Shortly after the war, another period of importance in general education was both marked by and inspired by Harvard University's study of the curriculum known as the "Red Book."[27] Officially, the "Report of the Harvard Committee on the Objectives of General Education in a Free Society," the document was sweeping in its perspective and recommendations and only partially successful in reforming general education at Harvard. It recommended that at least six year-long courses be set aside for general education and that all students be required to take a humanities course entitled "Great Texts in Literature" and a similar social science offering. Not infrequently today, such courses are found only in honors curricula. Also specified were introductory courses in the sciences and other broad and interdisciplinary classes across the curriculum. In some ways, the Harvard model hearkens back to the curriculum and goals of the colonial colleges by suggesting that all liberally educated individuals should share a rather broad introduction to the range of general knowledge. From the perspective of the twenty-first century, this vision of collegiate education appears to have lost momentum over at least the past fifty years.

Through the 1950s the United States as a nation also enjoyed a time of economic well-being, and in that era of the GI Bill and Eisenhower aura, all of the nation's institutions of higher education seemingly had nowhere to go but up—up in size, up in budget, up in mission expansion. Colleges and universities could lavish resources on academics and athletics; they could build gymnasia and art galleries. The market for young people who aspired to a career in college teaching seemed unlimited. Graduate programs flourished along with undergraduate instruction, and graduate schools and professors developed the shortsighted habit of boasting about how large a number of doctorates they could produce. Moreover, the startling launch in 1957 of the Russian *Sputnik* space satellite guaranteed a boost in prestige and in funding for higher learning in general and especially for the sciences in American colleges and universities. This heightened emphasis on science and engineering is seen by some scholars, like Burtchaell, Marsden, and Sloan, as entailing a corresponding decrease in interest and status in issues of faith, values, and the spirit.

Although big-time collegiate sports continued to flourish, students of the mid-twentieth century were on the whole less enamored of the non-curricular aspects of college life than their pre-war predecessors.

College costs escalated more rapidly in the final quarter of the twentieth century than did family income. According to the National Center for Educational Statistics, annual tuition and room and board at all accredited two- and four-year public and private institutions averaged about 15 percent of family income in 1976; by 1999 it was 21 percent (National Center for Educational Statistics). This trend has continued unabated through the first decade of the twenty-first century, with the gap being met largely by student debt and increased financial aid.

Also in the 1950s and 1960s, racial integration at long last came to the nation's universities, sometimes peacefully and uneventfully, sometimes accompanied with raucous rancor, as when the governors of Alabama and Mississippi defied court orders to admit African American students to the flagship public universities in their states. Private colleges, including religious institutions, also moved, some smoothly and some with controversy and confrontation, towards racial integration.

A similar step for women's rights at the nation's colleges occurred with the passage of Title IX of the Education Amendments of 1972, an action that continues to generate dramatic and often controversial repercussions, especially in athletics. Title IX evolved out of the Civil Rights Act of 1964, with strong advocacy by many women's organizations such as the National Organization of Women (NOW). Title IX, of course, had a profound effect on women's intercollegiate athletics and on gender-equity issues across the collegiate world. The notion that female collegiate athletes were entitled to equal treatment with their male peers sent shock waves through higher education's athletic establishment and indeed through higher education as a whole. While most students, faculty, and administrators supported and continue to support equity for women and women athletes, questions quickly arose, and continue occasionally to arise even today, four decades after Title IX, about what equal treatment really means.

- Does it mean equal budgets for the women's athletics department and the men's?
- Does it mean there should not be separate departments at all?
- Does it mean an equal number of intercollegiate sports opportunities for both genders?
- Does it mean equity in salary for coaches and athletics administrators across the line of sex?
- Does it mean an equal number of participants among men and women?
- Does it mean a balance in facilities and equipment?

Many of these questions are rendered much more difficult by the continued importance of men's football as a college sport. Football teams not infrequently have between 50 and 100 members, even in smaller institutions, and the cost of equipping a football squad is shockingly higher than, say, a track team, volleyball squad, or basketball program. Clearly, Title IX and, more generally, the women's movement brought female competitive athletics, intramural, and fitness activities into the mainstream of American collegiate life. Today, female varsity athletes are a familiar constituency of virtually all campuses. In the years after World War II, they did not exist in any significant numbers and were seen as curiosities by many until the final quarter of the century. Virginia Hunt, in an unpublished dissertation on the history of womens' collegiate sports, shows how those sports grew in importance and budget. As a direct consequence of that growth, the NCAA, which had formerly represented only men, moved, unilaterally, to supplant the former Association of Intercollegiate Athletics for Women (AIAW). Tracing its origins to the early 1940s, the AIAW flourished briefly after the passage of Title IX, but once it became clear, Lee observes, that women's athletics could be a profitable venture, the NCAA aggressively began staging tournaments in direct competition with the AIAW, and by 1982, the latter was out of business (341). The opening of intercollegiate athletics to women is important to honors education since the percentage of female honors students on most contemporary campuses is 60–70%.

Beginning in the 1960s, higher education also paid attention to the opportunities for Hispanic Americans. In California, the National Hispanic University website reports that both the university system and the state college system created programs designed to promote Hispanic access to higher learning (National Hispanic). By 2004, Shilpa Banerji says some 1.8 million Hispanic students were in college, about 11% of the total student enrollment in colleges and universities—but still only 25% of college-age Hispanics were enrolled, compared to 42% Whites, 32% African-Americans, and 60% Asians (Banerji).

Although contemporary popular culture has sanitized and romanticized the 1960s, it was in reality a difficult time on many of America's college campuses. The civil rights movement radicalized many young people and taught them effective means to challenge previously unquestioned authority, on and off campus.[28] Increasing African American populations in student bodies intensified rather than lessened demands for better treatment. The expansion of an unpopular war in Southeast Asia exacerbated these tensions, and campus after campus exploded in protest and conflict as the decade neared its conclusion. At many mainline Protestant-affiliated campuses, the student activism of the 1960s led to the demise of many of the religious characteristics that had still been vital and important early in the twentieth century: required courses in religion and required chapel survived the Second World War on most private Protestant-related campuses, but they did not survive Vietnam. Sloan contends, perhaps somewhat dramatically, that "by the end of 1969, along its entire front, the major twentieth-century engagement of the Protestant church with American higher education had collapsed, and its forces were in rout" (206). Faculty, too, heartened by the activism of the students they instructed (many of whom are today's faculty themselves) lobbied, often with success, to do away with faculty and admissions quotas, which had protected founding denominations, as well as other religious requirements and customs.[29] Finally, college campuses were shocked when students were slain at Kent State University and Jackson State University: student protest had turned into riot and armed warfare.

So, for a range of reasons, America's colleges and universities after World War II became more diverse in their populations with regards to race, ethnicity, gender, and religion, and they moved to sever or redefine their links to their Christian, largely mainline Protestant, origins. Just as it could no longer be assumed that sports heroes were males, it was no longer the case that the overwhelming majority of all college students were white Christians; public and private colleges and universities no longer saw the promotion of sectarian Christianity as a core element of their missions. But, as the work of the Astins and others have amply demonstrated, college-age young men and women did not grow less engaged in eschatological questions, in the age-old mulling of the meaning and purpose of life (Foreword, *Encouraging*). Fascinatingly, in a 2002 survey by L. J. Sax et al., 46% of students prior to entering college found "integrating spirituality into my life" very important or essential; after the first year, that number rose to 55%, and at the same time the proportion of those students who attend formal church services declined (Sax et al.). As formal religion waned at many colleges, a compensating student attention to non-sectarian spiritual formation grew. While many institutions reacted by moving towards increased student control over college life and decreased curricular and social requirements, a contrary development, which sought clear classroom and behavioral expectations, was developing among some students and parents. As a large proportion of public and private institutions moved further away from strong intellectual and personal guidance, the small number of schools that clung to such standards enjoyed a revitalized popularity among a constituency who sought them. Many observers, such as Ringenberg, Sloan, and Burtchaell have noted, in American culture in general and in colleges and universities in particular, a similar simultaneous decline of the mainline Protestant churches and rise of evangelical Protestantism. From the 1970s on, evangelical Christian colleges have emerged as an increasingly successful, popular, and noteworthy segment of the American higher educational panorama.

Thus, it was not only experiments on the political, theological, and cultural left that flourished during the mid-century period. This period was also the time when several new small colleges with deep Christian commitments, such as Westmont College and Thomas Aquinas College, both in California, were launched. This was, perhaps, both a consequence of a revival of evangelical Christianity and a reaction to the perception that many colleges had drifted to the political Left, had simultaneously moved away from a strong program of direct ethical guidance of students, and had weakened or even severed connections with the religious bodies that had created them.

An opposite and different legacy of the 1960s is an atmosphere of open educational experimentation that had consequences large and small throughout higher education. At all but a handful of colleges, curricula expanded to include topics and areas that had hitherto been off-limits, such as Black Studies. Interdisciplinary honors seminars became increasingly common. Early in the decade, when resources still seemed abundant and the winds of change were gusting, several significant collegiate experiments were launched. Some of the public liberal arts colleges that are now a fixture on the U. S. educational landscape were founded during this period. Some of these and other small colleges, like Evergreen State College, Simon's Rock, and New College, which were reinventing themselves or newly created, offered dramatic alternative educational philosophies and style. Other older, more traditional institutions initiated curricular revisions and experiments alternately lauded and decried.

In some ways, honors programs and colleges, as well, have benefitted from this renewed interest in a personalized, interactive undergraduate experience. The pages that follow examine some of the forms that effort has taken. How are honors students today encouraged to ask the "big questions" that probe the meaning and purpose of their lives? How can the honors curriculum and extracurriculum help them grope their ways towards tentative answers?

In the last decades of this period, fitness and amateur sports enjoyed a boom. In the 1980s, the fitness movement, which featured the running craze, aerobics, and for-profit health clubs, flourished, and on many college campuses, Thelin reports that the "dank, sweaty gymnasia were replaced by state-of-the-art health and fitness centers that rivaled Club Med" (327).

In the final quarter of the twentieth century, the expansion of the college student population slowed, and for the first time in memory there were more college teachers than there were jobs to be had teaching college. This sense of increased competition for declining resources both strengthened and weakened collegiate religiosity. One collegiate historian, Julie Reuben, puts it bluntly: "economics became the overwhelming preoccupation of higher education. This manifested itself in several ways, including institutional policies, student attitudes, and the curriculum" (47). As noted above, some institutions that maintained or created anew strongly religious traditions flourished by appealing to a particular niche of higher education consumers. Others took the opposite tack and lessened their religious emphasis to appeal to a broader clientele. Thus, for example, the College of New Rochelle, which had been established as a Catholic women's college in 1904, added a graduate school in 1969, a school of nursing in 1976, and a School of New Resources for adults in 1972. Noting that, taken altogether, the student population of the College of New Rochelle is no longer primarily Catholic, Burtchaell states, with some venom, that "New Rochelle survives, but it is not the same college," and "'Catholic' had come to evoke everything the college was happy to have left behind" (363, 366).

During the second half of the twentieth century, most colleges and universities, public and private, dropped the physical education requirements that had been ubiquitous at midcentury when a 1953 survey showed that over 90% of American colleges offered physical education; in 1960–61, 84% of colleges had some sort of PE requirement, and nearly half had a swimming test (Turner and Hurley 1–21).[30] While some institutions maintained and still maintain today gym requirements, that number steadily shrank. But from a somewhat removed perspective, it is clear that required physical activity ebbed just as involvement in personal fitness was growing. This trend was clear both in the general population and among college students. For example, Cornell University dropped the physical education requirement in the late 1990s, only to see enrollments in gym classes increase! (*Physical Education*).

In addition to increased demographic pressures, colleges and universities at the beginning of the twenty-first century found themselves ensnared in a continually escalating pattern of ever-higher expectations in such diverse areas as information technology, state-of-the-art facilities, outcomes assessment, regional economic development, and workforce preparation. They were coping with exploding technological needs and costs at a time of declining enrollment and reduced tuition revenue and, in the public institutions, ever-lessening shares of pinched state budgets. By the turn of the new century, finding much viable evidence of the ebullience of the postwar period, with the notable exception of the evangelical institutions, was difficult. It was impossible to find a college or university, from Harvard, Stanford, Grinnell, and Wellesley to the tiniest and least prestigious junior college, that would consider itself to be financially comfortable.

Even in these comparatively lean times, significant collegiate culture change has occurred. If women and people of color still sometimes seem to be treated as less than equals, in education as throughout the culture, the progress of both in the past half-century is breathtaking and gratifying. Gay, lesbian, and bisexual students, faculty, and staff have gone from being unmentionable to being, on many campuses, unremarkable. White students attend historically black colleges and vice versa; women often comprise the majority at most undergraduate institutions, especially in honors courses, and female and minority faculty and administrators are no longer a curiosity. Non-Christian students are welcome at the great majority of institutions, and nobody looks twice at a student wearing a yarmulke or burka; some campuses that once admitted only Protestants have today officially recognized student organizations of atheists.

The honors movement enjoyed steady growth during this period. At the end of the Second World War, there were only honors programs, no honors colleges. Today dozens of the latter exist; often they have their own deans, faculty, facilities, graduation requirements, and names (e. g., the Calhoun Honors College at Clemson University). Early in the second half of the twentieth century, the annual meetings of the NCHC could take place on college campuses; William and Mary and Kent State University were hosts and were attended by a few hundred faculty and students. Today those meetings are held in major convention hotels in large cities, and around 2000 honors enthusiasts are present.

Perhaps most importantly and dramatically, in the final years of the twentieth century and on into the twenty-first, postsecondary education has become the universal standard in the United States. At the beginning of the twentieth century, nearly all Americans had some schooling. At its midpoint most graduated from high school. At its end a postsecondary option existed for virtually every high school graduate, be it a conventional college or university, a two-year institution, distance education or a proprietary school, a military training facility, or a post-secondary educational experience within a corporate setting. According to A. Cohen, today over two thirds of high school graduates matriculate directly to a formal postsecondary educational setting. Thus, for most Americans, in the first years of the new century, high school graduation is not the end of the educational career. America is the first nation in the world to be entering an era of universal higher learning. If educators do not yet know exactly what this means or how they need to handle it, it is nonetheless a dramatic and significant moment not just in the history of American higher education, but in the history of human enlightenment.

This historical sketch suggests the pattern by which today's profile of American higher education has evolved. From origins that were wholly religious in the colonial era, educators have created a system that includes public and private, non-sectarian colleges and universities, and a remarkably diverse range of institutions with religious traditions and connections. In less than a century, nearly 1000 colleges and universities have created formal honors programs that are members of the National Collegiate Honors Council. There have been dramatic fits and starts, ebbs and flows in the patterns of piety and religious affiliation. Similarly, from quiet and informal patterns of collegiate physical endeavors, a huge intercollegiate sports structure has grown and flourished, and institutions have made intramural sports and individual and group fitness activities for college students universal.

In the first years of the twenty-first century, then, holistic higher education in America was at a paradoxical crossroads. Religion requirements, both curricular and as chapel attendance, were commonly abandoned except at strongly religious institutions. Yet research shows that college students wanted and sought spiritual sustenance at and from their schools. Physical education requirements, too, fell by the wayside even as institutions vied to construct the most impressive and state-of-the art fitness centers. Intercollegiate athletics became an ever bigger business, and the participation of women in wellness, intramural activities, and competitive sports expanded radically. It was—it is—for the education of the student as a whole, integrated person, the Dickensian best of times and worst of times.

INTERVIEW ONE

Dr. Richard Chess

Dr. Richard Chess works in honors as the Roy Carroll Distinguished Professor of Honors Arts and Sciences at the Asheville Campus of the University of North Carolina. He is an admired classroom teacher, a highly regarded and productive poet, and a thoughtful student of literature. Dr. Chess is also deeply interested in exploring a more holistic model of collegiate education, with a particular emphasis on classroom contemplative practices. I asked him to introduce himself briefly, including his connections to the spiritual and religious life of his public liberal arts university.

I earned my BA in Communications from Glassboro State College in 1976. I earned my MA and PhD from the University of Florida, where I worked on both my creative thesis (a collection of original poems) and my scholarly dissertation (a study of American-Jewish Poetry) under the direction of Donald Justice.

I have published three books of poetry. My work has been included in a number of anthologies, including *Telling and Remembering: A Century of American-Jewish Poetry*, *Best Spiritual Writing 2005*, and *Bearing the Mystery: 20 Years of Image*. I am currently at work on a book of prose (short essays) on the practice of reading the daily Psalms as included in Jewish liturgy.

I direct UNC Asheville's Center for Jewish Studies (CJS). I also serve as the advisor to our small Hillel group. At times over the course of my twenty-three years here, I have participated in meetings of a group of campus ministers. I am not a rabbi, not a minister; however, I do try to help Jewish students get what they need as Jews, sometimes by hosting them for Sabbath dinners at my home, sometimes by helping them establish relationships with local rabbis or other leaders of the Jewish community, sometimes by offering them guidance and financial support from the CJS for programs they develop or undergraduate research on topics related to Jewish civilization.

I am also deeply involved in a project of exploring the place and use of contemplative pedagogy and practice at UNC Asheville. I tend not to think about the potential spiritual values of these practices, but I know from talking to some of my students that they are very enthusiastic about the benefits—academic and other—they have gotten from being introduced to and given an opportunity to engage in these practices in class and out of class.

What, I asked, is your sense of the role spirituality can/should/does have in the public sector of higher education?

Rather than talk about "spirituality, I would like to talk about "spirit," as in the sense of an animating or vital principle in us. If it is not our responsibility, as educators, to awaken our students' spirits, then it is at least an opportunity we have, an opportunity that should not be missed. No less than the private sector, the public sector of higher education should and often does work to create an environment that encourages, stimulates, and supports the spirit of inquiry, an open-ended process that can, and sometimes does, lead to discovery, insight, and understanding. Of course, genuine inquiry involves risk, and risk includes the possibility of failure. By creating and sustaining a culture of inquiry, we in higher education offer students a place where they can inquire into the subjects in which they are interested as well as into the full range of inner experience.

Of course, there are methods of inquiry, different for each academic discipline, that students must be taught. Students can be evaluated on their ability to apply those methods skillfully to their investigations. But students can also be given the opportunity to explore their inner experiences of the process of inquiry, experiences that may include hope, confusion, frustration, fear, disappointment, determination, surprise, and satisfaction. They can be given guidance on how to inquire into these feelings as well as physical sensations experienced during the process of inquiry. They can be invited to consider the possibility that there might be some connection between their inner experiences—physical and emotional—and the external work of, say, collecting and analyzing data, examining primary sources, working in the field, or composing a poem. Guided by a skilled educator, students may come to see a connection between feeling or physical sensation and, say, thinking and communicating one's insights and ideas to others. They may find, in fact, that their understanding of or insight into something under investigation—say, the behaviors of a nomadic African tribe or the unfolding of a poem—may in some ways be shaped or limited by their emotional or physical responses to their engagement with the material.

Let me offer just one example from my personal experience in the classroom. In a class called "Readings in Poetry," I ask students to reflect, informally and in writing, on their experiences reading, for example, the work of Emily Dickinson. I give them an opportunity to admit to frustrations they have when they encounter lines or images whose "meaning" eludes them. I also give them a chance to say something about what gives them pleasure as they read Dickinson, Whitman, and other poets. When students report that they feel frustrated, that they cannot relate to the work of one poet or another, we then have an opportunity to examine their experiences of frustration—physically, emotionally, and intellectually—as well as their responses to the experience of frustration. By directing our attentions to students' actual lived experiences in working with sometimes difficult, demanding poetry, I hope that students might overcome a sense of inadequacy, a sense of alienation that will prevent them from learning to encounter deeply work that might initially seem alien to them. To get there, we have to look away from the work itself and direct our attentions instead to the actual experiences of those reading the work. And we have to resist the temptation of judging the students' actual experiences—pleasant and unpleasant, receptive and resistant—in response to the work at hand.

Whatever else might come of it, when students are given the opportunity to consider the means by which they come to experience and know something—the workings of their minds, hearts, and bodies—they may come to feel a sense of wholeness they had not experienced before in an academic setting. That experience of wholeness may be the very thing that excites and inspires them to keep exploring, keep inquiring, keep investigating.

What I am talking about here is creating an educational environment that takes a student's inner life into consideration, no matter what the student happens to be studying. It is unrealistic to expect that students can leave their inner life outside the door when they enter the lab or the classroom. It accompanies them wherever they go. So, it is something that should be worked with and can be integrated into a class in which students also receive guidance on how to read the tone of a poem or how to determine the economic and environmental benefits and costs of buying local food.

Inner life: spirit. Not soul, not the theologians' soul.

Spirit, enthusiasm. Enthusiasm: if not the experience of being possessed by a god, then a rapturous intensity of feeling, the kind of feeling that, once experienced, one wants to experience again and again. That is what we want to inspire in our students, or, to help our students discover for themselves: enthusiasm for learning—the whole process of learning.

One way to create the possibility that students will develop enthusiasm for learning is to validate their inner experiences as they attempt to master the material—to learn the methods, the primary sources, the theories, the procedures, the practices of our various disciplines. Validate their inner experiences and help them learn to work with those experiences, however challenging, unsettling, unnerving they may be.

Perhaps it is impossible to quantify the level of enthusiasm in students, the level of their spirited engagement with the work of inquiry. But, as Astin, Astin, and Lindholm have shown in their study *Cultivating the Spirit*, when a college student's inner life is engaged, when students feel a sense of purpose and meaning in what they are studying, they perform better academically: in exams, research projects, and other measurable ways.

Public colleges and universities could and probably should do more in the classroom itself—not just in student life or student affairs—to engage the whole student, to help students develop the skills to work effectively with their emotional and physical experiences, both of which contribute in significant ways to their ability to learn. Those emotional and physical experiences may even determine what can be known by any individual student.

So what about the spirit? The spirit, the enthusiasm for learning may come to life when students discover, in an environment created in part by faculty, the power of bringing their whole self to the project of inquiry.

Please focus on some ways in which this work is particularly relevant and/or valuable to honors students.

An honors class is the perfect place to experiment with designing and delivering courses that engage the whole student. In my experience, honors students arrive in the classroom with a certain amount of academic and intellectual discipline. The honors students I have worked with also seem to be engaged with ambitious academic projects as well as student organizations, community service, and many other worthwhile endeavors. These students are driven—as much by their personal desires to succeed as, it seems to me, by their sense of responsibility to others. Consequently, their calendars are full!

As wonderful as this is, it may also mean that these students have very little time and very few opportunities to reflect on what they are learning and what they are doing. This may be one reason why honors students in several classes I have taught recently have told me how much they value the practice of two, three, or even four minutes of silence with which I begin many classes.

I do give the students some simple instructions on what to do with these brief periods of silence. I invite them to close their eyes or soften their gaze. I ask them to direct their attentions to their breath, the physical experience of breathing, or to another strong physical sensation. I ask them to return their attention, once they notice it has wandered, to their breath or other prominent physical sensation: "Direct your attention, notice when it has wandered, bring it back to the original object of concentration." That's it. When the time is up, I invite them to spend a few minutes writing informally in their journals about what they noticed during the period of silence.

So many students have told me they look forward to coming to my classes in part because they know they will have an opportunity to settle in before we begin dealing with the course "content." They have told me that this simple activity enables them to pay closer attention to our discussions in class, closer attention to each other, and closer attention to the literary text or film or work of art under consideration. And with close attention comes, as they report, the possibility of new insights. Perhaps because they are so driven, honors students may need an opportunity for settling, directing their attention inward, and using informal writing for the purpose of self-reflection more than other students.

[*Note: I realize that some instructors may feel that such a practice takes valuable time away from other classroom activities more closely related to the formal content of the course. The counter argument, I suppose, is that forty-five minutes of high quality time is better than fifty minutes of distracted student attention. I have occasionally tried this with good results. I have also begun a few classes with several of minutes of physical activity—stretching or gently moving about with equally positive effects*—à chacun son goût.]

As the students learn to listen differently and more closely to one another, a result of the initial silent practice at the beginning of the period as well as a result of other contemplative exercises used during the class, they report feeling a greater sense of community among their classmates. This then enables them, so they say, to offer ideas and opinions in class that otherwise they might not have felt safe enough to share with others.

Honors students also may tend to be perfectionists. This commitment to perfection may result in a student's reluctance to take risks—intellectually, artistically. One student told me that she felt like a failure when doing the required brief meditations outside of class. Because she was an honors student and was unlikely to just stop doing this assignment, she had to figure out a way to get through this part of the class. So, she decided to just accept her failure, to give herself permission to fail as a meditator. What surprised and delighted her and her peers and me was how her willingness to allow herself just this one imperfection made it possible for her to turn in written work—original works of poetry and non-fiction prose—that she considered imperfect. And as soon as she was able to see her writing as imperfect, she became receptive to the practice of deep revision, a kind of revision that involves radical transformation of drafts of work-in-progress. She wound up as one of the strongest writers in the class. Her work went further than the work of some others because she was willing to risk everything in her revisions. Her experience with meditation transferred to her experience with writing.

I can offer many other examples of remarkable insights my honors students have gained as a result of being given an opportunity to and some simple guidance on how to explore their inner lives in the context of an academic course.

At the beginning of Edward Hirsch's *How to Read a Poem and Fall in Love with Poetry*, he recalls Nicolas Malebranche's maxim: "Attentiveness is the natural prayer of the soul." I think that in these honors classes, and probably in all of my classes, I am trying to teach students how to be more attentive, how to be more aware—both to things that they may find pleasant and reasonable and understandable, and comforting as well to things they may find unpleasant, disturbing, disorienting, strange, and maybe even threatening. Attention, the experience of paying attention, of giving one's entire attention to something: that gives one a sense of wholeness, which, as I said earlier, arouses the spirit.

Honors students in particular, given that they arrive at the university with pretty good academic preparation and motivation, may benefit more from the opportunity to move beyond merely wanting to do their best, to please their instructors, to earn the best grades, to master the material. They may find that learning to be, at times, less goal oriented in their work actually enables them to see more widely and deeply into themselves and the world around them.

Spirituality, then, may be experienced as a process, not a product: a process engaged in throughout their lives, not just in their churches, synagogues, temples, or mosques. Spirituality is not something to be attained. Nor does it lead to irrational, sloppy thinking. Though all students can benefit from such an understanding and experience of the spirit if not spirituality itself, honors students might be especially prepared to broaden their sense of what spirituality is and to discover that it can be an integral part of their academic lives.

CHAPTER 3

Mens Sana in Corpore Sano

The focus of this section is the physical and the ways in which physical cultivation interacts with intellectual growth and spiritual deepening. I begin with a personal tale.

AUTOBIOGRAPHICAL NOTE

When I was a little boy, I always wanted to be a gym teacher when I grew up.[31] Physical Education was my best and favorite class in grade school, and the vision of eternal vocational access to swimming pools, basketball hoops, indoor tracks, and trampolines seemed to me a glimpse of earthly paradise.

Like all such visions, alas, I outgrew this one sometime during high school and my early college days at Grinnell. My sweaty Eden receded and was eventually replaced by a tamer and more scholarly career. Locker rooms became library carrels; gym classes turned into PhD seminars in "Problems in Shakespearean Biography"; track meets were transmuted into the race to complete a dissertation on Jacobean tragedy. I became not the burly recreationalist of my boyish fantasy but a professor of Renaissance drama, then an honors director, a chief academic officer, and finally the chancellor of two fine public liberal arts colleges.

Childhood aspirations die hard, however. In the midst of my administrative career, I had the opportunity to fulfill my old wish: I taught my first gym class.[32] Being a gym teacher (at last!) was a rewarding and instructive venture for me. Here are some reasons why.

Faculty who see students exclusively in classroom-related activities know these young adults only in a very partial way. This observation is, of course, a truism, but it is one that is more commonly apprehended rationally than emotionally or behaviorally. Educators affirm this fact, but most of the time they do not truly act as if it was either true or relevant. So, for example, when instructors say student X is "quick," or Y is "slow," they are referring to the speed with which they learn facts or grasp abstract concepts. Out on the track, "quick" and "slow" mean very different things, and sometimes the student who is quick in one of these settings is not in the other.

In my class, it turned out that some of the high-achieving scholars in the classroom were not only less physically talented, but they were also less physically inventive, creative, imaginative, and clever learners. I developed a respect for some students' kinesthetic intelligence, students who, in the circumstances in which I would normally have come to know them, would not have attracted much favorable attention from their instructor. Moreover, I saw how some classroom superstars were far from leaders outside the intellectual circles in which I usually taught them.

Both of these revelations are helpful and humanizing. This experience helped me to learn to appreciate and to interact more comfortably and positively with students whose primary gifts are non-intellectual. Also, I more easily understand the self-image and peer image of students whose principal gifts are scholarly.

Of course, not only did I see students differently but, perhaps even more importantly, their perceptions of me altered dramatically as well. All teachers are somewhat two-dimensional characters to their pupils, and upper-tier academic administrators even more so. A sharp shift of context is a fine way to upset this ultimately unproductive, fragmented, and dehumanizing view. Suddenly, I became not only someone who knew the name, date, and locale of the first theater built in Elizabethan England or who could control administrative budgets or decide the fate of errant students: I became also a fleshly creature who owns and wears ugly T-shirts, who sweats when it is hot and shivers when it is cold, who curses when he steps into a puddle, and who could derive an intense and wholly irrational joy from a fast last lap. Because all these characteristics are true and are important to my nature, I am able to be a more effective teacher and administrator if those with whom I am working grasped them. Parker Palmer suggests throughout his book *The Courage to Teach* that we teach who we are, and one of the things I am is an athlete.

As a PE instructor, I consorted with other gym teachers. This interaction gave me an increased understanding of and feeling of collegiality with a little-known but universally present campus constituency. It turns out that pedagogical problems and puzzles exist in the PE Department just as they do in the honors program.

How, for example, is one to grade fairly a class that focuses upon a physical activity? Should one give an "A" to the fastest runner? The one who is most improved? The one who worked hardest? What the heck does an "A" mean in a running or racquetball or swimming class, anyway? These are hardly new issues, but they are ones that most faculty members rarely think about in the context of the field house. But the issues are real, and physical education professors are thinking hard and carefully about them as teachers, advisors, and members of a college community. How different are these questions from those I ask myself as a literature teacher? Do I reward the students who came into class so far ahead of their fellows that they finish the course still ahead of them, even if they have not done much or learned anything (not an unfamiliar problem in honors)? What does an "A" mean in a Shakespeare class? Some physical educators, certainly, are not intelligent or sensitive or diligent. Surely the same could be said of instructors in philosophy or physics or English. By and large, most of my co-workers in the gym were thoughtful, caring, hardworking, intelligent, and engaging women and men, and I was thankful for an opportunity to get to know them better.

Finally, and most importantly and surprisingly to me, my stint as a jogging teacher presented me with an opportunity to live up to an institutional promise too often "more honored in the breach than the observance," the promise that colleges teach *values*. Institutional statements of purpose or mission often proclaim that they seek not only to make students more knowledgeable, but better men and women. I found that my gym class was an excellent forum for that lofty goal. I saw my students learning important things about the following values:

- *Diligence*. The successful inauguration of a personal fitness program demands and rewards persistent, steady, consistent, and continued attention to clearly defined goals.
- *Hard work*. Joggers and other fitness participants certainly have a direct opportunity to learn the virtues of working hard. They quickly understand the ethical axiom that the fruits of one's labors are usually in proportion to the effort one chooses to apply to them.
- *Courage*. My students learned something, I am pretty sure, about the ability to override pain or embarrassment, and they learned to do a thing they were afraid to do.
- *Honesty*. Certainly, a physical education class teaches some clear lessons about honesty, the most basic of academic values. When ten or fifteen folks are running together, there is no way to disguise the moment one has to stop or drop back. If students have not done their "homework" consistently in an activity class, there is no way to "BS" through a test of cardiovascular fitness.

Some other worthwhile academic and human characteristics also come to mind as being cultivated in this setting: modesty, realism, a sense of pace, and time management. These values are perhaps simpler than those that emerge from a close reading and discussion of *King Lear* and because they are simpler, they are perhaps less fully true to the complexity of human psychology and social interaction. I would not, however, be dissatisfied if all the graduates of America's honors programs and colleges were diligent, hard-working, courageous, cooperative, honest, and straightforward.

Michael Allen Gillespie, the Jerry G. and Patricia Crawford Hubbard Professor of Political Science at Duke University, notes that informal, intramural, and intercollegiate sports can teach the values of skill, hardness, stamina, courage, loyalty, rule-abidingness, justice, moderation, endurance, and teamwork (298ff).

My enthusiasm for this new pedagogical role was, of course, controlled and finite. I did not permanently transition from being a teacher of Renaissance drama or an academic administrator to serving as a jogging coach, nor would I particularly encourage (or discourage!) my colleagues to contemplate such a shift. My experience as a physical education teacher, however, did for me what any good class should do for students and instructors: it changed and broadened my view of myself, my students, and my world. It enlarged my sensitivity to some of my fellow humans and expanded my appreciation of the multiplicity of their talents and potentials. It taught me much about the interpenetration of the intellectual and the physical. And I never had to wear a tie.

NEUROSCIENCE AND EXERCISE

Since antiquity, there has been a general belief that physical and mental cultivation go together, that there is something mutually reinforcing about bodily vigor and intellectual acuity. Only quite recently, however, has some fascinating and intriguing scientific research demonstrated compelling links between these aspects of human nature. It turns out, to put it bluntly, that hard physical exercise can make people smarter! Popular science writers have broadcast that conclusion. Barbara Strauch writes: "In one rigorous study after another, exercise has emerged as the closest thing we have to a magic wand for the brain" (126). John Medina concurs: "Exercise can result in a sometimes astonishing elevation in cognitive performance" (14). This discovery, that physical fitness and mental achievements are related, challenges some contemporary stereotypes: that intellectuals tend to be inactive; that people who work hard physically are not bright; that there are those who work with their brains and those who work with their muscles and never the twain shall meet. These stereotypes have had some impact on the image of honors programs and honors students, both from within and from without. Of course, a visit to the swimming pool, fitness center, or racquetball court at noontime at any college or university would already do much to dispel these biased notions, but now actual evidence confirms that quite the opposite is true. Moreover, that evidence comes both from animal experimentation and from research on human subjects. Clearly, this link should be of keen interest to all educators, including honors educators at the college level.

One line of research has been pursued by Scott Small, MD, a professor of Neurology at Columbia University (ctd. in Strauch 127–128). Small and his co-researchers disproved a central dogma of neuroscience, namely that the brains of adults are, in effect, finished, and while they can lose capacity, they cannot add to their fixed structure. In other words, the number of brain cells was fixed in adulthood. When Small and his colleagues put a group of mature laboratory mice on a regimen of regular, rigorous aerobic exercise and then injected them with a chemical dye that tracks the creation of new brain cells, or neurogenesis, they discovered dramatic activity. Exercise was stimulating the creation of these new cells. The control group of mice, which did not exercise, produced only half as many new cells. Small remarked, "To see it so clearly, new brain cells that came with exercise, it was impossible to ignore" (qtd. in Strauch 126). He goes on to note that once exercise was clearly linked to the formation of new brain cells, his colleagues dashed off to put on their sneakers (ctd. in Strauch 126). One commentator, Gretchen Reynolds, in the *New York Times* sums up: exercise "prompts the brain to remake itself" (Reynolds). In another related study, Henriette Van Pragg and her co-researchers conclude: "Our findings demonstrate that voluntary running [of mice] results in long-lasting survival of BrdU-positive [brain] cells, improved performance in a water maze, and a selective increase in dentate gyrus LTP [long term potentiation]" (Van Pragg, "Running Enhances").

Where do these new cells come from, and how does exercise stimulate their creation? New brain material is generated in an area of the brain called the "dentate gyrus" (a locale that sounds to this non-scientist as though it should produce spinning teeth), which is a region of the hippocampus particularly associated with the ability to remember things. Neurogenesis is stimulated by substances such as epidermal growth factor (EGF) and fibroblast growth factor (FGF), but in the adult brain, these substances do not easily cross from the brain's blood vessels into the brain itself. Exercise appears to enhance the number and size of those blood vessels and to make them more permeable to the neurogenetic chemicals, thus enabling the brain to create new neurons.

Does this link between exercise and neurogenesis really work? Does exercise not only produce an observable boost in brain cell growth in lab animals, but also make them smarter? Here, another important laboratory experiment conducted by Fred H. Gage is illuminating.[33] Gage, like Small, is a highly respected academic scientist; he is Adler Professor at the Salk Institute for Biological studies in California, a past president of the Society for Neuroscience, a fellow of the American Association for the Advancement of Science, and the recipient of numerous prizes and awards. Gage and his research team took two groups of genetically identical mice, allowing one the opportunity to exercise and depriving the second group of that benefit. Then they gave both groups the Morris water navigation test. In this experiment, mice are put into a container of murky water that is over their head; the murky water hides a platform that is invisible to the swimming mice but enables them to stand up. The experiment is used in a variety of settings to test memory and cognition: how long does it take the lab animal to find the platform in the second and subsequent dunkings? Does the animal easily remember where the escape is located and swim directly and quickly to it, or does the bedraggled rodent have to find the platform by randomly swimming about all over again? What Gage and his group discovered is that the mice that exercised performed far better than their genetically identical siblings on this test. This result demonstrates conclusively that exercise made the mice smarter: they could think faster, and they had better memories (Gage). Gage concludes: "If more people knew that . . . exercise can increase the number of neural connections in specific regions of the brain, thereby improving memory and reasoning ability, they would take better care of themselves" (Gage).

If college students were just swimming around, looking for, and needing a resting place, previously engaging in exercise would have been beneficial to them. Of course, they are not. Obviously, conducting this sort of experiment on the brains of fit humans is not possible and is inappropriate, to say the least, but other experiments, both in the laboratory and in the field, have produced similar results. At Columbia University, Reynolds reports, the neurogenesis researchers made use of a type of MRI machine, called a "functional MRI," that can measure blood flow as well as the size and shape of the brain. A group of test subjects, male and female, aged 21 to 45, embarked upon a guided exercise program. After 12 weeks, the researchers found that their blood flowed at a much higher rate to the hippocampus, where neurogenesis takes place. The scientists hypothesized that that heightened blood and oxygen flow was facilitating the creation of new neurons (ctd. in Reynolds). At the University of Illinois, Charles H. Hillman and his colleagues produced similar results: they tested high school students before and after a hard workout on a treadmill. They found that both reading and math scores rose significantly (Hillman et al.).

Finally, in what is perhaps the most practical test of the exercise/cognition link, Central High School in Naperville, IL, with a population of about 3,000 students, launched an extensive, and carefully documented, program of cardiovascular fitness for all its pupils. This program is documented at some length in John R. Ratey's *Spark*. He notes that at a time when too many school systems are trying to save funds by dropping or reducing physical education, the Naperville system has profoundly enhanced student performance by going in exactly the opposite direction. For several years and across the student population, scores in the basic skills of reading and math have risen dramatically. Gym for the Naperville students no longer consists primarily of games of skill such as baseball or volleyball; it requires sustained fitness exercise. Students have a choice of activities, but they are graded NOT on how good they are at some sport, but by how hard they work at it. They are issued heart-rate monitors that record how much they challenge themselves. Thus the well-coordinated natural athlete who can hit and throw better than anyone in his or her class might fare less well than the uncoordinated, somewhat overweight student who really works at a fitness activity. What is measured and rewarded is value added rather than innate talent. Not surprisingly, the Naperville program has received national attention, for example appearing on ABC News in April, 2010, in a story entitled (perhaps unfortunately) "Bikes, Balls in Class: How Phys. Ed Transformed One School" and subtitled "Flab is Down, Scores Up at Illinois High School That Puts New Emphasis on Physical Education" (Wright and Siegel). The Naperville program was also featured on PBS, on a segment available on YouTube (YouTube). Mary Carmichael's article in *Newsweek* magazine proclaimed: "Kids with the fittest bodies were the ones with the fittest brains" in the Illinois test (Carmichael). Ratey sums up this research:

> Exercise improves learning on three levels: first, it optimizes your mind-set to improve alertness, attention and motivation; second it prepares and encourages nerve cells to bind to one another, which is the cellular basis for logging in new information; and third, it spurs the development of new nerve cells, from stem cells in the hippocampus. (53)

While much of this research, according to Stanley J. Colcombe et al., promises to be useful in a wide variety of areas such as recovery from brain injuries or disease and Alzheimer's disease research, the primary interest here is its implications for higher education. About a half-century after most colleges and universities ceased requiring students to exercise regularly, hard scientific evidence suggests that regular exercise makes them better students. Does that mean that colleges need to reinstate the old gym requirements? Hardly. But the evidence does mean that this connection should not be ignored by those people working in higher education.[34] Given what scientists have discovered, merely making available to students intercollegiate athletics, intramural sports, and fitness opportunities is inadequate. Institutions of higher learning must cultivate some middle ground where students are strongly motivated to engage in physical exercise and are given a range of attractive opportunities to do so. Here are a few suggestions:

- Set aside some time in the daily/weekly academic schedule of the entire institution specifically for exercise. If, for example, from 11:00–12:30 MWF were designated the "activity period," a range of activities could be made available during that time: pick-up basketball or volleyball games, bike rides, runs of various distances at various speeds, and open lap swim. Perhaps more importantly, this exercise period could be made into an institutional cultural imperative: nothing else would be scheduled during those times—no committee meetings, no classes, no office hours, and no departmental or administrative conferences. Nobody would be required to exercise during the activity period, but doing anything else would be frowned upon.

- Institute a more modest variation for honors colleges or programs: designating some particular times for physical activity, such as Tuesday and Thursday evenings from 8:00 to 9:30 and/or Saturday morning from 10:30–12:00, and making available some attractive facilities, like the swimming pool or volleyball court, for honors students at those times. Perhaps a weekly baseball, basketball, or volleyball game could be scheduled at one of those times. Some honors programs/colleges have formed intramural teams to compete against other campus units.

- Encourage faculty and staff to exercise. Students frequently seem surprised to find faculty members in the campus fitness facility. All university staff, including everyone from the grounds crew, housekeeping, and food service to the president and provost, could be given release time to exercise; if this arrangement is impossible at the institutional level, perhaps the honors program or college can be a testing ground for this initiative. Giving honors staff three one-hour periods each week, over and above lunch hours, to be away from the office for exercise would produce a powerful model for students, and it might have such a positive effect on efficiency and morale that it would outweigh any time lost. If honors deans or college presidents told their students that they were going on a 3-mile jog every morning at 7:30 and anyone who wished could come along, surely some would. People who work at colleges and universities tend to see themselves as outrageously busy, and, indeed, their days are full, but they could be encouraged to re-set their priorities to make regular exercise an essential feature of their lives, not an extra.

- Give credit for exercise. Perhaps every college and university in America could offer students one credit hour towards graduation each year they affirmed that they had exercised, say, 50 times during the academic year. This practice, at maximum, might amount to four credits out of some 120–130 required, which is not an outrageous expenditure for better brain and body health. If only a few students on every campus took advantage of such an offering, that would mean that thousands were improving their fitness each year.

- In a somewhat similar venture, easily copied, the University of Indianapolis offers students the chance to earn, through its kinesiology department, a healthy diploma, which combines fitness with diet/nutrition, instruction, and counseling. Students sign up for the program during their first or second year, and those who complete its requirements are awarded the certification. The University of Indianapolis contends that, in addition to promoting better physical health and fitness, this program will help students improve their GPAs and make them more employable since prospective employers know that fit workers cost less than couch potatoes. Nothing would prevent an honors program or college from offering some sort of similar wellness certification (University of Indianapolis).

- One mechanism that does not seem to have worked very well was Lincoln University's requirement that any student with a Body Mass Index (BMI) over a certain level (30) had to take an exercise course to graduate. Students felt that this was intrusive, reports Jennifer Epstein in the online journal *Inside Higher Ed*, and they were unenthusiastic about it. Indeed, according to Jacqueline Seaton and Nicole Lockley, writing in Lincoln's student newspaper, the criticism was "fierce," and the faculty subsequently overturned the decision (Seaton and Lockley). In general, the carrot works much better than the stick when it comes to exercise and fitness. (See the discussion of Lincoln's experience below in Chapter 5.)

- Improve facilities and access. Many colleges and universities have built state-of-the-art exercise facilities in recent years, often as recruitment incentives. This development is positive, but many schools, particularly smaller ones, have quite restricted hours for facilities such as swimming pools or weight rooms. The slight cost of increasing hours by hiring a few extra minimum-wage student workers would be a price worth incurring. A few schools have experimented with, for example, setting aside all or part of their cardiovascular health-club facilities for special groups such as residence halls, clubs, or staff and students focusing upon weight loss at certain hours of the day or night. Perhaps the honors program could be one such group. At larger campuses, placing a few exercise machines like treadmills, stationary bikes, or elliptical machines in locations other than the central campus exercise area could encourage students to take a few minutes for some activity without trudging all the way across campus to check into the gym.

- Pair fitness activities with course work. Perhaps an honors seminar discussing Chaucer's *Canterbury Tales* should take a vigorous walk. An honors psychology class on testing and measurement could conduct its own experiments on exercise and cognition. At many Christian colleges, students and teachers begin each class with a few moments of prayer;

could one not also begin each class with a few minutes of exercise?

- Expand competitive opportunities in fitness sports across campus. Adding intercollegiate opportunities is expensive, but in some sports such as cross-country, swimming if a pool already exists, or soccer, the expense does not hold a candle to football. Between intramural sports and intercollegiate ones are so-called "club sports," which are almost always quite economical, can be offered in a huge range of areas, and might involve only a few competitions with nearby schools in any given year. Many young women and men enjoy competition, but they are not eager, during their college years, to make the commitment to regular intercollegiate athletics. Club sports would attract those students. At the very least, any institution could make it clear that it encouraged, assisted, and supported student efforts to launch such endeavors.

FACULTY AND FITNESS

Unfortunately, some preliminary studies are showing that those who work in the academic world, who should cherish most deeply and understand most profoundly these links between physical vigor and mental acuity, are neglecting their own bodily welfare. Two Canadian research scientists from the University of Victoria, Megan A. Kirk and Ryan E. Rhodes, have studied the fitness habits of new assistant professors. They cite the "vast array" of benefits of a physically active lifestyle, including reduced risk of many chronic diseases, improved psychological well-being, an overall lower risk of mortality, and reductions in work-related burnout and stress, reduced absenteeism, and, especially, improved focus and concentration (Kirk and Rhodes). When 267 assistant professors responded to their survey, Kirk and Rhodes discovered that only 30.7% were meeting the activity level of 20–30 minutes of moderate-to-vigorous physical activity on most days of the week. That figure compares to 49–54% in the general population of individuals in the same 25–44 age group (Kirk and Rhodes). Young faculty, pressured to move forward in their profession and simultaneously often beginning family life, decreased their physical activity by, on average, two days per week upon making the transition from graduate school to professional life. The characteristics that distinguished those who continued fitness activity from those who did not were attitudinal. Kirk and Rhodes report that those who believed that physical activity took time from other obligations and that it was a hassle or an inconvenience stayed away; those "who expected exercise to complement and enhance their work-life balance were more likely to continue with exercise" (Kirk and Rhodes).

The researchers conclude by reaffirming that physical activity leads to positive physical and mental outcomes, including work productivity and performance. They make a number of recommendations for young faculty:

- Accumulate 20–30 minutes of exercise daily.
- Find an activity you enjoy doing.
- Take a 10-minute walk break at lunch.
- Park your car far away and walk the rest of the way to work.
- Bike to work.
- Enroll in a fitness class with colleagues.
- Engage in a fun fitness competition with colleagues.
- Enter a charity run.
- Incorporate physical activity in time spent with your family.
- Establish a support system that encourages being active. (Kirk and Rhodes)

Dan Berrett, reporting on this research in *Inside Higher Ed*, suggests that this Canadian research has drawn the attention of some American professors. Thus, for example, the blog "Tenured Radical" of April 29, 2011, contains some comment about the study and several reactions, mostly from younger faculty members citing and lamenting the difficulty of maintaining physical wellness while building an academic career. Two distinguished American scientists suggested that these findings resonated with their experience and anecdotal information. Dale. R. Wagner, president of the American Society of Exercise Physiologists, notes that he has "observed the same pattern in university professors in the U.S.A." (ctd. in Berrett). And Cathy A. Trower, research director of the Collaborative on Academic Careers in Higher Education at Harvard, has surveyed assistant professors and noted that many talked about stress, weight gain, and the lack of time for healthful activities (ctd. in Berrett). This research suggests that if academics wish to encourage their students to adopt and maintain a healthy holistic model of living that balances mental and physical activity, they need to make sure that they model that balance in their own busy daily schedules.

SPORTS POSITIVES

When most Americans think of physical challenges at colleges and universities, they do not think of work programs or wellness/fitness opportunities. They think of Knute Rockne and Michael Jordan. They think of New Year's Day football and Final Four basketball: intercollegiate athletics.[35] Although colleges and universities develop and support intercollegiate athletics programs for many reasons, some of which are quite pragmatic, many reasons also exist for viewing such development and support with suspicion. At Division III schools, often a quarter to half of the student body is engaged in competitive athletics, compared to percentages more in the 1-in-15 student athlete ratio at major Division I powers.[36]

Anecdotally, these fractions apply, at least roughly, to honors programs at small and large institutions as well.

Sports programs help with student recruiting, including honors student recruiting, which is certainly a pragmatic, fiscal rationale for maintaining them. On the other hand, they can be incredibly costly in many ways, including in time commitment and raw dollars: one of those things most college faculty members do not really want to know is what it costs just to outfit each of 40–80 football players, much less coach them, transport them, and feed and house them. Of course, the central mission of colleges is not fiscal well-being: it is education. Thus the question becomes: what is it that young women and men learn during their athletic careers? Since many schools see their enterprise as *liberal learning*, what sorts of liberating collegiate experiences might colleges be providing their student athletes to reinforce or complement the learning that goes on in the honors seminar, laboratory, library, faculty office, or elsewhere in the extracurriculum? One major and important caveat: the positive lessons of college sports will occur when a sensible, balanced, and appropriate institutional perspective on the relationships between athletics and academics exists and where strong, solid collegiate leadership from presidents and provosts, athletic directors, and coaches steadily affirms that productive link. When institutions lose that good sense and leaders do not seek and reward it, positive results are unlikely, and negative ones can readily take their place.

Two benefits and lessons from athletic careers are obvious. Everyone declares that participation in sports teaches young people (and older ones, too) the value of teamwork and the value of hard work. While agreement appears universal, perhaps a slightly more nuanced way to think about these two lessons is necessary.

Teamwork

One truism of contemporary culture posits that much of the work being done is actually teamwork. Lone scientists hatching astounding discoveries in isolated labs, brilliant corporate executives making millions of dollars on their own, solitary medical practitioners, these are all probably pretty anachronistic or at least rare. Even college teachers and administrators cooperate on some things, some times. Athletics teaches individuals how to work in groups. Obviously, this quality varies from sport to sport. The teamwork component of a volleyball or basketball team is much more ambitious than that of a wrestler or cross-country runner. Of course, many faculty across many disciplines have discovered that the practice of dividing their classes sometimes into small groups and having students work on class activities together is valuable. All human beings are, finally, as Vladimir Nabokov reminds readers in *Speak, Memory*, prisoners of their own solitary consciousness, pounding on the walls of their individual cells, trying to make connections with each other. Studying history or literature or psychology or evolution helps; so does playing soccer.

Hard Work

All educators want honors students to understand that easy accomplishments are often cheap and that hard work is often necessary to do things that are truly valuable and important. Athletics certainly requires and rewards working hard. Steve McNamara, a regional director for the Fellowship of Christian Athletes, stresses that a principal spiritual value of competitive athletics is that it challenges students to maximize their abilities, to learn what it means to be "all in," to live up to their expectations for themselves.[37] Competitive athletics demands a particular kind of work: persistent and consistent labor. No one becomes a good distance runner by working out once every few weeks, no matter how hard. No good pitcher goes very long without throwing the ball. Just as a violinist or a dancer or a reader has to practice, practice, practice, so too do athletes. Here, remembering the lesson of Milo of Crotona, who is well known to all college athletes, is valuable. Milo was the ancient Greek wrestler who trained for the Olympics by picking up and carrying a baby bull the same distance every day for four years. At the end of the four years, and in time for the next Olympic competition, the bull was huge, and Milo was powerful and victorious. Athletics teaches that persistence trumps irregular flashes of brilliance or labor.

Below are three more lessons from college sports:

Talent Diversity

College athletics provide a stark reminder that very few people are good at everything, and almost everyone is good at something. As I remarked at the beginning of this chapter, when I taught a fitness class it was an important revelation to me that students I knew from the classroom as "quick" were sometimes "slow" on the track, and some students who were not sharp at literary analysis were smart indeed when it came to physical conditioning. Chaucer writes that "God clepeth folke to him in sundry wise, / And everich hath of God a proper yifte. . . . " (WBP 102–103). (God calls folks to him in various ways, / And everyone has from God his own gift. . . .) Even Michael Jordan was not much of a baseball player.

Human Capacities—Part 1

Competitive sports can teach everyone, athletes or spectators, the amazing capabilities of the human creature. It can be astonishing and inspirational to witness the strength of a linebacker, the leaping ability of a volleyball spiker, or the endurance and speed of a runner. The athletes who are willing to work hard and persistently learn what they are capable of, and it is often far more than they would have dared believe. Those who watch them grow and improve from year to year are equally awestruck as they reach higher and higher goals that might never have been imagined possible a few years ago. Liberal learning should teach the admiration of humanity: William Shakespeare's or Jane Austen's brilliance with character and language; Albert Einstein's expansion of the understanding of the way the universe works; Ludwig van Beethoven's music and Michelangelo's art; Charles Darwin's and Jane Goodall's insights into the structure of life. To grasp and understand and revere what women and men are capable of is one of humankind's joys. Sports help.

Human Capabilities—Part 2

Perhaps the ultimate lesson of college sports is that all human capabilities are, finally, limited. One of the key lessons of Shakespeare's most majestic tragedy, *King Lear*, is that, at the end, everyone is only a "poor, bare, forked animal" (3.4.106–107). Next to British Renaissance drama, athletics is the best teacher of this lesson. In this imperfect and broken world, even the best people are ultimately frail and flawed. Even as people admire Roger Bannister for breaking the four-minute mile barrier, people realize that nobody will ever run it in three. Nobody is ever going to pitch only no-hitters. Seeing 41-year-old Dana Torres in the Beijing Olympics was wonderful, but she could not make the team for London. College athletes test how much they can do and how good they can become; what they can achieve is remarkable. But it is even more important that they learn the great, tragic, and wonderful liberal lesson of our common flawed humanity. Nothing can be learned in college that is more important than universal human nature: that people can achieve great things and that they will always be imperfect. Indeed, it is only in recognizing human limitations, I think, that people can push so close to them as to become only a little lower than the angels. One can find that recognition and that push in a great college basketball game, in an all-out finish at a cross-country meet, or in a wrestling match or a volleyball game where nobody has anything at all left at the end. College sports, like *The Canterbury Tales* and *King Lear*, can teach what it means to be human.

SPORTS NEGATIVES

Of course, the preceding section focuses on a positive and, unfortunately, only partially accurate depiction of collegiate athletics. Intercollegiate athletics can do much for colleges and for athletes, but not all of it is always good. There have been a number of well-researched, scathing indictments of university sports.[38] One of the most cogent statements of the case against big-time athletics was written by Gary Bell, the former honors dean at Texas Tech University. Bell makes the following arguments:

- Intercollegiate and professional sports have become "one of the true catastrophes of American culture" in that they have turned us into "a society of observers" rather than participants. (61)
- Only a very small minority of collegians participate in varsity athletics—at Texas Tech, 350 out of 30,000. (62)
- Universities spend obscene amounts of money supporting athletics that might better be spent on academics. Bell notes

that at Texas Tech, the athletic budget jumped to $54 million in 2009, not counting a campaign to build a $25 million addition to a $100 million stadium, a new $65 million basketball arena, and a new baseball field. All this expense occurred at a time when the academic budget has been cut by 10% in two years. (63)

- Rather than encouraging positive school spirit, athletics fans have become rowdy, irresponsible, alcohol-fueled hooligans. (63)

James L. Shulman and William G. Bowen have argued that abuses such as these are not the exclusive problem of large universities with national-level programs of big-time intercollegiate sports. Writing about elite liberal arts colleges, they contend that "intercollegiate programs in . . . academically selective institutions are moving steadily in the direction of greater intensification, increased tension with core educational values, and more substantial calls on the tangible and intangible resources of their host institutions" (172). Critics of the NCAA, now the dominant governing body of intercollegiate athletics, observe that report after report has documented efforts at reform for nearly a century and have warned against the commercialization of college sports. Despite these reports, Thelin protests that the NCAA has been able to do little or nothing to curb "the excesses of recruitment, athletics scholarships, and special privileges as corruptions of the student-athlete ideal" (*Games* 197).

Gillespie notes three influences on contemporary American sports. The Greek tradition emphasizes "radically individualistic" competition and the development of a semi-religious heroic ideal (300). The Roman model was quite different: for Roman citizens, "the only appropriate physical training was military and sports were left to slaves" (301). Finally, sports in nineteenth-century Great Britain, including those at Oxford and Cambridge, aimed to cultivate vigorous outdoor activity. They were predominately team-oriented, and their goals included team play, sportsmanship, and strict adherence to rules (Gillespie 302). While lauding the potential for ethical learning in college sports, Gillespie deplores their

"Romanization," in which "the university even begins to market itself not as an academic institution but as a sport experience," and resources are diverted from academics as well as informal and intramural sports to intercollegiate athletics (311).

The College Sports Project (funded partially by the Mellon Foundation) studied the academic performance of student athletes at NCAA Division III institutions: eighty-four institutions participated, of which 24 were highly selective colleges (College Sports). Information on over 83,000 students was collected. This research showed that, in terms of GPA, athletes "underperform": they earn GPAs below what would be predicted in comparison to non-athletes (College Sports). Males underperform more dramatically. Recruited athletes underperform at a higher rate than walk-ons. Non-recruited athletes of both genders have slightly lower GPAs than non-athletes, and the disparities among recruited male athletes are highest at the highly selective colleges. Retention statistics, however, show that student athletes persist at rates comparable to their non-athletic peers (College Sports). I have not seen any comprehensive information on the academic success of honors students who are varsity athletes, but this would be fascinating material to collect.[39]

A valuable philosophical perspective on intercollegiate athletics is provided by Dr. John DeGioia, writing as President of Georgetown University. He suggests that two models of human excellence contend in the realm of athletics and in the university setting generally. What DeGioia calls the Aristotelian model "holds that human excellence is best understood as a balance, an integration, of the various dimensions of our humanity" (56). Those dimensions include the physical, intellectual, artistic, communicative, emotional, religious, and moral. The second model, which DeGioia terms the "Nietzschean" ideal, suggests "that human excellence is best demonstrated in boundary-breaking achievements. . . . This form of excellence requires that one sacrifice well-roundedness and harmony to the focused, unyielding pursuit of truly unprecedented discovery or performance" (56). Major universities have pursued the Nietzschean model particularly in major sports such as basketball and football. DeGioia observes that major research universities similarly pursue that model of human excellence in the realm of faculty research by seeking professors who will push beyond the limits of prior knowledge in the areas of their expertise. He suggests that overall universities encourage both these models and that managing this philosophical conflict is a major challenge of contemporary universities (58).

Surely, the record of intercollegiate athletics is mixed. Competitive sport has the potential to contribute much to students and to institutions. College sports can teach cooperation and teamwork, it can reinforce the importance of hard and persistent labor, and it can teach much about human potential. At the same time, abuses in college sports, especially in the most visible sports, have certainly often worked against the highest aspirations of American colleges and universities.

INTEGRATIVE DISCIPLINES

One development that testifies to the interest of today's college students in matters of the mind, body, and spirit is the popularity of various integrative disciplines, mostly of Asian origin. Literally hundreds of American colleges and universities now offer courses in such practices as yoga, taekwondo, karate, kung fu, and tai chi. Many of these disciplines involve both an exercise component and a meditative element.[40] The varieties of venues in which such work is offered are fascinating. Some are housed in academic departments, some in extracurricular clubs or programs, and some in student life.

Sometimes these offerings are part of the Physical Education Department, for example at Cornell University, which offers a PE course in tai chi (*Physical Education*).[41] Sometimes classes are offered through college or university health centers, like the one at the University of Minnesota Twin Cities Boynton Health Center or the Medical Wellness Center of the University of Miami. The honors program at the University of North Carolina Asheville has appointed a term-endowed professor, Richard Chess, with the goal of bringing contemplative practices into the honors classroom. (See the interview with Chess above.) Often instruction in these disciplines is available, like the yoga course taught at the University of Wisconsin, Milwaukee, through continuing education or an adult education division. A class entitled "Tai Chi: Spirituality in Motion" is offered by Southern Methodist University's Perkins School of Theology (Southern Methodist). At the University of Maryland, the medical college offers medical professionals a course described as follows:

> We know how hard practicing medicine has become—how the hand holding, the personal touch, the one-on-one connecting that first inspired us to work in the health care profession has gradually been pushed into the broom closet. . . . That is why we hope you will join us in the Healing Pathways class. We will bring you back to a deeper sense of peace, balance and comfort that will benefit you and your ability to help your patients. (University of Maryland)

At other colleges and universities, student clubs sponsor the study and practice of these disciplines. This is the case at institutions as various as Rice University, the University of Chicago, Ohio State University, Hope College, and Wheaton College.

In virtually all of these cases, the attraction of these practices clearly involves a combination of physical activity (poses or movements), spiritual cultivation (meditation, philosophical outlook on life), and mental education (mindfulness or centering the mind). They stress helping practitioners to achieve a balance of mind, body, and spirit, often by using carefully controlled bodily exercises with an inward focus on mental processes and spiritual self-awareness. Although these disciplines differ, at the simplest, broadest, and most general level they share a core belief that through activities designed to heighten attention and focus on one's body, mind, and spirit in the undistracted here and now, one achieves internal balance that leads to personal peace.

WORK

There are a number of programs and some thoughtful research on the subject of *work*—that is, hard, physical labor—and its relationship to cognition. In this section, I examine one stimulating study of restaurant work by Mike Rose, Professor of Social Research Methodology at UCLA's Graduate School of Education and Information Studies, and then look at one college, Deep Springs College, that has made work programs an important part of its overall undergraduate educational offerings.

Working as a waitress at family restaurants may seem quite remote from the honors classroom, but Rose's "The Working Life of a Waitress," originally published in the journal *Mind, Culture and Activity*, suggests that the distance is not as far as it may appear. My curiosity about Rose's work was stimulated by an interview on the National Public Radio program *Speaking of Faith*, broadcast on 7 January 2010. The article focuses upon the career of the author's mother, Rose Emily Rose, who worked as a waitress for much of her adult life. The essay is in one sense a personal homage, but it is also a scholarly study of "the cognition involved in various kinds of work" (3). A blending, from the author's perspective, of reminiscence and science, the study relies upon the author's personal observations of the working life of a waitress, interviews with Rose Emily Rose and other waitresses, and a thorough review of the scholarly literature on subjects like "expert memory." Rose describes in some detail the cognitive demands of the work of a waitress:

> Consider the restaurant in terms of multiple streams of time and motion. Customers enter with temporal expectations: They will be seated without much delay and, once seated, a series of events will unfold along a familiar timeline, from ordering through salad, entrée, dessert, delivery of the check. Their satisfaction—physical and symbolic—is affected by the manner in which these expectations are met. But, of course, customers are entering the restaurant at different times, each with his or her own schedule, so tables (or places at the counter) proceed through meals at a different

pace. This staggering of customers facilitates the flow of trade, but also increases the cognitive demands on the waitress: what she must attend to, keep in mind, prioritize, etc. This situation intensifies during peak hours, for the number of customers expected can be estimated, but not known—family-style restaurants do not take reservations—and if the numbers swell beyond capacity or an employee calls in sick, is late, or quits, then, as the younger waitresses I interviewed vividly put it, you're "slammed," abruptly pushed to the limits of physical and mental performance.

Another timetable kicks in as soon as an order is placed with the cook. Different items have different prep times, and once the item is prepared, there is a limited amount of time—quite restricted for hot items—during which it can be served. As well, the serving area needs to be cleared quickly so that the cook can deliver further items. The waitress, therefore, is aware of the kitchen as she moves among her customers.

Finally, both the waitress and the management work by the clock. Profit is related to time; the quicker the turnover, the more revenue for the company, and the greater the number of tips. There can be exceptions to this principle for the waitress (but not the management); for example, the regulars who may hold a table or stool longer but tip more. Still, generally, the waitress—like her manager—is ever mindful of clearing a plate, closing out a tab, moving the process along. Imagine these streams of time and motion as co-occurring and related but not synchronous. Any given customer may hem and haw over an order, or want a refill while the waitress is occupied, or send an item back. The cook may deliver a waitress's hot dish while she is in the middle of taking an order and is being summoned by two other customers. Tables may be full with variously contented customers while the manager feels the press of new customers gathering inside the door.

> [Rose reminds us that] no matter how efficiently designed the physical layout of the restaurant, the waitress's motion will be punctuated by the continual but irregular demands made of her. For example, all requests for coffee do not come at the same time or in regular intervals. So one request comes during an order, and another as she's rushing back to get extra mayonnaise, and another as she's clearing a table. The waitress must learn how to move efficiently through a vibrant environment that, for all its structural regularities, is dynamically irregular. A basic goal, then, is to manage irregularity and create an economy of movement. She does this through effective use of body and mind. The work calls for strength and stamina, for memory capacity and strategy, for heightened attention, both to overall configuration and specific areas and items, for the ability to take stock, prioritize tasks, cluster them, and make decisions on the fly (5–6).[42]

Rose notes the exceptional demands upon memory that this work creates: features of the menu and foods, orders, names and characteristics of repeat customers, routines, and physical layout of the restaurant itself. He reports on several techniques, including "visual, spatial and/or mnemonic techniques" that his mother developed to facilitate these complex tasks (12). He notes the relevance of various psychological studies of attention to the particular demands of this work. The cognitive requirements and skills of waitressing are inseparable from the nature of the job itself; the physical labor and the mental skill are not two distinct aspects of the profession: they are unified. Rose writes:

> Evident throughout this article is the fact that the waitress's thinking is situated in a complex, interlayered physical-social-economic field of activity. Her memory skill and other cognitive processes—attending, sequencing and clustering of tasks, etc.—are functional and purposive, both emerging from and structuring her work. (10–11)

Rose observes that American culture would define the work of a waitress as a relatively unskilled, lower-class occupation but concludes, convincingly, that "skill, like intelligence, is a socially constructed notion," and that "without the cognitive dimension, the service provided by the waitress would be impossible" (13).[43]

Rose concludes, then, that this physically demanding work entails mastering important cognitive skills, especially memory and attentiveness; that it teaches and enhances those intellectual abilities; and that success in this work is directly related to complex thought processes. Surely the same could be said for other kinds of physical labor. The automotive mechanic who diagnoses the causes and cures of some car problem, which likely baffles the PhD car owner, has learned a complex process of posing and testing various solutions to a problem. That process replicates what professors would call, in the classroom if not the garage, critical thinking. The pipe fitter learns how to envision, in the abstract, before he or she actually touches a pipe, the most direct and efficient plan for connecting, say, a source of water to the point of its utilization such as a fountain.[44] Good work involves good thinking; good thinking can result from good work. This lesson is certainly relevant for educators whose work is helping young women and men to become more skilled thinkers.

WORK COLLEGES

Some American colleges have tried to build educational programs that combine physical work with intellectual activity. At several institutions, like Berea College, Warren Wilson College, and Blackburn College, the initial impetus of such programs was fiscal: having students do a significant portion of the labor necessary to build and maintain the campus or having students engage in money-making ventures, such as agriculture or crafts or hotel operations, keeps the costs of attending low, thus enabling students of modest means to attend.[45] In every case, however, the work element has grown to be more than a pure financial arrangement. It has become integral to the overarching educational philosophy and goals of the colleges.

Deep Springs College is both highly idiosyncratic throughout its program and emblematic of the ways in which physical labor can connect to high academic achievement and a spiritual quest. The college was founded in 1917 by a wealthy and entrepreneurial business man, L. L. Nunn, who had worked with the Westinghouse Company to develop long-distance transmission of alternating current electricity needed for mining operations in the American West (Deep Springs College). Nunn founded, in addition to Deep Springs, the Telluride Association, which today maintains houses on the campuses of the University of Michigan and Cornell University. Nunn's educational goal was to produce men who would be intelligent, creative problem-solvers, self-motivated, capable, and physically and technologically skilled. (Deep Springs decided to admit women in 2011.) Thus, Deep Springs College rests on three pillars: academics, labor, and self-governance. To the founder, these pillars were deeply linked to a spiritual base. In the 1923 Deed of Trust establishing the legal organization of the institution, Nunn writes that its purpose is "the need and opportunity for unselfish service in uplifting mankind from materialism to idealism, to a life in harmony with the Creator . . ." (Deep Springs Board). Elsewhere, in a letter to the students of the college, dated 5 April 1921, the creator of the college writes, in a comparison that may strike some as immodest, "The purpose of Deep Springs, as identical with the purpose of God, which is the well-being of the universe, must be recognized" (Deep Springs Letters). In a brochure written in 1957, an anonymous description of the college affirms that each student

> can come to understand himself better at Deep Springs and thereby can further his understanding of his relations to his fellow-men and to his creator. . . . In short, he can further to an unusual degree his progress toward maturity and wisdom, toward high achievement tempered by a sense of obligation to God and to man. (Deep Springs Brochure)

The same brochure notes that students "should develop a high sense of spiritual values." Today, students and staff tend to see the founder's overtly religious emphasis as somewhat anachronistic;

nevertheless, some of the students continue to meet for Bible study one evening a week.

The college is tiny by almost any collegiate standard: there are about twenty-six students and three regular continuing faculty members, supplemented by a handful of rotating temporary teachers. Students attend for two years. The academic qualifications of Deep Springs' students are impressive: they would more than satisfy the entry profile of any honors program in the country. On average, they present a verbal SAT score in the upper 700s and a math score of about 700. Over the past ten years, Deep Springs graduates have completed their undergraduate careers at some of America's most prestigious institutions: 16% have transferred to Harvard, 13% to the University of Chicago, 7% to Yale, and 7% to Brown. Thanks to the founder's endowment and subsequent gifts, all Deep Springs students attend with a full scholarship, regardless of need. The academic year, which is the whole year, is divided into six terms of about seven weeks, and students are expected to be on campus for 11 of the 12 terms of their two years. The academic program, not surprisingly, stresses small, intense courses.

The labor program at Deep Springs is primarily agrarian, but with some significant additional community work, such as maintenance, repairs, and cooking. The college maintains, with student labor, a garden with over 100 rows of organically raised vegetables, a farm that cultivates 152 acres of alfalfa, and a herd of 300 cattle. Maintaining such an operation is demanding, both physically and in terms of time commitment: for example, feeding the cattle has to be done very early in the morning before the remainder of the day's activities begins. As a general rule, students attend class in the morning and work on the ranch in the afternoon. Students work a minimum of 20 hours per week.

The mission and goals of the labor program were reviewed and rearticulated in 2009. The revised Mission Statement notes that "the labor program creates a distinct pedagogical environment" that helps "develop in each student the character, skill, maturity, accountability, and leadership that is essential to the school's mission of educating effective servants to humanity" (Deep Springs

Forum). A series of goals are articulated. The work program seeks to help each student develop

- An honest understanding of himself;[46]
- A good work ethic;
- A positive community membership;
- Self-reliance;
- Problem-solving ability;
- Technical skills;
- A high level of stewardship;
- A perspective on labor and its role in society;
- A perspective on service to humanity. (Deep Springs College)

Clearly, Deep Springs' labor program is deeply and thoroughly integrated with a concern for the spiritual development of its students (self-understanding, communitarianism, service to humanity) and the intellectual work of the college (problem solving, skills acquisition, stewardship of nature). A former faculty member at Deep Springs, Dr. David Schuman, who is now a judge on the Oregon Court of Appeals comments:

> The work program serves two purposes: first, to introduce some practical thinking into the abstract, idealistic, and theoretical frame of mind that bright college students naturally cultivate; and second, to demonstrate in tangible ways that we all depend on each other. The academics and the work are not hermetically sealed from each other. The aspiration is that they inform each other. ("Re: Deep Springs")[47]

D. Schuman writes that Deep Springs is set against the more common collegiate tendency to create "an environment that isolates and fragments the individual" ("Education" 133). He asks, "Why can't college education . . . take place in an environment that not only allows, but that demands moral, ethical, and emotional growth? An environment where values must be discovered and tested as part of everyday life?" (134).

Honors programs and colleges are unlikely to launch work programs like that of Deep Springs, Warren Wilson, or Berea, and most do not particularly hope that their graduates aspire to careers as waitresses. But honors has grown deeply involved in service learning and volunteerism in recent years, and at the very least, seeing the service aspect of such endeavors as involving serious physical labor might be worth considering.

A popular book of the early 1970s was the feminist classic created by the Boston Women's Health Book Collective: *Our Bodies, Ourselves*. The pages above certainly testify to the wide range of ways in which our physical selves interact with our intellectual and spiritual natures in the collegiate context. From gym classes to brain chemistry to the cognitive demands of blue-collar jobs to university athletics to meditative disciplines to work colleges, the body is, in fact, an inseparable aspect of the whole self. Not surprisingly, during the college years and through the experiences at college, many people move from youth to adulthood. They enter university as teens and depart as grown-ups. A core element of that maturation is the care and cultivation of the self as a physical creature. Singh Khalsa Gurucharan, a member of the faculty at MIT, who also happens to be a Sikh minister, sums it up: "We can no longer separate thought to a rarefied mental realm and the body to an earthly prison" (Khalsa Gurucharan 155).

INTERVIEW TWO

Two Honors Student-Athletes: Natalie Pearson and Heide Overton

Here are some contrasting comments by two outstanding student-athletes. The first, Natalie Pearson, was an international student who excelled in track and field. Her comments reflect a largely secular perspective. And yet, she sees her athleticism as "a kind of faith." The second student, Heide Overton, speaks from a deeply religious point of view. She grew up in a clerical family, and it is clear that a traditional Christian faith is deeply important to her. Both of these women were exceptional honors students as undergraduates as well as accomplished varsity athletes.

NATALIE PEARSON

In July 2011, Natalie Pearson, University of North Carolina Asheville (UNCA) senior sprinter, was named the Female Student-Athlete of the Year by the NCAA Division I Big South Conference. She is the first athlete in the university's history to win the female honor. Pearson is a native of Sheffield, England, and was the only Big South Conference women's athlete to qualify for the NCAA track meet. In the Big South Conference championships, she won the 100-meter dash and the 200-meter dash. Pearson was also named to the United States Track and Field Cross Country Coaches Association All-Academic Team. I asked Ms. Pearson to tell me about her background, her athletic record, and her ideas about the connections between sports and studies.

I grew up in Sheffield, England, which is in South Yorkshire. There I played field hockey and netball. I started running because my parents both ran and my mum used to take me to the track when I was little.

By the time I had finished my A-Levels, I didn't really know what I wanted to do at university. A friend from my track club was recruited to go to America to run, and she gave me the information as to how to go about it. I had four schools show interest, but UNC Asheville sounded the nicest. I got on really well with the head coach, and he sent me some really nice pictures of the area including the [Blue Ridge] Parkway, which immediately made it my mum's favourite choice. Haha. So I guess I came because it looked the prettiest! (Don't judge me!!!)

I am a member of the honors program. My majors are Literature and Mass Communication with a journalism concentration. My GPA is 3.64 right now, and I graduate this May [2011]. I think looking back at both my majors, Appalachian literature sticks out in my mind as a favorite area of study, and seeing as though UNCA is in Appalachia, I find it fascinating. I had no idea to what extent coal mining is damaging the area until I started studying the literature, and because I wrote my thesis on stereotypes in Appalachian literature, it definitely holds an important place in my heart! I also work for the school newspaper as the Sports Editor, and I really enjoy sports writing and the design aspect of laying out newspaper pages.

I do the sprints in track—the 60m and 200m indoors, and the 100m and the 200m outdoors (unless the coach blackmails me to do the 400m). I started doing multi events when I was small, but I eventually narrowed my events as I realized I probably could jump further than I could throw, and I always won the sprint races. So I have specialized in the sprints for as long as I have been a competitive athlete. I have been lucky to have a wonderful coach here, and so I have managed to accomplish a lot of things I am proud of. I got to race in the UK Olympic trials three years ago, which was an awesome experience! Since then, and probably my biggest accomplishment was qualifying for the NCAA Div. I Outdoor Track and Field Nationals last year in the 200m. I got to fly to Eugene, Oregon, (Track Town, USA!) and being there was awesome. Track is such a big deal there, and I was so proud to be representing our school in a competition only 24 athletes for every event get to compete in. I will never forget racing at Nationals, and I hope I get to do it again this year!

I work out for about 17–20 hours a week for track, 4 hours or so Monday, Wednesday, and Friday; 2 hours Tuesday and Thursday; and then about 2 hours over the weekend. The 17–20 hours per week is mainly from August to June. Normally, I finish competing in June because I go home to compete in some of England's meets too. After I finish competing for the year, I take three weeks completely off, which is when I normally go on holiday or fly out to see my boyfriend and then one week of alternative sport. This is my OFF off season when I go on holiday for a week, or fly out to see my boyfriend play baseball (and eat cheesecake). Then, it transitions into the off season, which is when we train but don't compete—I get back into regular training hours here. Track is weird because you literally can't afford having a lot of time off. Three weeks is probably the most because you start losing fitness after two, and then speed after four. Track transitions a lot more from season to season than other sports, so my training volume is always pretty high. But in the first month I usually get the weekend off. So those weeks I may only be practicing 15 hours or so.

I think being an athlete has helped me tremendously in my academics. Being a competitive athlete who has received success, I understand the concept of working hard and working towards goals. From track I have learned that hard work pays off, and the benefits always outweigh the cons for every task. I have also learned how to manage tasks, prioritize workloads, and manage my time. Being so busy all the time never lets me take the foot off the gas, but

I find that I can do my best work in this situation because I always have a clear schedule and definite to-do list—I never have time to be lazy and wasteful. I also always want to be the best I can, and that applies to my school work as well as track. Finally, track has taught me how to push myself, which is incredibly helpful when dealing with deadlines and enormous, daunting projects. I let people down when I don't give my best in track, and so I have transferred this attitude into my academics also.

I do have to make sacrifices when it comes to missing certain classes or field trips, but I can always make up lost time and my grades haven't suffered either. Making sacrifices is something that comes in the territory of track and field, and so I have learned to realize what is important and what is not so important. I do get tired, but again, I know that my hard work pays off and have evidence to prove it, and so I always look to the positive in every instance. Time pressures can get a little stressful, especially when it comes to the end of the semester when I have back-to-back class, meetings, group projects, track practice, etc. to go to, but everything seems to work out, and I never remember the stressful things in the end.

I am definitely not a religious person, nor do I really see myself as a spiritual person, but I am certainly an open person. I think there can be a spiritual dimension to anything in the world, be it athletics, work, or school, but I don't think it's absolutely necessary. It's personal preference. For me, I feel being spiritual or religious serves as motivation for people, but I get my motivation from *people*. I value the importance of good relationships between people higher than anything else, and I know that I couldn't have achieved as much as I have without the help of others.

I once read an article about Willie McCool, one of the astronauts who died on the *Columbia* spacecraft. He also ran, and he said that he believes "every one of us has some sort of faith and the trick was in recognizing it, in seeing it." This really stuck with me, and for me, being a competitor in track is my faith. I give it all I have, and it gives me back happiness. In turn, I can relate this to academics, and I feel like being an athlete has grown my intellectual capacities enormously. I wouldn't be complete losing either one of them. I am open to the world around me and encourage new experiences, instead of being defined by a religious group or depending on only ideas to help me progress.

I guess I think running and working out serve as something like meditation in the sense the focus is entirely on my body, what is the next step athletically, and learning how far I can push myself every day. But it is not tranquil or peaceful exactly. I always have to be sharp, listening to what my body is saying and learning to adapt to it. Having said that though, going to practice every day serves as a little break from whatever else is going on. I can retreat from stressful school work, annoying situations, complicated relationships, etc., and just focus on what I need to do. Running is something I want to be good at, and so I am willing to invest a great deal of energy into it. Even if I'm having a bad day at the track, it still serves as a place that's different from everything else. Like a little island of track and field! Investing so much energy into it has taught me to understand myself better. I have learned how to control my emotions, how to listen to when something isn't right in my body, how to push myself through pain, how to respond to criticism, how to adapt to the criticism, and all these things relate to life in general and academics.

I feel like track has taught me how to be in tune with how I feel, and I understand that what goes into my body, or how I treat it, affects the output it gives back to me. For example, if I eat nothing but ice cream a week before a meet, I'm going to run slowly. At the same time, I have learned from this that if I stay up all night, working on something I could have done two days ago, I am not only going to run badly, but I am going to do badly on whatever I am working on. Finally, I think the nature of working out helps me solidify my goals. A lot of the time when you are running, you are at one with your thoughts and no one is there to disrupt them. There's something supernatural about running and thinking, maybe it's being surrounded by the outside? Maybe it's because you can feel so much power that you are creating through your strides? But it helps me organize my priorities and concentrate on my goals and the steps needed to achieve those goals.

I have enjoyed school tremendously, but I think five years of higher education is quite enough (haha). I am definitely continuing my athletics with my coach. My target is to make Great Britain's Olympic track team over the next few years. *[Natalie competed in the tryouts for both the 100 and 200 meter sprints for the London Olympics, and she did credibly but did not make the team, alas.]* I also would love to combine my academics and athletics and work in the field of sports communications. I have a couple of paid internships for the summer, one of which is for our school's athletic sponsor, and so I hope one of them will unfold into something full time. I also hope that I get sponsored for track to help me accomplish my goals. I plan to run for at least another 3 or 4 years, getting my international vest for GB, and then I would like to start a family with my boyfriend. And so in a few years, I would like to have a bit more freedom so I can start a new chapter with him (not intended to be cheesy! Haha). I also still love literature, and so I have toyed with the idea of being a literary critic, but I think that job is a dying breed, sadly, so we will see what happens!

HEIDE OVERTON

Heide Overton is a 2011 honors graduate of the University of New Mexico in Albuquerque. She was an outstanding athlete and an outstanding student. She is currently attending medical school. Here are some of her thoughts on the ways that athletics, faith, and academics connected during her undergraduate experience.

I was born in Cortez, CO, and moved to Durango a mere ten days later for my dad to become the minister of a small Christian church. Durango was where I first fell in love with Jesus, first learned how to ski, went hunting, rode horses, and spent lots of time with family. We moved to Carlsbad, New Mexico, when I was four years old so my dad could become the pastor of a church there. Carlsbad was the place where I grew in my faith, started playing soccer and softball, learned how to swim, attended kindergarten through second grade, and made my first friends. We moved to Gallup, NM, when I was eight years old, again so my dad could pastor a church there.

Gallup became our home and my true roots. I played soccer, basketball, and softball throughout all of grade school and middle school and became very involved in church activities. The older I got the more I decided to focus on what was important to me. I chose soccer as my predominant sport and, while I stayed involved with other sports, it was my focus. My goal was to play soccer in college so I joined a club soccer team in Albuquerque (130 miles from Gallup) and traveled twice a week for practice and games during the spring season. We attended elite tournaments and camps, and I became a better goalkeeper. I was the four-time MVP of my varsity high school soccer team, but my senior year provided a choice between sports and academics. I began receiving full-ride academic scholarships for college but none for soccer. This made my choice easy, and I accepted my position in the Combined BA/MD Program at the University of New Mexico.

Within my first week of college, I was asked to try out for the rugby team. The structure of the team as well as the benefits of staying physically active contributed greatly to my early academic success in college. However, I had to have two shoulder surgeries in two years as a result of injuries sustained playing rugby so I quit playing rugby after my sophomore year. The end of my rugby career was timely because my junior year as an undergraduate required more focus and time than the previous years, especially in preparation for the MCAT. I remained involved with the rugby team as an honorary coach and enjoyed teaching new players all that I had learned about the game. My faith remained at the center of my life during this time and was my foundation and motivation for both school and athletics. I graduated Summa Cum Laude from UNM and received a scholarship for medical school. After my first month of medical school, I have returned to playing recreational soccer when I have time to gain the benefits of exercise and competition. I thank God every day for all the blessings in my life and live each day to glorify Him.

I absolutely believe there is a spiritual dimension to both athletic and academic work and success. There are two Bible verses that I strive to live my life by that have influenced this belief. The first is Colossians 3:23, which states: "Whatever you do, work at it with all your heart, as working for the Lord, not for men." The second is Matthew 5:16: "Let your light so shine before men, that they may see your good works and glorify your Father in Heaven." These verses are my motivation to work hard in everything I do. The understanding that I am working for the Lord in the classroom and on the field gives me the foundation and perspective I need to find value and worth in every endeavor. Thus, I do things in excellence for the glory of God, not for the praise or approval of men. My hope is that people will see the good things I do and give glory to God for his loving-kindness and faithfulness towards us. My spiritual development is therefore the primary influence of my physical and intellectual development.

CHAPTER 4

College Spirit

THE SPIRITUALITY OF TODAY'S COLLEGE STUDENTS

Understanding and putting into perspective the importance of spiritual development in higher education necessitate recognizing the spiritual nature and needs of today's college students, including, of course, honors students. The college years, observes Andres G. Nino, are "a time which produces a fundamental turning point in the life cycle as young adults move away from parental homes and fairly well-defined roles and frames of reference into rather uncharted territory where they begin to build a provisional life structure" (48). A century ago, people generally assumed that most college students were solid, practicing Christians, perhaps with a smattering of non-believers and other-believers. As Chapter 1 noted, today, encountering assertions of just the opposite predisposition is not uncommon, although, as we shall see, often with no supporting evidence. For example, Riley cites the "spiritually empty education of secular schools . . . the sophisticated ennui . . . the intellectual relativism of professors and the moral relativism of [students]" (*God* 214). Similarly, in Page Smith's popular attack on higher education in the 1980s, he castigated what he called the "spiritual aridity" of American campuses (20).[48] Of course, others, such as C. John Somerville, have refuted this assessment of American colleges and students.

Happily, an understanding of the spiritual proclivities of American college students and their teachers no longer needs to rest upon anecdote, political inclination or polemics, thanks to Astin, Astin, and Lindholm and to the research of the Higher Education Research Institute at UCLA and its "Spirituality in Higher Education" project to study and describe the spiritual status of contemporary students. The HERI team did not seek to prove that offering college students opportunities to deepen their spiritual lives would cause them to have greater success in their classroom endeavors; however, they do establish a convincing correlation between those activities that enhance students' sense of spiritual nourishment and those that enhance academic achievement. The pedagogical practices that encourage and allow students to grow spiritually are also those that increase the odds of academic success, and those same practices tend to be those that characterize honors programs and honors work.

The Spirituality in Higher Education project began with a pilot survey of 3,700 students in 2003, followed by a full 2004 survey of 112,000 first-year undergraduates at 136 colleges and universities. A subset of 15,000 of these students completed a follow-up study at the end of their junior year in 2007. Examining the findings of the Spirituality in Higher Education project is helpful for understanding why and how cultivating the spiritual development of today's college students is a vital aspect of holistic higher education. Although several brochures, electronic sites, and presentations have reported on the results of the project, the definitive documentation is the 2011 book by Astin, Astin, and Lindholm, *Cultivating the Spirit: How College Can Enhance Students' Inner Lives.*

To reiterate its key definition, the project defines "spirituality" in the collegiate population as the "inner" aspect of students' lives, the "big questions" such as "Who am I? What are my most deeply felt values? Do I have a mission or purpose in my life? Why am I in college? What kind of person do I want to become? What sort of world do I want to help create?" (Astin, Astin, and Lindholm, *Cultivation* 1). It is "the values that we hold most dear, our sense of who we are and where we come from, our beliefs about why we are here—the meaning and purpose that we see in our work and our life—and our sense of connectedness to each other and to the world around us" (*Cultivating* 4). Spirituality can also refer to "such things as intuition, inspiration, the mysterious, and the mystical" (*Cultivating* 4). Although, the authors note, for many decades spirituality and religiosity were more or less the same thing, they are now usually understood to be different. Religiousness currently implies "adherence to a set of faith-based beliefs (and related practices) concerning both the origins of the world and the nature of the entity or being that is believed to have created and govern the world" (*Cultivating* 5). Many faculty members, however, "associate spirituality with religion, and since most of our colleges and universities are secular, they assume that spirituality (religion) has no place in the academic environment, except possibly as a subject . . . in departments of religious studies" (*Cultivating* 6). It is my personal experience that a great many of my faculty colleagues, some of whom I know to be deeply spiritual and/or religious persons, are very uncomfortable discussing or contemplating such matters in the context of their professional lives.

Students come to college with high expectations in these matters:

> More than eight in ten report that 'to find purpose in life' is at least a 'somewhat' important reason for attending college (half say it's a 'very important' reason), and two-thirds of new freshmen say that it is either 'very important' or 'essential' that college 'helps you develop your personal values' and 'enhances your self-understanding.' (*Cultivating* 3)

The study found that, while students' level of formal religious engagement declines somewhat during the college years, "their spirituality shows a substantial growth" (*Cultivating* 10). And, even more revealing, "that spiritual growth enhances other college outcomes, such as academic performance, psychological well-being, leadership development, and satisfaction with college" (*Cultivating* 10). Key experiences such as study abroad, service learning, and interdisciplinary work contribute to student spiritual growth (*Cultivating* 10). Note, once again, that these are *exactly* the experiences that often characterize the curriculum and extracurriculum of honors programs and colleges.

The pilot survey enabled the research team to devise a set of queries that would yield key information in ten areas, five in the realm of spirituality, five having to do with religion. The paragraphs below briefly highlight the study's findings.

Spiritual Quest—searching for meaning and purpose. This measure assesses the students' interest in finding answers to "the mysteries of life, attaining inner harmony, and developing a meaningful philosophy of life" (*Cultivating* 20). For students who score high on this measure, seeing answers is an important reason to go to college: 71% indicate that "finding my purpose in life" is either a "very important" or "essential" rationale for university enrollment (*Cultivating* 30). This search for purpose and meaning grows stronger during students' careers: "At the end of their junior year in college, students are more inclined than they were as entering freshmen to rate 'integrating spirituality in my life' as 'very important' or 'essential'" (*Cultivating* 31). The research team concludes "that for many young adults questions of meaning and purpose become increasingly more salient over the course of their undergraduate careers" (*Cultivating* 31). Among the factors that increased students' search for meaning and purpose were professors who "encourage them to explore questions of meaning and purpose" (*Cultivating* 37). An important finding is that 62% of students "report that their professors 'never' encourage discussions of religious/spiritual matters" (*Cultivating* 37). Students were unanimous in not being receptive to being directed by their professors about what to believe on spiritual matters; in fact, "many students seemed to presume that faculty members characteristically have little, if any, interest themselves in these matters" (*Cultivating* 38).[49]

Equanimity. Do students feel at peace, centered, able to deal with hardship, believe each day is a gift: do they feel good about how their lives are going? The study team began with the sense that "equanimity was something that highly spiritual people were likely to exhibit" (*Cultivating* 49). They thought about actual people exhibiting that trait, such as the Dalai Lama, Nelson Mandela, and Coretta Scott King, all of whom seem "characterized by calmness, serenity, centeredness, and seeming imperturbability" (*Cultivating* 49). I would observe that one could find many examples of highly spiritual people, such as Martin Luther and Sir Thomas More, who do not exhibit this trait. They also noted that this characteristic is not the same thing as passivity, placidity, or complacency; indeed, individuals embodying this quality are often highly engaged and effective social activists. The study found that students with high equanimity scores achieve better grades in college, report higher levels of psychological well-being, and are more satisfied with their college experience. Scores on the equanimity measure increased during the college years: 19% of entering first-year students scored high on this item; 23% had the same result after the third year (*Cultivating* 53).

The major facilitator of students' sense of equanimity was inward-looking activity: meditation, prayer, or self-reflection. The study found that about one in six college students meditate at least several times a week; half never meditate at all (*Cultivating* 54). This characteristic is further strengthened by leadership training, student groups, and group projects in class, which leads to the conclusion that "equanimity appears to be enhanced by engaging in group activities that have constructive ends" (*Cultivating* 59). One such group activity that led to a 15% increase in this measure was participation in intercollegiate football or basketball (*Cultivating* 59–60). It seems to me possible to explain this correlation by a link between demanding physical activity, which is an outlet for anxiousness and stress, and the reinforcing support of being a member of a close-knit team. Students who score high on equanimity study more hours per week than those who do not, although which of those factors is cause and which is effect is not clear. Are students who study diligently more likely to increase their equanimity, or do students whose equanimity grows then tend to study more? What is revelatory to note here is the correlation of students' sense of spiritual centeredness and their heightened study habits for students engaged in intercollegiate sports.

Ethic of Caring. This measurement is of students' "degree of commitment to values such as helping others in difficulty, reducing pain and suffering in the world, promoting racial understanding, trying to change things that are unfair in the world, and making the world a better place" (*Cultivating* 20). The ethic of caring measure assesses *feelings*, not deeds. The study found that this aspect of spiritual development shows the most growth during the college years, with 14% of entering students scoring high on this quality and 27% of the juniors. Women score higher than men, but the amount of growth is just about the same. At evangelical institutions the initial level and the final level are both higher: "growing from 17% of students who scored high as freshmen to 33%" (*Cultivating* 66).

Charitable Involvement. This item measures such activities as participating in community service, charitable financial donations, and helping friends with personal problems (*Cultivating* 21). It is the behavioral counterpart to the Ethic of Caring measure. Overall, this item slightly declines during the college years, from 12% receiving high scores, to 9%, but with some variance between different activities. So, while the percentage doing volunteer work goes down, those helping friends or donating money to charity goes up (*Cultivating* 70). Twice as many women as men score high on this measure, both as first-year and as third-year students. Students at all kinds of institutions except evangelical campuses show an overall decline in charitable involvement during the college years, perhaps, the research team speculates, because they just become too busy as college students (*Cultivating* 69–70).

Ecumenical Worldview. This measure indicates "the extent to which the student is interested in different religious traditions, seeks to understand other countries and cultures, feels a strong connection to all humanity, believes in the goodness of all people, accepts others as they are, and believes that all life is interconnected" (*Cultivating* 21). (See the discussion later in this chapter of religious pluralism.) Here, too, growth occurs between the first and third years, with 13% of beginning students scoring high, and 18%

in that bracket by the end of the junior year (*Cultivating* 67). Particularly dramatic is that on the item "understanding other countries and cultures": 42% of entering students consider this objective very important or essential, and 54% do so as juniors (*Cultivating* 67). Again, women score higher than men, but both genders show about the same growth during the college years

The study found a positive correlation between several college experiences and the development of the three measures of "spirituality in practice" (*Cultivating* 72–4). These include majoring in "more person-oriented fields" such as the social sciences (*Cultivating* 73); interactions with faculty who favor a student-centered pedagogy (again, a characteristic of honors classes) and encourage student spiritual exploration (*Cultivating* 76); meditation and contemplation (*Cultivating* 77); living on campus (*Cultivating* 79); and interdisciplinary courses and studying abroad (*Cultivating* 80). The research team reports on an as-yet-unpublished study that finds "that meditation enhances cognitive and academic performance, assists in the management of academic-related stress, and contributes to the development of the 'whole person'" (*Cultivating* 77). The one behavior that had a negative impact in all three areas was watching television (*Cultivating* 79–80).

The religious life of college students shows some similarities and some important differences to their spiritual development. Most of today's college students enter higher education with strong religious backgrounds: 80% "attended religious services during the year prior to entering college . . . ; more than three-fourths (77%) say they believe in God . . . ; and more than two-thirds pray" (*Cultivating* 83). The study measured three aspects of religiousness: religious commitment (an "internal" quality measuring the extent to which students' religious beliefs play a central role in their lives); religious engagement (an "external" measure involving religious behaviors such as attending religious services and praying); and religious/social conservatism that weighed such items as students' opposition to casual sex and abortion and their commitment to proselytize. (84).[50] They found little change in the level of religious commitment, with a strong correlation between externalized behaviors of religious engagement and internal commitment. The activities associated with declines in this characteristic are playing video games, consuming alcohol, and partying, but here again causation may move in either way: students may party more if they lose religious commitment, or vice versa. Religious engagement, especially attendance at religious services, "shows a steep decline during college" (*Cultivating* 89). The rate of frequent attendance at religious services declines from 44% to 25%. Overall, other aspects of religious engagement also decline but in a less dramatic fashion. The level of religious and social conservatism also declines during the college years. So, for example, 48% of entering students oppose abortion, but only 40% of the third-year respondents. Similarly, in the initial survey, 55% of students disapproved of sex between people who have only known each other for a short time, but by the third year, the level of disapproval had dropped to 48% (*Cultivating* 92).

The study proposed a number of factors to explain some of these findings. These include denominational preference, with the highest levels of engagement being shown by Baptists and Mormons and the lowest levels occurring among Buddhists, Jews, Unitarian/Universalists, and unaffiliated students. One denomination, Islam, showed an increase in frequent attendance at religious services. College type, not surprisingly, had an effect upon measures of religiousness, with evangelical colleges showing the strongest levels of religious engagement.

The project examined issues of religious struggle for college students. For many of them, these years "are a time for reflection about one's faith: What do I really believe? What is the meaning of life? Why is there suffering, evil and death in the world?" (*Cultivating* 101). Overall the percentage of students scoring high on measures of religious struggle rose from 9% for entering students to 13% for the third-year respondents. Increases were shown in students' struggle to understand evil, suffering, and death; in questioning their religious beliefs and feeling disillusioned with their religious upbringings; in feeling distant from God; and in "feeling unsettled about spiritual and religious matters" (*Cultivating* 103). Rising levels of religious struggle were seen at all kinds of institutions, with the highest increase at evangelical colleges.[51] Certain majors, particularly in the humanities and social sciences, seem to increase the likelihood of such struggles, as do such common honors experiences as study abroad or interdisciplinary courses, which, obviously, expose students to perspectives different from their own. The research also uncovered a "strong positive association between Religious Struggle and Charitable Involvement" (*Cultivating* 107). Perhaps the experience of helping those suffering or in need intensifies questions of divine mercy, goodness, and loving-kindness.

The final characteristic measured by the project on Spirituality in Higher Education was religious skepticism. That skepticism is negatively correlated with religious commitment and engagement is not at all surprising. During the college years, the research uncovered, religious skepticism in college students shows very little overall change. About one fifth of students, first and third year, score high on these items (*Cultivating* 109). Religious activities and participation in football and basketball reduce religious skepticism. It is increased by "partying, alcohol consumption, watching television, study abroad, participation in ROTC, and having parents go through a separation or divorce" (*Cultivating* 112). The researchers are puzzled by the ROTC association. Finally, the report notes the dramatic difference between religious struggle and religious skepticism: "highly skeptical students tend to be nonreligious, students who are heavily engaged in a religious struggle are often highly religious" (*Cultivating* 113). Thus students at evangelical colleges show a sharp increase in religious struggle during the college years but a decline in religious skepticism. In my personal experience, both as a teacher and a student, many college professors see as a part of their mission imbuing their students with a healthy dose of skepticism.

The researchers also investigated the practices that lead to spiritual growth in college students and how those practices influence traditional indicators of academic success.[52] The research revealed: "When it comes to the college GPA, the most striking finding concerns the spiritual quality of equanimity: when college students show significant growth in equanimity, their GPAs tend to improve" (*Cultivating* 119). Several of the academic practices that enhance students' equanimity and spiritual development turn out to enhance their academic performance. These include service-learning courses, study abroad, interdisciplinary courses, volunteer work, and charitable giving (*Cultivating* 129). The first four of these are common, often defining attributes of honors work. Faculty attitudes and practices that enhance spiritual development, such as student-centered pedagogy and encouraging contemplative practices, have a favorable effect on academic performance (*Cultivating* 134). Overall, the conclusion is that "educational experiences and practices that promote spiritual development—especially service learning, interdisciplinary courses, study abroad, self reflection, and meditation—have uniformly positive affects on traditional college outcomes" (*Cultivating* 135–36). This conclusion should keenly interest honors faculty and administrators. Honors programs and colleges seek to improve those traditional outcomes—e.g., retention and graduation. So, they should consider how to enhance the opportunities available to their students to participate in these sorts of experiences and practices.

The study concludes by reaffirming the "large gap in our understanding of how college students develop and a corresponding lack of appreciation on the part of colleges and universities of the need to address that gap" (*Cultivating* 137). Higher education needs to find a "more purposeful role [it] . . . can and should play in enhancing students' spiritual development" (*Cultivating* 138). Faculty, obviously, need to play an important role in that development, and the study reviews its findings regarding faculty spirituality: 53% think it essential or very important to help students develop their personal values, and 60% similarly rate enhancing students' self-understanding; 81% consider themselves spiritual and 64% religious; 60% indicate that they engage in meditation or prayer; and about 70% say they seek opportunities to grow spiritually. Just under half consider integrating spirituality into their own lives as very important or essential, but only about 30% support any focus on students' "spiritual development," as contrasted with "personal" development, confirming that the word "spiritual" is an anathema to many professors (*Cultivating* 141). (See the discussion later in this chapter.) Among the major conclusions of the study is the suggestion that "one of the surest ways to enhance the spiritual development of undergraduate students is to encourage them to engage in almost any form of charitable or altruistic activity" (*Cultivating* 147). Another major finding is that "contemplative practices are among the most powerful tools at our disposal for enhancing students' spiritual development" (*Cultivating* 148). Astin and his colleagues point to the Center for Contemplative Mind in Society, founded in 1997, and a decade later the Association for Contemplative Mind in Higher Education. (A later section of this chapter focuses upon this issue and this organization.)

What can colleges, universities, and honors programs do to encourage spiritual development on campus? Some suggestions from this study include:

- Offering opportunities for spiritual reflection at events such as new student orientation;
- Discussing spiritual development at new faculty orientation;
- Creating relevant professional development programs;
- Establishing physical places on campus for reflection and dialogue;
- Providing an interfaith forum on spirituality and religion;
- Creating guiding principles for conversations on this topic;
- Integrating discussions of spirituality in living and learning centers and residence halls;
- Hosting guest speakers;
- Incorporating spirituality into mission and vision statements. (*Cultivating* 152)

The report concludes by affirming that "the findings of this study constitute a powerful argument in support of the proposition that higher education should attend more to students' spiritual development" (*Cultivating* 157).

The HERI results have been duplicated and verified in other similar but smaller studies. For example, Cornell College's Office of Institutional Research and Assessment did a study entitled "Pathways: A Study of Spirituality and Vocation at Cornell College."[53] A group of students at this small Iowa liberal arts college, historically affiliated with the Methodist Church, were researched, both by survey and focus group. (See the interview with Cornell's chaplain at the conclusion of this chapter.) Students from thirty-three faith traditions responded. Between half and two thirds said that they participate in prayer of some sort, 87% indicated they believed in "the sacredness of life," over three fifths said they were involved in matters of spirituality, and over half reported their belief that they have had a connection with God or a higher power (2). A majority reported having religious/spiritual questions and having been able to find meaning in times of hardship (2). Over half indicated that it was very important or essential that the college enhance their self-understanding, help clarify personal values, and explore their sense of self and meaning and purpose (3). At this small, private, traditionally faith-affiliated college, over one-third indicated that they had participated in a Chaplain-sponsored or Office of Spiritual Life event. Over half reported that they had taken or planned to take a Religious Studies course (4). The authors concluded:

> Cornell College students are interested and engaged in spiritual exploration. . . . Furthermore, students indicated it was important to them that the College help them explore and clarify their sense of meaning, help them clarify their connection to others, and provide voluntary opportunities for spiritual exploration. (4)

One valuable research project used the HERI data to study a very particular issue: the variable of race in the levels and patterns of spirituality at evangelical Christian colleges. Kristin Paredes-Collins and Christopher S. Collins noted that most evangelical colleges, the members of the Council for Christian Colleges and Universities, were predominantly white, despite "the evidence that suggests the great value of integrating multiple forms of diversity into the learning environment" (80).[54] In spite of years of effort, a great many honors programs and colleges are less diverse than the institutions that house them, so this study is not without some relevance to honors. The findings of the study indicate that white/Caucasian students scored high on the HERI "religious commitment" scale, both in the initial survey of 2004 and subsequent follow-up in 2007. The scores of both groups dropped during those three years, indicating that the effect of going to college, even in evangelical schools, slightly diminishes overt religious commitment. Conversely, the non-white students scored higher than the white ones on the ethic of caring aspect of the HERI survey, and both groups showed some increase between 2004 and 2007. One conclusion supported by the study is that "students of color would be more prone to the social justice-oriented aspects of faith and spirituality" while the white students were more deeply attached to the often socially conservative tenets of Evangelical Protestantism (*Cultivating* 93).

A recent study by Philip Schwadel of the University of Nebraska suggested some interesting correlations between education level and religion, in particular, liberal religion (ctd. in Grossman). Schwadel found that each year of education raises by 15% the odds that respondents will say that there is "truth in more than one religion" (qtd. in Grossman). For each year of schooling beyond the seventh grade, Americans are 15% more likely to have attended religious services in the last week, 14% more likely to say they believe in a "higher power" rather than a personal God, 13% less likely to say that the Bible is the literal word of God (ctd. in Grossman). Education, in other words, increases skepticism about some conservative religious principles—such as belief in a personal God or the literal truth of the Bible—but increases conviction in some common beliefs of a more liberal religious bent, for example that many religions capture spiritual truths.

A contrastingly personal and anecdotal article from the perspective of an undergraduate student is Madeleine Schwartz's "The Most Important Course," written at the conclusion of the author's junior year at Harvard. Schwartz writes that she has come to wonder: "Was Harvard encouraging us to think about the meaning of our lives?" (Schwartz). She notes that Gale Professor of Education Richard Light has been interviewing Harvard students on the brink of graduation, and he observes that many feel unprepared to take on life's bigger questions. Schwartz recalls: "One student told Light that although his classes had equipped him for work in chemistry and physics, 'Harvard forgot to offer the most important course—a course in how to think of living my life'" (Schwartz). Light has established a first-year course on "reflecting on your life," that has proven strikingly successful, with some 150 students enrolling annually. Schwartz notes that even in philosophy courses:

> Conversations are subsumed in the substance of course requirements. . . . When reading the fourth century "On the Pythagorean Life" for class, the most immediate question is not 'What does this mean for me?' but rather 'Can I write five pages on this before next week?' It's still schoolwork. (Schwartz)

She concludes that "if Harvard is to fulfill its promise that a liberal-arts education can form individuals, not just prepare them for careers, it needs to push its students in a way that Introductory Economics cannot" (Schwartz). These observations seem to me richly suggestive for honors, as well as Harvard.

THE SPIRITUALITY OF TODAY'S COLLEGE FACULTY

The first decade of the twenty-first century produced valuable research on the spirituality and the religiosity of American college and university faculty as well as students. The research team at HERI surveyed over 40,000 professors at 421 institutions as part of the Spirituality in Higher Education project (Astin, Astin, and Lindholm, "Spirituality").[55]

The HERI study found that a significant majority of college and university professors consider themselves to be spiritual individuals, but they were sharply divided about whether higher education should emphasize students' spiritual development. For example, 81% of faculty members responded "to some or a great extent" that I "consider myself a spiritual person" ("Spirituality" 3). Nearly half said that they are spiritual "to a great extent" (3). Similarly, 69% said they seek out opportunities to grow spiritually, and almost half have "integrating spirituality in my life" as a goal ("Spirituality" 3). More specifically, over 60% consider themselves to be religious persons while only 37% describe themselves as "not at all" religious ("Spirituality" 3). One would expect professors who considered themselves spiritual beings more likely to work in religious colleges. That is, in fact, the case, although the gaps between various kinds of institutions are not as large as one might suspect. The highest proportion of self-described spiritual faculty are found at colleges that are mainline Protestant, Baptist, and evangelical affiliated; the lowest in public universities:

- Religious Colleges—64% self described "spiritual"
- Roman Catholic Colleges—50%
- Two-Year Colleges—50%
- Nonsectarian Colleges—43%
- Public Colleges—41%
- Private Universities—36%
- Public Universities—33% ("Spirituality" 5)

While none of these profiles is shocking, I find it somewhat surprising that only half of the professors at Roman Catholic schools consider themselves to be spiritual persons and, conversely, that fully a third of those at public universities do.[56] Not at all surprising is the fact that a substantial majority of those who consider themselves to be highly spiritual also self-identify as highly religious: 70% to a great extent, 18% to some extent ("Spirituality" 7).

There are revealing correlations between high scores on spirituality and a number of other characteristics. Thus, for example, the HERI researchers found that 59% of those who were high scorers on spirituality reported a "positive outlook in work and life" while only 36% of the low scorers so described themselves ("Spirituality" 7). Similar dramatic differences emerge on other issues such as "focus on students' personal development" (43% high scorers on spirituality vs. 5% low scorers); civic-minded values (41% vs. 16%); diversity advocacy (33% vs. 21%); and student-centered pedagogy (26% vs. 12%) ("Spirituality" 6–7). Highly spiritual faculty utilized much more than their lower self-ranked peers such pedagogical practices as cooperative learning, student self-evaluation, reflective writing, group projects, community service, and student evaluations of each other's work. Several of these practices characterize much honors pedagogy.

How do faculty regard the role of spirituality within the college community? The research team found a considerable division of opinion on this issue:

> For example, when asked whether "colleges should be concerned with facilitating students' spiritual development," only a minority of faculty (30%) agree. This is consistent with the finding . . . that most college juniors report that their professors have never encouraged discussion of spiritual or religious matters, and never provide opportunities for discussing the meaning or purpose of life. However, many faculty also believe that the following educational goals for undergraduate students are "essential" or "very important": enhancing self-understanding (60%), developing moral character (59%), and helping students develop personal values (53%). ("Spirituality" 9)

Professors are most likely to endorse facilitating students' spiritual development if they are in the social sciences or humanities and the least likely if they are in the biological sciences, physical sciences, or agriculture/forestry. In the mainline and evangelical protestant colleges, 68% of faculty endorse this goal and 62% in the Catholic schools, whereas only 23% in public colleges and 18% in public universities do so ("Spirituality" 5). These statistics reveal that significantly more faculty at Catholic institutions believe in facilitating students' spiritual development than describe themselves as highly spiritual beings, while in public universities the exact opposite is the case: about half as many seek to help students cultivate their spirituality as describe themselves as highly spiritual. A slight majority of all faculty responding (57%) *disagreed* with the statement that "the spiritual dimension of faculty members' lives has no place in the academy" ("Spirituality" 10). Those who work in the faith-based institutions disagreed in greater proportions than faculty in public universities.

In sum, college faculty, like college students, consider themselves to be spiritual persons, and the majority describe themselves as religious beings. They seek to cultivate students' self-understanding, moral character, and personal value systems, but they are sharply divided on the place of overtly spiritual matters on campus and, according to their students, often avoid raising spiritual issues in the workplace.

In contrast to HERI's broad focus upon spirituality, the study by Gross and Simmons, which was noted earlier, is narrowly aimed at assessing the religiosity of college and university professors. Gross and Simmons begin by briefly recapitulating the secularization theories of Emile Durkheim, Karl Marx, Max Weber, and others that suggest "an association between modernization and the withering away of religious institutions and belief" ("Religiosity" 101). In the mid-twentieth century, students of American higher education such as Laurence Veysey, Richard Hofstadter, Christopher Jencks, and David Riesman saw "the professionalization of the professoriate and the institutionalization of academic freedom, as a triumph of science and Enlightenment ideals over religious dogmatism" ("Religiosity" 102). The assumption, write Gross and Simmons, was that "professors in the modern era, as carriers of Enlightenment values and agents of secularization, would themselves tend to be religious skeptics" ("Religiosity" 103). In fact, this is not the case, and the majority of college faculty members, even those at the major research universities, are not skeptics on issues such as "belief in God, views of the Bible, spiritual identity, religious orientation, and attendance at religious services" ("Religiosity" 103). Gross and Simmons review the growth of the American graduate-research university and the opening of the doors of access to elite higher education to non-Protestants, chiefly Catholics and Jews, after World War II. Later in the century, women and people of color also penetrated the ranks of academe in far greater numbers. This shift led, observe Gross and Simmons, to an "erosion of Protestant numerical dominance," with the proportion stating their religious identity as Protestant shrinking from 49.6% to 41.2% between 1969 and 1984 ("Religiosity" 107-108). They note the lamentations of writers such as Marsden and Burtchaell, who see the withering of traditional Christian ties of many colleges and universities in the second half of the twentieth century. Others, however, such as Nicholas Wolterstorff and John Schmalzbauer have affirmed that secularization has ebbed, even failed, and that the contemporary world of higher learning is witnessing a reinvigoration of interest in religion. Writers such as these two note that many opportunities exist for students to "engage in mainstream forms of religious worship," and that many of them are religious seekers, not religious dwellers (Gross and Simmons, "Religiosity" 110). There remains a widespread and firm conviction that, as one correspondent wrote me, the "established dogma" of secular universities is agnosticism, and if one is, in fact, a religious believer, "you'd better keep your mouth shut if you want to be taken seriously."[57]

To assess the religious status of today's professors, Gross and Simmons examined data from the "Politics of the American Professoriate" study that they undertook in the spring of 2006. Their survey, funded by the Richard Lounsberry Foundation, of faculty from two-year colleges, four-year institutions, and non-elite and elite PhD-granting institutions, had a 51% response rate representing 1,471 individuals.

On the issue of belief in God, Gross and Simmons report in "Religiosity" that professors exhibit greater levels of atheism and agnosticism than the American population as a whole, with 9.8% affirming non-belief and 13.1% responding, "I don't know whether there is a God." On the other hand, one in five say they believe in a "higher power," and 4.3% believe in God some of the time; 16.6% say that while they have doubts, they do believe in God; and 34.9% "know God really exists and have no doubts about it" ("Religiosity" 114). In short, three quarters of American college professors affirm some sort of faith in a divine entity. Close to 65% of professors at the elite doctoral institutions are believers, 36.5% either atheists or agnostics ("Religiosity" 103). Of American professors who identify themselves as religious, a bit over one-third see themselves as "progressives," a fifth as "traditionalists," and the largest number, 42.4%, as "moderate" ("Religiosity" 115). In terms of affiliation, overall about 38% identified themselves as Protestant, 16% as Catholic, and 5.4% as Jewish ("Religiosity" 119). Nearly one in five said the term "born again Christian" describes them, but that proportion drops down to about 1% at elite doctoral institutions ("Religiosity" 118). In this study, just about half (49.9%) of American professors overall say that the term "spiritual person" describes them, a figure slightly less than that reported in the HERI study ("Religiosity" 121). Four in ten report regular attendance at religious services ("Religiosity" 110).

Gross and Simmons observe that the culture of the contemporary academic world "is secular in orientation despite the personal religiosity of the majority of the faculty overall" ("Religiosity" 122). They conclude that American faculty are more religious than is commonly assumed and that even at the most elite institutions, there are "more professors who are religious than who are nonbelievers" ("Religiosity" 124). They note that this observation, in turn, suggests that secularization has led to the privatization of religion in the academy, not to its elimination. Colleges and universities are secular institutions not because the faculty is irreligious, but despite the fact that they are religious believers ("Religiosity" 124). Indeed, the bulk of teaching in American colleges and universities, across the spectrum of higher education, "is being carried out by academicians who are personally sympathetic to religion" ("Religiosity" 125). Gross and Simmons conclude that "religious believers are more common in the ranks of the American faculty than many strands of social-scientific analysis—and much popular discourse—would suggest" ("Religiosity" 126). In sum, the study by Gross and Simmons suggests that college professors' religiosity is somewhat more liberal and somewhat less conservative than that of the general population, but that they are hardly the irreligious, even anti-religious, group they are sometimes portrayed as being by pundits of the political ultra-conservative persuasion.

The picture that emerges clearly from the barrage of statistics generated by these studies is a provocative and, on the surface at least, a somewhat puzzling one. Students overwhelmingly see themselves as spiritual seekers and wish their collegiate experiences would help them with that quest. Faculty members tend, as well, to self-identify as spiritual. Across the spectrum of contemporary American higher education, a significant percentage of both students and faculty also understand themselves to be religious people. Nevertheless, students report that their professors do not encourage spiritual cultivation in class, and a majority of faculty believe they should not do so. One might conclude aphoristically that, when it comes to spirituality in today's colleges, the students want something that the faculty apprehend and have experienced but are reluctant to share with them. That is, we seem to have somehow created a culture in the world of academia that does not actually reflect the beliefs and values of the inhabitants of that world. I am not entirely sure how this came to pass. I speculate that perhaps as American higher education moved away from its earlier, sectarian, roots, we let the pendulum swing past a center point. We perhaps concluded that any attention to the spiritual dimension might be, or might seem to be, backsliding.

An important and different perspective on professorial spirituality is found in the influential and popular work of Parker J. Palmer, especially his book *The Courage to Teach: Exploring the Inner Landscape of a Teacher's Life.*[58] Palmer's core thesis is as powerful as it is simple: the most important element in good teaching is the teacher: it is not technique but the human heart that is the essential source of good teaching, not school buildings, legislative appropriations, assessment protocols, teacher-training courses, or restructured curricula. Palmer calls this essential factor the "who" question: who is the self that teaches? How does the quality of my selfhood form—or deform—the way I relate to my students, my subject, my colleagues, my world? How can educational institutions sustain and deepen the selfhood from which good teaching comes? (*Courage* 4). The act of teaching—in college and in any school from kindergarten to post-doctoral institution—is one of connection. The integrity and identity of the teacher are essential to that linkage. Palmer analyzes how different fears, such as the fear of a genuine, live encounter unprotected by a professional persona, threaten inner wholeness and balance. He suggests that embracing some of the paradoxes inherent in teaching spaces, like the tension between solitude and community, and creating a community of truth-seeking and truth-telling individuals enable teachers to overcome fear-based fragmentation and find the courage to teach (*Courage* 35–62). Palmer writes elsewhere about how "objectivism" has become the dogma of the modern university. This academic orthodoxy "insists that we can know the world only by distancing ourselves from it, by separating our inner lives from the external objects we want to know" (Palmer, "Vision" 17). Amusingly, Palmer deconstructs the nearly universal collegiate catalog phrase suggesting the university is dedicated to the pursuit of truth by exploring the conceit hidden in this phrase:

> Truth is imagined as an evasive fox, fleeing from us as fast as it can, tearing across the fields and hiding in the hedgerows, while we—nobly mounted on horses, blowing our horns and urging on our hounds—are passionately trying to track truth down, to capture it, and, of course, to kill it! It's a very odd image, at best . . . [because] truth is not evasive. We are. We are the ones running across the fields and hunkering down in the hedgerows. . . . We are the ones who are hiding from truth's claims on our lives, even as truth actively seeks us. . . . ("Vision" 21)

Palmer is suggesting that the truths of our lives as teachers and of our students, including the truths of the spirit, are not always obtuse or out-of-bounds; they are accessible and they are important.

Going one step further, a few observers of college faculty have even seen some connections among the intellectual work of teaching, spirituality, and the body although these linkages still seem more anecdotal than scientifically verifiable. For example, in a commentary in *The Chronicle of Higher Education*, Professor Laura Sloan Patterson discusses "using the entire body from head to toe. . . . Our bodies and our passions—intellectual, emotional, corporeal—contribute to the excellence of our teaching" (B20).[59] Patterson discusses "that magic moment when a course takes flight, when intellectual sparks fly in a way that creates a bond between student and teacher that feels more than cerebral. That moment feels almost spiritual, encompassing us as total beings so that we are not even capable of dividing brain and body" (B20). Such magic moments are not, of course, going to happen on a M/W/F—10:00–10:50 basis. But most educators have experienced them, and they help to transform teaching jobs into vocations.

MEDITATION

One area in which the spiritual, physical, and intellectual seem to converge on many campuses and for many college and university students, faculty, and staff is the realm of meditation and similar contemplative practices.[60] A 1996 book on Buddhism and mindfulness by Sylvia Boorstein was cunningly entitled *Don't Just Do Something, Sit There.* A significant number of college students and faculty have concluded that just sitting there can be doing something that is actually quite powerful. The last two decades have seen a striking growth in the interest in various contemplative practices and their relationship to higher learning. What the literature seems to prove is not necessarily that meditative practices demonstrably enhance scholarly and academic achievement, but that a great many practitioners of various forms of contemplative practices are convinced that those activities have made a positive difference in their lives as teachers, students, and scholars.

The case for attending to the "inner liberal arts" is argued by Tobin Hart, Professor of Psychology at the University of West Georgia, in the Garrison Institute electronic newsletter (Hart). Noting that "education is preparation for a future not yet determined," Hart wonders if "our current emphasis on information acquisition and on basic literacy and numeracy [is] sufficient to prepare our charges for the reality to come" (Hart). He contends that an adequate education will require "integration: science and spirit, art and technology, reason and feeling, mind and body, forest and tree, mystery and certainty, inside and outside, self and other" (Hart). While classical Greek philosophers sought the good life "by developing the mind and the soul through reflection, study and practice," today people require, Hart asserts, a liberal arts that "represent the necessary inner arts and technology needed to balance mastery over nature with mastery over ourselves" (Hart). Contemplative education utilizes a wide variety of approaches, observes Hart, "that are designed to quiet and shift the habitual chatter of the mind in order to cultivate a capacity for deepened awareness, concentration and insight" (Hart). Simple contemplative practices, he suggests, "engender a host of significant states such as mental clarity and calmness as well as traits like emotional resilience, flexibility, and compassion" (Hart). (I would be very comfortable with course work that offered students such contemplative opportunities but uncomfortable with a class that required them, unless, of course, they were advertised in the course bulletin as such.)

A group called "The Center for Contemplative Mind in Society," originating in 1991–92, has defined one of its core areas of interest as education. It created an academic program area, and in 2008, that program in turn became The Association for Contemplative Mind in Higher Education. Its founding director is Dr. Arthur Zajonc, long active in various activities involving contemplative practices and Professor of Physics at Amherst College. Since 1997 several dozen academics have received Contemplative Practice Fellowships to study and implement the use of such practices in their teaching and research. In 2008, Mirabi Bush and Zajonc edited a draft handbook entitled *Contemplative Practices in Higher Education: A Handbook of Classroom Practices*, for the Center for Contemplative Mind in Society, and the following paragraphs have been drawn from that text.

Nancy C. Sharts-Hopko describes contemplative practices as "an array of modalities that . . . have as a primary aim the enhancement of mindfulness and calm" (91).[61] "Contemplative pedagogy," asserts Zajonc, "makes conscious use of a wide range of practices for two essential ends: the cultivation of attention and emotional balance; the development of faculties required for insight and creativity" (9). The range of activities subsumed under this heading is daunting. A partial list includes meditation (in several variants); mindfulness (that is, focusing upon being in the present moment, not the past nor the future); yoga and various martial-arts disciplines such as tai chi; breathing exercises; controlled walking disciplines; journaling; labyrinth activities; contemplating works of art such as paintings or music; chanting; pilgrimage; and visiting sacred places. Often these practices are combined in various ways. What is important to note about several of these activities, such as yoga, walking, and breathing exercises, is that they invoke the spiritual through the physical and thus are deeply connected to many of the subjects of the preceding chapter.

Those people affiliated with the Center for Contemplative Mind in Society and its academic program certainly hold the opinion that these practices do, in fact, enhance learning, in at least two ways. First, writes Zajonc, they quite simply make students better learners: "Emotional balance can lead indirectly to improved performance in school" (9). Just as advocates of physical cultivation believe that exercise and fitness improve intellectual performance, believers in contemplative practices affirm that their activities enhance cognitive skills. One professor, Brian Stock, speaks of Greek meditative philosophical exercises that "were intended to develop the intellect" (66). Another professor, Robert A. F. Thurman, describes how "transforming meditations" are "most important in psychological, intellectual, and spiritual development" (69).[62]

Second, advocates of contemplative practices in higher education believe that they not only enhance cognitive learning skills but complement them as well. In the words of Mirabai Bush, the ancient contemplative methods being pursued by contemporary teachers offer "their students a way to make learning more meaningful and education more integrated" ("Compassionate" 78). Some instructors (for example, Professor Chess in Interview 1 above) have found that devoting class time to meditation helps students to focus upon and reflect on class work (ctd. in Bush and Zajonc, "Contemplative" 15). Noting that critical thinking is one of the most important flowers of Western civilization, Steven C. Rockefeller, Professor of Religion emeritus at Middlebury College, wonders:

> Whether the education of the undergraduate college in America today fails to put science and discursive reason in proper perspective and whether it tends to encourage a character orientation that is too head-centered as distinct from heart-centered, more interested in information than appreciation, more concerned about the knowledge which is power than wisdom and ethical values, more oriented toward I-it than I-thou, more skilled at striving for future ends than living a fulfilling life in the present. (58)[63]

Contemplative learning, asserts Stock, "insists that education deal with the whole person" (65). Thurman claims that it combats the "dualistic alienation of body from mind, emotion from intellect, humans from nature, and art from science" (71). In other words, Bush argues, they promote "wholeness, unity, integration" ("Compassionate" 78).

From the perspective of a sympathetic outside scholar, I would note that most of the evidence of this link between contemplative activities and intellectual growth seems more anecdotal than quantitative or scientific. While the literature seems full of claims that meditative activities enhance learning, the actual evidence of this link is scarce. For example, one meditation website asserts: "Meditation and learning work very well together. . . . [T]hrough training the mind to focus more effectively you can take learning to a higher level. Thus you can learn subjects faster and to a deeper level" (Mastermeditation). Obviously, one must ask "higher," "faster," and "deeper" than what, and by how much? George A. Boyd similarly suggests that meditation enhances the ability to learn and the effectiveness of study, but that well-meaning suggestion is unsupported by any objective evidence. In this respect, the advocates of blending contemplative exercises into higher education occupy a position similar to that of advocates of physical education perhaps a quarter-century ago: they are confident that the connection exists, but they have not yet proven it in a laboratory setting. As Rockefeller notes, meditation needs to be demythologized in American culture, and "the truth about meditation should be carefully researched and studied" (59).

One area in which some scientific research has been done concerns the effectiveness of meditative techniques in improving the learning of students with learning disabilities who are usually younger than college-age students. One small study actually measured the results of five weeks of meditation on thirty-four adolescents with learning disabilities. At the beginning of the study, those individuals initially showed heightened levels of anxiety and stress when contrasted with their peers, but the practice of meditation lowered those levels, and "outcome measures showed significant improvements, [including] academic outcomes" (Beauchemin, Hutchins, and Patterson 34–45).

One theme that runs through much writing about contemplative practices in contemporary higher education is the concern that such activities might be perceived as proselytizing for some particular religious perspective, especially in the context of secular colleges and universities. While many advocates of meditative pedagogies are quite involved in Asian spiritual traditions, there are also many who believe that contemplative techniques can be fruitfully undertaken without seeking the religious conversion of participating students or converting them to a belief in religion.

Bush and Zajonc's manuscript cites numerous ways in which college teachers are integrating this spiritual dimension into their teaching. Here are a few brief summaries of some of those techniques that could easily be adapted to honors courses:

- In the field of Architecture, Professor Ekaterini Vlahos at the University of Colorado at Denver takes students on a three-night camping trip during which they immerse themselves in a wilderness site, away from the technological distractions of daily life, in order to sharpen their perceptions of space. They follow up on this experience by reflecting about it in writing, drawing, or photos.[64] (ctd. in Bush and Zajonc, "Contemplative" 14–15)

- Marilyn R. Nelson began a poetry class at West Point for cadets with five minutes of meditations of various sorts. The goal was to teach the cadets "the gifts of interiorization and humanization, and learning to confront their vulnerabilities and weaknesses through meditation." (qtd. in Bush and Zajonc, "Contemplative" 19)

- A professor of visual arts at the College of Holy Cross, Joanna Ziegler, has her students look at two paintings, one from the Renaissance, one an abstract modern work, for thirteen weeks. Each week, they say what they have seen in the paintings that time, and each week, they report something new. She believes this exercise is a form of meditation. (ctd. in Bush and Zajonc, "Contemplative" 21)
- At the CUNY Law School, a labyrinth was constructed with the goal of teaching law students how to deal with the stresses of their schooling and their profession. (ctd. in Bush and Zajonc, "Contemplative" 25)
- At Westmont College, an evangelical Protestant Christian college, Professor Marilyn Chandler of the Department of English had her class participate in a Quaker dialog process. The class was silent, and then individually "speaking from the silence," students said what they had understood and learned from a work they had been reading. (qtd. in Bush and Zajonc, "Contemplative" 33)
- Professor Bret Wallach of the Department of Geography of the University of Oklahoma led students on a pilgrimage to the grave site of Geronimo in a course on "The Power of Landscape: Place-induced Contemplation." (qtd. in Bush and Zajonc, "Contemplative" 41)
- A course in "Contemplative Practices in Health and Illness" was offered by Professor Nancy C. Sharts-Hopko, a nursing educator. The class followed a retreat format—it met all day long for five days in a row. Each day a guest speaker spoke on a topic such as art therapy, tai chi, etc. Many honors programs and colleges include a similar retreat experience in their annual schedule (91–100).

In addition to particular courses devoted in whole or in part to contemplative practices, Bush notes that some colleges and universities have established institution-wide programs that focus upon this area (Introduction 7). These include the Program in Creativity and Consciousness Studies at the University of Michigan. This program "argues that two emergent areas of academic inquiry—creativity and consciousness—warrant a fundamental place in the educational landscape of the future." Bush and Zajonc cite several fascinating initiatives. The Contemplative Practice Program at Brooklyn College cultivates a contemplative educators' network within the institution and New York City. It features contemplative practices courses, a study group, and a network for students to focus upon contemplative issues. At Brown University, the Contemplative Studies Initiative links faculty from across the disciplines who are interested in the study of "contemplative states of mind, including the underlying philosophy, psychology and phenomenology of human contemplative experience" (qtd. in Bush, Introduction 7).

EDUCATION AS TRANSFORMATION AND BEYOND TOLERANCE

Two noteworthy national programs that address the role of spiritual life in contemporary undergraduate education sprang from Wellesley College in the late 1990s. Given their origin, both these programs, although not specifically connected with honors, were created with above-average students in mind. These are "Education as Transformation," and "Beyond Tolerance." The latter is, to some extent, an offshoot of the former, but it has taken on an identity of its own.

"Education as Transformation" offers this description of itself on its website:

> An international organization that works with colleges, universities, K–12 schools and related institutions exploring:
>
> 1. The impact of religious diversity on education and strategies for addressing this diversity.
> 2. The role of spirituality in educational institutions, and particularly its relationship to teaching and learning

> pedagogy; the cultivation of values; moral and ethical development; and the fostering of global learning communities and responsible global citizens. ("Education as Transformation")

This endeavor began with a conference at Wellesley in September 1998. The conference was opened by then-President Diana Chapman Walsh, who said:

> we seek to envision a whole new place . . . for spirituality in higher education, not as an isolated enterprise on the margins of the academy, not as a new form of institutional repression and social control, but as an essential element of the larger task of reorienting our institutions to respond more adequately to the challenges the world presents us now. ("Transforming" 1)[65]

The project continues its work by sponsoring a number of conferences, both domestic and international, and sending participants to the academic meetings of other organizations, such as the AAC&U and Conference of Independent Colleges. Its founding president is Victor Kazanjian, Dean of Religious and Spiritual Life at Wellesley College, and its current director is Peter L. Laurence. It offers a consultation service that helps to facilitate retreats, plan facilities, and create campus programs. Another offshoot of "Education as Transformation" besides "Beyond Tolerance" is the "Education and Spirituality Network," an online organization of educators who are exploring issues involving religious and spiritual diversity/pluralism in various educational settings. This electronic resource has information about publications and activities, events, and organizations in the area. "Education as Transformation" also publishes an electronic newsletter, which appears at irregular intervals throughout the year, featuring articles and information relevant to this subject.

Working with the National Association of Student Personnel Administrators (NASPA), the professional organization of student affairs administrators in higher education, "Education as Transformation" has developed a campus diversity kit that includes a video and a study guide for use at institutions seeking to explore the sometimes-hard questions and issues that surround religious pluralism in today's colleges. In collaboration with the Peter Lang publishing company, "Education as Transformation" has generated several books on this subject, beginning with a collection of essays edited by Victor H. Kazanjian, Jr., and Peter L. Laurence entitled *Education as Transformation: Religious Pluralism, Spirituality, and a New Vision for Higher Education in Americ*a. This volume features a huge range of voices, including a variety of essays written by practitioners offering the perspectives of their own particular religion. For example, Suheil Badi Bushrui and James Malarkey's piece, "Education as Transformation: A Bahá'í Model of Education for Unity," notes a "broad vision of education [that] entails cultivation of the full range of human potential: intellectual . . . moral . . . spiritual . . . and, not least, physical. . ." (93). A chapter by Arthur Green on Judaism speaks of "the breach that deeply underlies the entire Western academic enterprise, but one quite alien to Jewish tradition. . . . the bifurcation between sage and scholar, between the quest for wisdom and the pursuit of knowledge. . ." (115). In his essay, Douglas C. Bennett, President of Earlham, argues that "truth seeking should involve both intellect and spirit, and that the conversation between intellect and spirit can be unusually fruitful" (187). Other essays are written by Roman Catholic, Buddhist, Sikh, Muslim, Quaker, Protestant, Hindu, and Native American authors.

The book series sponsored by "Education as Transformation" is called "Studies in Education and Spirituality" and includes a rather wide and diverse collection of writings:

- *Integrative Learning and Action: A Call to Wholeness*. Ed. Susan M. Awbrey et al. This volume is a diverse collection of essays by educators, writers, various professionals, thinkers, and practitioners.
- *Transforming Campus Life: Reflections on Spirituality and Religious Pluralism*. Ed. Vachel W. Miller and Merle M. Ryan. As the title suggests, this book focuses upon campus life; it argues that neglecting religious and spiritual development and exploration leads to personal fragmentation and disconnection from the social and physical environments.

- Two works in the series are written by Robert J. Nash, a professor at the University of Vermont. *Religious Pluralism in the Academy: Opening the Dialog* discusses the necessity of initiating and maintaining sometimes challenging discussions of multiculturalism and pluralism on campus. *Spirituality, Ethics, Religion and Teaching: A Professor's Journey* is a more personal look at Nash's development as a teacher and his ideas and pedagogy in the area of spirituality.
- *Minding the Light: Essays in Friendly Pedagogy*. Ed. Anne Dalke and Barbara Dixson. This text is also a more personal approach, recounting the authors' experiences in Quaker institutions. The book grew, in part, out of an annual meeting of the Friends Association of Higher Education held at Earlham College. Professor Dalke, who teaches at Bryn Mawr College, is also the sole author of *Teaching to Learn, Learning to Teach: Meditations on the Classroom*. Focusing upon teaching the liberal arts, this collection of personal stories is about pedagogy that incorporates religious and interactive dimensions of the process.
- *Spirituality, Action, and Pedagogy: Teaching from the Heart*. Ed. Diana Denton and Will Ashton. This collection of essays, many involving the various arts and communications areas, offers specific examples of integrating spirituality into classroom practice.
- James Gollnick is Professor of the Psychology of Religion at the University of Waterloo in Canada, where he also serves as Director of the Spirituality and Personal Development Program. His book, *Religion and Spirituality in the Life Cycle*, focuses upon the contemporary changing nature of the relationship between religion and spirituality and how these changes have led to an evolving conception of the nature and growth of human personality.
- One book in this series focuses upon pre-college learning and spiritual formation: *Gateways to Spirituality: Pre-School through Grade Twelve*. Ed. Peter W. Cobb.

Taken together, these books and the multitude of essays in them make a multifaceted case for the importance of including spiritual development in the work of today's colleges and universities. They offer numerous stories, models, and examples of those who have followed this path.

Overall, the "Education as Transformation" project seeks to understand and promote the role of spirituality in the development of today's college students. In a sharp break from the sectarian roots of religion in American higher education, discussed in Chapter 2 above, this endeavor does not seek to promote any one religious or spiritual tradition over others. It is, in this sense, non-sectarian, almost at times contra-sectarian, embracing of spiritual diversity, including those who reject particular religions or even any religion as being necessary for spiritual cultivation. In that spirit, "Educational Transformation" developed, first at Wellesley College, but later for a larger community, a sub-project entitled "Beyond Tolerance." In the views of the founders of this program, the word "tolerance" connotes a mainstream tradition—in this case, a spiritual or religious tradition—that tolerates individuals and groups that fall outside that mainstream. In the case of most U.S. colleges, including Wellesley, that mainstream tradition would be Protestant Christianity. "Beyond Tolerance" began as a presentation piece produced by a group of Wellesley women of differing religious beliefs and backgrounds; its website describes, the original goals of the program:

> "Beyond Tolerance" explores the possibility of people of different religious traditions celebrating their religious diversity and affirming their common humanity as they work together to build a multi-faith community. Through this experience participants are invited to share in the story of the women of the Wellesley College multi-faith student council, a group of 21 women representing diverse religious traditions (Bahá'í, Buddhist, Christian, Hindu, Jewish, Muslim, Native American, Pagan, Sikh, Unitarian Universalist, and Zoroastrian), who have engaged in a three year process of building multi-faith community. ("Beyond Tolerance," *Wellesley*)

Ten women from the Wellesley Multi-Faith Student Council presented a different faith tradition at the 1998 conference at Wellesley that initiated the "Education as Transformation" program. Each of the students tried to describe what she saw as the essence of her religious tradition and tried to listen to what others said was most important to them in their faith.

The "Beyond Tolerance" project at Wellesley has grown beyond the borders of that particular institution. I have already mentioned that the project generated a campus diversity kit designed to help other institutions initiate similar programs. Several have: Juniata College, for example, offers an annual "Beyond Tolerance" series of presentations, workshops, films, and travel opportunities. Mt. Holyoke College, through its office of Diversity and Inclusion, has also created a "Beyond Tolerance" Program.

The "Beyond Tolerance" movement has also created a website that has an online sanctuary in which participants can explore cultural and religious understanding (*Beyond Tolerance*). The site includes a roster of participants, a listing of resources, options to engage in dialogs with other participants, and an area where electronic visitors are invited to express their own reactions to a series of questions about multicultural issues.

One particularly influential study of contemporary religious pluralism, cited often in writings about both the "Beyond Tolerance" project and "Education as Transformation," is Diana Eck's *Encountering God: A Spiritual Journey from Bozeman to Banaras*. Eck, who holds and has held several distinguished positions at Harvard University, describes her personal journey from Montana to India, her transformative encounter in Banaras with Hindu polytheism, and how that experience has deepened her Christian roots while it has broadened her understanding of the multitude of ways in which diverse human cultures have encountered the divine. Of particular importance is her careful analysis of the exclusivist, inclusivist, and pluralist positions. Exclusivists affirm that their religion is the sole truthful tradition and that all other faiths are false. The inclusivists say that many faith traditions include partial insights into the divine that can be subsumed under the inclusive umbrella of one particular tradition. The pluralists see different faith traditions as all embodying some aspects of a truth that is finally unknowable in its entirety, and proponents of any religion can deepen their own faith by seeking dialog and understanding with other pathways (166–99).

In sum, the "Education as Transformation" project has as its overarching goal to reaffirm the important place of spiritual exploration and development in the culture of today's colleges and universities. The "Beyond Tolerance" program focuses upon the interactions between individuals of differing faith and spiritual traditions, practices, and beliefs.

MORAL EDUCATION

Beginning around 1990 and continuing unabated through two decades, a lively debate has evolved concerning the notion of moral education as a function of contemporary colleges and universities. For some educators, moral education is not necessarily linked to the spiritual; for others they are indivisible. Certainly issues of ethics, virtue, and morality engage those same big questions of meaning and purpose in life that define the essence of spirituality.

Of course, affirmations that higher learning instills virtue have been a significant part of the American scene since the founding of Harvard in the 1630s. Elizabeth Kiss and J. Peter Euben write:

> Educators in the American colonies and the young United States embraced a tradition going back to Aristotle and the Greeks that linked liberal education with the development of moral and civic virtue. A concern for character formation and citizenship, intertwined with Christian and civic republican conceptions of duty and virtue, dominated American higher education throughout the nineteenth century." (Introduction 6)

Indeed, as I was writing these words, I was listening to NPR in the background, when I heard an advertisement for Bryant College in Rhode Island, which described itself as devoted to "the development of intellect and of character."[66]

A remarkably high percentage of honors programs and colleges mention moral education in their mission statements. An almost random sampling of vocabulary includes:

- Illinois State University: "promote civic engagement."
- Loras College: "moral inquiry."
- Owens Community College: "ethical reasoning," "civic engagement and leadership."
- Mount Union College: "emphasizes social responsibility and civic virtue."
- Schreyer Honors College at Pennsylvania State University: "creating opportunities for civic engagement and leadership," creating "men and women who will have an important and ethical influence in the world."
- Bloomsburg University: "integrity, character, moral responsibility."
- University of Colorado, Boulder: "moral and ethical leaders of the future."

A number of important higher education organizations have, in recent years, drafted statements that testify to a renewed ethical commitment in colleges and universities, especially in the area of social morality. The "Wingspread Declaration on the Civic Responsibilities of Research Universities" states:

> From one campus to another, there is increasing interest in efforts to better prepare people for active citizenship in a diverse democracy, to develop knowledge for the improvement of communities and society, and to think about and act upon the public dimensions of our educational work. (Boyte and Hollander)

The Association of American Colleges and Universities drafted a "Core Commitment to Educate Students for Personal and Civic Responsibility," which "aims to reclaim and revitalize the academy's role in fostering students' development of personal and social responsibility. The initiative focuses national attention on the importance of students exploring their ethical responsibilities to self and others" (Association of American). Since it was drafted in 1999 by Thomas Ehrlich and Elizabeth Hollander, 565 college presidents have signed Campus Compact's "Presidents' Declaration on the Civic Responsibility of Higher Education." "We must teach the skills and values of Democracy" (Campus Compact). A number of organizations are devoted, in whole or part, to this topic. These include the Association for Moral Education, founded in 1976, which sponsors an annual conference and publishes a journal, and the Center for Applied Christian Ethics, housed at Wheaton College. Some blurring of the lines between moral development and civic engagement obviously exists. Some institutions are clearly focusing upon the responsibilities of students as citizens; some heed their growth in terms of personal ethical behavior. Many lump together civic and moral character building.

This contemporary effort to heed the inculcation of moral values as part of both public and private higher education has not been without its articulate critics; perhaps foremost among them is Stanley Fish. In a series of articles, mostly for *The Chronicle of Higher Education,* Fish asserts that today's colleges cannot effectively shape the morals of today's students, and even if they could, they should not. Fish himself describes his position as an "insistence . . . that college and university teachers should hew to the line dividing academic from nonacademic activities . . . and refrain from any kind of partisan advocacy, be it political, economic, civic, or social" ("I Know It" 76). He defends his refusal to answer the question, "If colleges and universities don't think about how their curriculum and climate is likely to shape student values and behavior, then who should?" with the response "Beats me! But I don't see why that's a question I have to answer" ("I Know It" 90).[67]

Among the objections that are often raised to moral higher education are these:

1. It does not work. Gillepsie notes wryly: "We academics want to believe that our students are deeply influenced ethically by what they learn in our classes and from our inspiring

examples. However, this conclusion tells us more about our own wishes than about our actual effect on our students" (297). Students are influenced by their families, their peers, and the cultures in which they were raised. There is not much evidence that their ethical profiles are altered dramatically by college. James Bernard Murphy writes: "Both political philosophers and political scientists seem to agree, then, that deliberate instruction aimed at inculcating civic virtue is strikingly ineffective" (171).[68] The evidence that those profiles change during the college experience is, however, considerable.

2. Whose ethics do we teach? For the first three centuries of American higher education, the overwhelming spiritual and cultural ethos of American higher learning was that of prosperous white male Protestants. Today, most American higher education is far more diverse in gender, color, ethnicity, and religion. Lawrence Blum writes: "It was easier to teach values, it is sometimes thought, when student populations were more homogeneous" (140).

3. Moral education or indoctrination? When does teaching ethical values cross the line between a valuable and appropriate collegiate responsibility in a pluralistic culture and the mere promulgation of the particular set of morals, ethics, beliefs, and values of the particular instructor, department, college, sponsoring body, or cultural milieu?

4. The virtues that should be engendered by higher education are academic virtues—honesty, thoughtfulness, openness, and thoroughness—not personal ones. John Mearsheimer told the first-year students at the University of Chicago in 1997 that the purpose of the university is to teach students to think critically, to broaden their intellectual horizons, and to stimulate self-knowledge. Mearsheimer posits: it does not "provide you with moral guidance. Indeed, it is a remarkably amoral institution" (qtd. in Kiss and Euben, Introduction 4). It does not and should not be a place "where you discuss

ethics or morality in any detail," and it should not help students to deal with the ethical issues they face or will face in their lives (qtd. in Kiss and Euben, Introduction 4). Murphy is equally blunt: "attempts to use schools for moral and civic education almost always corrupt the appropriate moral purpose of academic education: to inculcate the intellectual virtues" (162).

5. There is, as well, considerable variance of opinion even among those strongly favoring moral education regarding what should be done in and out of the classroom to promote this cause. What is the role of experiential learning in moral education, for example? Should texts and issues that raise ethical questions be taught? Should those questions be highlighted, for example, by studying *Hamlet* and focusing on the morality of revenge? Should there be classes that center explicitly on ethical issues, like many business or medical ethics classes? What is the role of international education, service learning, or multicultural emphases?

While critics like Fish argue that colleges are ineffective at moral instruction, others, like David A. Hoekema assert (persuasively, in my opinion) that the collegiate experience cannot avoid ethical instruction: "Whether consciously or unconsciously, whether systematically or haphazardly [instructors] serve as moral guides to students. . . . [It is] the conduct of classroom discourse that shapes the students' conceptions of how to conduct their lives" (258). In an even larger context, writes Elizabeth V. Spelman, "whether or not we explicitly teach ethics or otherwise foreground morality in our curricula, we are ethical animals, always in the thick of ethical experience" (109). More particularly, Hoekema spotlights three sources of ethical instruction in today's colleges: faculty, student life staff including coordinators of religious life, and fellow students, which is the group he believes is the most effective (260). Professors who read all their students' work carefully and comment upon it thoughtfully and at length are instructing students in thoroughness and interpersonal care and respect. Student leaders who publically change their opinion on a campus issue after an open forum with other students are modeling the virtues of open-mindedness and interpersonal heedfulness. Campus chaplains who spend hours listening to the problems of students are teaching those students the ethics of humane caring. Conversely, twenty-first-century teachers of a course purporting to be an introduction to English language poetry who include only white, male, Christian poets, or who do not show up for posted office hours, are also demonstrating a moral position, in this case a pernicious one, to their students. Surely the pedagogy of a fine honors seminar offers instruction in careful heeding of a variety of perspectives, mutual respect, openness, responsibility, honesty, and similar virtues.

In response to the argument that cultural pluralism invalidates efforts to promote moral education, some people argue that pluralism itself inculcates certain ethical values. Blum, for example, notes that the values associated with *equality* are based on human differences. Similarly, the ethical position of appreciating and welcoming persons of difference presupposes a milieu that values being rich in those differences. Likewise, the appreciation and striving for community thrive in a multicultural setting (150–157).

Is moral education indoctrination? In many cases, it may be, especially in the weakest colleges and universities whose sectarian traditions are hidebound. There are religious colleges and universities that overtly endeavor to teach and to persuade students of the validity of the particular doctrines of their faith tradition. When I have visited religious colleges and universities, I have encountered institutions that explicitly include in their curriculum readings from Darwin and Machiavelli with the openly stated purpose of convincing students why and how those thinkers are in error. I have also encountered other, deeply sectarian faith-based institutions where both creationism and Darwinism are included in biology classes, but instructors encourage the students to weigh the alternatives. In other places that are also deeply faith-based, straightforward evolutionary theory is the sole option. Certainly not all moral education drifts into proselytizing, nor should the fact that an ethically aware curriculum or pedagogy can be abused deter efforts to develop educational experiences that will invite deepening and growing students' moral consciousnesses without seeking to lead them to particular spiritual conclusions. Of course, to some observers of American higher learning, it is the secular colleges and universities that have an orthodoxy of belief and practice, a monolithic definition of civic and personal virtues, into which they seek to indoctrinate all of their students. At the end of a long academic career as a student, a professor, and an administrator, I would disagree. The schools I know are hardly monolithic about anything. On matters of personal and civic virtues (and vices), I have often encountered deep and vigorous differences of belief and practice.

As more than one commentator has pointed out, it is not easy—indeed, it may be impossible—to draw a clear and unmoving line between academic ethics and personal morals. Is cheating on an exam only a scholarly flaw and not a personal failing? Is it possible to laud and to insist upon honesty in academic work without promoting a more general love of the truth? Are teachers who use their position to bully or to sexually harass students committing only an academic sin? Stanley Fish himself argues that separating the academic world and the real world is a fallacy since all worlds are real ("I Know It"). If the college classroom or residence hall has the same reality status as the corporate boardroom, hospital ward for the terminally ill, the situation room at the White House, a chapel, a dining table, or a street corner, it cannot have a separate and unique code of ethics or set of morals, and it certainly cannot be free of ethical matters. I believe "honors" is about acting "honorably" or being an individual of "honor." Educators will inevitably disagree about what the moral implications of what the subjects they teach may be and how we go about teaching or modeling them. But such disagreement is itself a valuable teaching opportunity that should be honored.

INTERVIEW THREE

Rev. Catherine Quehl-Engel

The Rev. Catherine Quehl-Engel serves as Chaplain of the College at Cornell College, Mt. Vernon, Iowa. Cornell is historically linked to the United Methodist Church (UMC), but Rev. Quehl-Engel is ordained as an Episcopal priest. She is a graduate of Cornell College and has been in her present role there since 1996. She also teaches courses in the Religion Department. She has held several positions within the Diocese of Iowa, including serving as a member of the Diocese Board of Directors. In addition to her Cornell College baccalaureate, she holds two master's-level degrees from the Pacific School of Religion. She is the author of several articles on a range of topics in religious studies. I asked her to reflect on her career, the role of a college chaplain today, and the connections between spirituality and academic development.

I am a Cornell College '89 graduate. I was groomed from childhood for a life in higher education. My father, Gary Quehl, was Dean of Men, then Academic Dean, then head of the Finger Lakes consortium, President of the Council of Independent Colleges and of CASE throughout my childhood and college years. He was Special Assistant to University of Iowa President Sandy Boyd during the student unrest of the 1960s and then stayed on as professor of Higher Education. He did his dissertation on United Methodist Church (UMC) related higher education in Iowa.

I went to seminary in Berkeley, CA, at Pacific School of Religion because there I could acquire my Master of Divinity while also pursuing an MA that would allow for my intellectual and inter-faith interests in Jewish-Christian history, Holocaust theology, and how artists act as theologians. I then entered a PhD program in Theology, Ethics, and Culture at the University of Iowa School of Religion to continue that research. My professional training was ecumenical and inter-faith.

My entering this profession was the culmination of a variety of realities from my youth: 1. A keen sense of awe/wonder mingled with the experience of transformative suffering as a child that piqued spiritual hunger and questioning. 2. Cross cultural and spiritual curiosities/adventures as well as witnessing/experiencing how religion can be used as both a sword and healing balm at individual and societal levels. 3. Love of learning, deep awareness of the need for social justice and inter-religious understanding/bridge building. 4. Glimpsing the sacred in the secular (sacramental awareness). 5. Interest in East-West inter-spiritual wisdom and practices, including meditation, that remained long after my parents' passing interest in them in the 1970s abated. (My current research interest and professional associations are in contemplative theory and practice including for higher education contexts.)

I asked Dr. Quehl-Engel to say a little about how Cornell, a school with, as she has written, "Methodism in its DNA," decided to select an Episcopal priest for its Chaplain?

Methodist DNA refers to the Wesleyan heritage of (a) valuing the life of the mind, (b) caring community, (c) uplifting the poor through access to education, and (d) like the Yale band of clergy who scattered colleges like good seed across this country in the nineteenth century, helping to usher in the kingdom or era of peace and justice on earth. Cornell sees education as a means of creating servant leaders for a more humane world. Honestly, there is not anything uniquely Methodist about that.

I am told that I was one of 200 or so candidates (and my father-in-law told me I did not have a chance because I was not UMC). I think I was selected for a variety of factors: (a) I knew the Cornell ethos; (b) I have an ecumenical and inter-faith background that is essential for any non-sectarian chaplaincy where there is one of you for religious, secular, and spiritual but not religious folk of various stripes; (c) I have the skills to easily flow across divisions in work with academics, student affairs, administration, alumni, and in town/gown relations; (d) I have an intensity that fits the one-course-at-a-time [at Cornell] context as well as a commitment to social justice—both of which are tempered by humor and humble lightness of being; (e) I look like I am about twelve years old but also like a professional who can easily connect with young people; (f) when I was a student here, I was mentored and nourished by United Methodists: my chaplain, Richard Thomas; Academic Dean Dennis Moore; the local UMC pastor; and the local UMC congregation the four of us engaged in; (g) I was willing to work for low wages. The Cedar Rapids Superintendent for the United Methodist Church was on the search team and Board of Trustees. He did not seem to mind my not being UMC. I was the only non-UMC finalist

I do not fit the box people put clergy in. Non-religious folks and folks from other faith traditions feel comfortable around me, perhaps because of my gender and small, unintimidating size. Folks call me "Fr. Cathy," which probably would not work in a parish context, but it is quirky enough to make me safe with college-age students. Gender has been a limitation on rare occasions with Christian fundamentalists, including a few female students. But keep in mind that I work closely with evangelicals, Roman Catholics, and others for whom women religious leaders can be an issue.

The UCLA Spirituality in Higher Ed research does a great job articulating much of what I do and why it is important. Cornell College President Garner and I revised my job description last year in order to reflect what it is that I actually do ranging from ceremonial to pastoral care and guidance to inter-faith exploration, social justice, mentoring, pre-seminary advising, and teaching. I have been rather spoiled at Cornell. Here I am able to flow into various secular and sacred contexts and across divisions of the college to the point where I am not sure whether I could work as a chaplain at a secular or sectarian school. Spirituality often gets put in a box in those contexts, either completely ignored all together as irrelevant or gets limited to just one specific religious expression. Here and elsewhere at historically affiliated, mainline Protestant schools, the chaplain must be able to extend care and wisely navigate amid a complex community including during ceremonial invocations and what is now an inter-spiritual baccalaureate service.

Regarding the range of concerns students bring to me—aside from exorcism requests for their computers: suicidal friend/roommate/family member or one's own thoughts of self-harm, parents' divorce, death, cutters, sexual abuse history or recent assault or accusation of assault, religious questing/identity, how to be more skillful with anxiety (I am a mindfulness meditation instructor), wanting to muse/ask the big questions about life and God, roommate conflicts, getting dumped by girlfriend, needing to dump girlfriend, forgiveness, low self-esteem, healing from religious-based hate or painful theology; healing from thin theology from high school church programming that turned them off to religion; premarital counseling, vocational discernment, interior life—learning to be on *being* mode and not only *doing* mode; learning to accept one's liabilities and limits. Also in the age of helicopter parents and most of our students being from several states away, I receive more phone calls from home. Much gets addressed outside of pastoral care contexts. That happens amid weekly ecumenical Christian chapel; programming and retreats; weekly meditation, mindfulness, and stress reduction sessions that include training the brain through non-attachment to ever-shifting thoughts that come and go, and awareness of how our sad/anxious thoughts are not who we are but rather like clouds covering a vast blue sky. Since my academic courses are about the big questions related to suffering, meaning, and purpose, the classroom is also a context for addressing this range of concerns.

We have used the HERI/UCLA instrument here at Cornell and confirmed that its descriptions and conclusions are valid for us. My on-the-ground experience in both the classroom and outside the classroom with extra-curricular work and pastoral care also backs up the claim. When our institutional research person and I presented our finding to faculty, they liked that we continue to shy away from discussing these matters in the classroom. Some faculty said they do not feel trained/comfortable doing this in the classroom. Some said that addressing these issues in the classroom is not appropriate. And a small number said they already do this, especially those teaching in the arena of religion and sociology.

In terms of human development and faith development theory, the vast majority of young people are in the critical thinking/deconstruction stage during the college years. At least that is so for the kind of student Cornell College attracts. They are supposed to be questioning and are often surprised to hear religious people say that they are to also do that with matters of faith and religion. As you know, some people, including faculty, never leave the deconstruction stage and thus fail to understand trans-spiritual, integral, and poetic ways of approaching religion. They are not able to see the difference between pre- and post-critical approaches. I agree with Ken Wilber's claim that most people in our society operate at a stage and state of consciousness that is not able to do integral spiritual/religious perception and awareness.[69] But those people who can do this make great chaplains because they are able to understand, navigate, and see the contributions of people with differing states and stages of consciousness.

I think most students and faculty consider themselves spiritual but not religious. Perhaps 50% claim to be religious or nominally religious. This was documented in our campus spirituality study.

An inter-spiritual course I taught in India was entirely about the uses of contemplative and meditative practices in academe—the theology and theory in both Hindu and Christian contemplative wisdom traditions, as well as experiential learning. I am also asked to give talks/learning sessions in psychology, kinesiology, and nature-writing courses. I am a member of the professional organization called "Contemplative Mind in Higher Education." It is a great organization reaching across the disciplines.[70] Research on these practices in and outside the classroom attests to increased concentration, mental health, anxiety reduction, and memory retention. There is extensive research in neuroscience and neuroplasticity with science catching up to what Buddhist and Christian contemplative practitioners have known for eons. In the fall, I am starting a Doctor of Ministry program that will feature this subject. I have also begun using assessment instruments. My office has completed a survey of students, faculty, and staff engaged in meditation, mindfulness, and stress-reduction offerings.

The religious studies course "Namaste: Meditation, Mysticism, and Servant Leadership" I taught in India last fall spends much time on the Hindu and Christian notions of the body as a temple for the indwelling of Spirit, Ruach, Atman, Chi/Eternal Life Force.

I asked about ministering to the needs of faculty and staff as well as students.

Last week I visited the dying mother of a longtime staff member and did pre-marital counseling for the daughter and fiancé of another longtime staff person. Tomorrow I am paying a pastoral call per his request to a first-year professor who is having a second major surgery. And Friday I am officiating the marriage of two faculty colleagues. Meanwhile, this precious town [Mt. Vernon, Iowa,] is coming unglued by grief from the three suicides of high school boys. Factions are forming on top of, or as a result of grief, and I have been in the thick of it, extending care to colleagues and townspeople. That should give you a taste of how, yes, my life is full of caring for non-students.

It is interesting that the increase of spiritual but not religious folks means more work for me. Increasingly people are wanting someone like myself who is not sectarian to walk with them through life-stage transitions/losses/marriages without organized religion.

CHAPTER 5

Snapshots

This section of *If Honors Students Were People* consists of an album or anthology of actual practices at a range of institutions.[71] Most are honors endeavors, but some enterprises from other institutions that seem relevant, helpful, and interesting are also included. None of these snapshots is intended as a model to be slavishly imitated although all of them teach valuable lessons for thoughtful contemplation by those working in honors. They represent institutions that are making a serious effort to touch the lives of their students both within and beyond the classroom in ways that integrate their physical, mental, and spiritual development. Chronicled here are successes and failures, and I doubt that anyone at any of these institutions would say they have arrived at their final and full realization of holistic higher education. By and large, however, they are moving—occasionally stumbling—down the right roads.

UNIVERSITY OF NORTH CAROLINA WILMINGTON HONORS COLLEGE

The Honors College at UNC Wilmington offers a course entitled "High Level Wellness" taught by Dr. Cara Sidman, Associate

Professor in the College of Health and Applied Human Sciences. The class overtly combines physical and spiritual development. According to Sidman's syllabus:

> Students will personally and collaboratively explore the dimensions of wellness (i.e., spiritual, emotional, intellectual, physical, and social) through self-assessments, experiential activities, critical-thinking exercises, and reflections. Classes will include mini-lectures, partner/group discussions, and hands-on learning all designed to improve knowledge, awareness, attitudes, and skills associated with healthy lifestyles and high level wellness (i.e., quality of life in all the dimensions). (Sidman)

Each student prepares a wellness self-assessment, sets goals, and keeps a journal. In-class activities include conventional honors seminar discussions as well as experiential wellness activities, such as meditation or walks. In addition, an outside-of-class experiential activity is required of each student, with an academic written reflection following the experience.

Students are enthusiastic about this course and its passionate instructor. One commented: "It really helped me with my problems handling stress, my emotional and physical stress, as well as social skills. The class helped me with all of my other classes, and it has changed the way I think about myself and other people. I'll remember what I learned in this class for the rest of my life." Another remarked that the class "was always helpful enough to make me feel better for the entire week." Several students commented that the class invited them to do things they would most likely not have done otherwise, such as yoga, a boat ride, and nature walk. While the physical activities were clearly the most popular aspect of the class for its students, several also found the discussions "interesting and enlightening." One student summarized the overall reaction: "Wellness is so important and I really learned a lot and challenged myself to grow as a person through this course."

LINCOLN UNIVERSITY AND COKER COLLEGE

In 2009, a controversy erupted at Lincoln University that ultimately received considerable national attention. The issue centered on a physical fitness requirement. This case raises a number of important questions about the degree to which colleges and universities should involve themselves in the physical wellness of their students and how to do so.

Lincoln was originally chartered in 1854, and it is one of the oldest African-American institutions of higher education in America. It has about 2,000 students and occupies an historic campus in rural Pennsylvania not far from Philadelphia.

Eric Hoover describes the controversial plan in *The Chronicle of Higher Education*:

> As part of the university's core curriculum, campus health educators weigh and measure all freshmen during the fall semester, and later calculate each student's body-mass index, or BMI. Those with a BMI above 30, which suggests obesity, must enroll in a one-credit course called "Fitness for Life" before they graduate. Students can satisfy that requirement if they "test out"—by subsequently earning a BMI below 30—or by passing a sports course. (Hoover)

This weight/obesity control requirement drew little attention until the first group of seniors reached the point where they were told that they were not going to graduate because they failed to fulfill it. Over a several year period, about 15% of Lincoln's students had a BMI [Body Mass Index] over 30. Their protest was reported in the campus newspaper, and coverage quickly became nationwide. From some distance, chronologically and geographically, this case seems a model of how sometimes two rights can make a wrong.

Lincoln had long required all students to take a two-credit-hour wellness course. At the time of a curriculum revision in 2006, according to the Chair of the Health, Physical Education, and Recreation Department, James L. DeBoy, an additional course was designed specifically for students with weight problems (ctd. in Epstein). It involved primarily walking and similar fitness activities. This course is the one required for students who failed the BMI test.

When considering this program, experts outside the Lincoln community disagreed in at least two areas: its legality and the BMI test. The Lincoln faculty itself raised some questions about the legality of using such a physical measurement and adding a graduation requirement selectively for some students. Legal opinions from around the country were mixed. As reported in *The Chronicle of Higher Education*, a number of experts in university law thought the requirement was within accepted legal practice; a number believed it was not (Hoover). The second, equally vigorous disagreement among outside experts concerns the validity of the BMI test itself as a sole or primary means of ascertaining unhealthy obesity. Stocky, muscular, well-conditioned individuals can sometimes have a high BMI even though their overall fitness level is satisfactory.

Not surprisingly, once this matter went viral, a number of other issues, even more knotty than those concerning the validity of the BMI or the legality of a graduation requirement surfaced. According to one school of thought, held by a significant number of Lincoln students as well as outside commentators, this test and requirement constitute a grievous invasion of students' privacy. Others argue that Lincoln, as an educational institution, should heed only students' intellectual size, not their waistline girth. One student, Tiana Y. Lawson, writing in the campus newspaper, cogently argues: "I didn't come to Lincoln to be told that my weight is not in an acceptable range. I came here to get an education which, as a three-time honor student, is something I have been doing quite well, despite the fact that I have a slightly high Body Mass Index" (1). Others, such as a blogger cited in *The New York Times,* like the requirement, but think it should be universal, not restricted to those with a high BMI ("Lincoln University Blog").

Perhaps most vexing, though, are the arguments that arose, probably inevitably, involving race. To some, this requirement seemed an effort to require African American students to present an "elite" image of slimness. For example, one respondent to the story in *The Chronicle of Higher Education* wrote:

> I think this has very much to do with the fact that the school is historically black and that it therefore has a more paternalistic attitude toward its students. . . . [W]eight is seen as a class marker, and if all the graduates from Lincoln are slim and "elegant" looking, they figure that the "value" of their degrees will go up. (qtd. in Hoover)

After about a month of heated exchanges about the BMI/weight graduation requirement, the Lincoln faculty in December, 2009, voted to curtail the program. *The Chronicle of Higher Education* reports:

> Under the new faculty proposal, campus health educators would not calculate each student's body-Mass index, or BMI. All students would still be required to take "Dimensions of Wellness," a two-credit course for freshmen and sophomores. Professors who teach that course would evaluate the students' health and physical fitness and, at the end of the semester, recommend that certain students take the additional one-credit course, which features walking, Pilates exercises, and fitness games. Students would not be required to do so, however. (Hoover)

The graduation requirement, thus, is no longer a requirement but a non-mandatory recommendation, based not solely on the controversial BMI test but on several measures. This case represents the story of an institution that tried to do something positive about students' physical well-being but went about it in a politically inept manner.

Recently, another institution, Coker College, with similar goals to Lincoln's but attempting to learn from its predecessor's mistakes, has initiated a universal fitness test, utilizing the BMI. Writing in *Inside Higher Ed*, Alan Grasgreen explains:

> All freshmen this year will take a mandatory "fitness assessment," in which they will—among other things—receive their body mass index (BMI) score, which measures body fat; do a one-mile run/walk; and see how many push-ups and sit-ups they can do in a few minutes. If time permits, the students may also do curl-ups, trunk lifts, and beep tests, in which they run back and forth between two cones at increasingly quick speeds.
>
> When Coker President Robert L. Wyatt gave his inauguration speech in March 2010, he suggested it was time for the college to make some changes. "For more than a century now, Coker has prepared students for the next step in their lives," Wyatt said. "Looking forward, Coker will greet students of a new century, and we must redefine what it means to prepare this generation. "
>
> One way he wants to do that is by educating students on "fiscal and physical fitness" so they can live "long, happily, and well." (Grasgreen)

Following the fitness assessment, Coker first-year students will, as part of Coker College 101, which is a universal introduction-to-college course, participate in at least four physical wellness activities, such as Zumba, kickboxing, or strength training.

OLIVET NAZARENE UNIVERSITY HONORS PROGRAM

Olivet Nazarene University is a small Christian college in Illinois and is affiliated with the Church of the Nazarene. The college has approximately 2,600 undergraduates on its main campus in Bourbonnais. Counting graduate students as well as undergraduates and branch campuses, the total student population is about 4,600. It has created an honors program that overtly seeks to integrate spiritual, physical, and intellectual work. In the words of the director of the honors program, Sue E. Williams:

The core of our program includes four interdisciplinary, general education courses that focus on the question, "What does it mean to be human?" The courses integrate the intellectual, spiritual, and physical dimensions and take the place of these general education courses: Christian Formation, Wellness, College Writing II, and Fundamentals of Communication. Sample topics of study are Exploring Faith and Humanity through Film; Human Disciplines; Exploring Faith and Culture in a Non-Western World; Myths and Messages in Advertising. In addressing the central question about humanity, the courses purposely take a holistic view of humankind, discussing intellectual, spiritual, and physical wholeness.

The four honors core courses (each three credit hours) are entitled

1. Exploring Faith and Humanity;
2. Human Disciplines;
3. Advertising;
4. Technology.

In the first course, the overall theme is "What Does It Mean to be Human?" which is explored through a concentration on film. Students view films; read works related to what they have seen; discuss those topics in the context of Christian formation and personal wellness; and in a "laboratory" linked to the class, engage in physical activities that connect to what they are learning. The Human Disciplines course is a team-taught, interdisciplinary seminar focusing upon five areas in human life: physical, emotional, intellectual, spiritual, and social. These seminars are linked to particular academic disciplines. Students seek to define their goals in these five areas, then work to meet them. The third course, taken in the first term of the second year, uses the thematic topic of advertising as an entry point, and the

> fourth course deals with technology. The other requirement of the honors program is an independent project, scholarly or creative, that may involve an internship or study-away option. (Williams)

I was able to ask an outstanding recent graduate of the Olivet Nazarine Honors Program some questions about her experiences at the college. Katie Eccles' responses were thoughtful and full. Here are some of her thoughts:

> My name is Kathryn Eccles, but I go by Katie. I grew up in Plainfield, Indiana, and graduated from Olivet Nazarene University in May of 2011 with a double major in geology and science education and a minor in biology. I was a member of ONU's first cohort of the university honors program and also graduated *summa cum laude* with departmental honors for geology and was recognized as the most outstanding female graduate through the presentation of the Maggie Sloan Crawford Award. [When the academic year 2011–12 arrives,] I am headed to Boston University to begin a PhD program in Earth Sciences.
>
> The four courses that my cohort took were entitled Exploring Humanity through Film, Human Disciplines, Advertising, and Technology. . . .
>
> The idea behind each class was to use a specific topic to integrate development of communication skills in both public speaking and writing, discussions on faith and morality, and exploration of personal wellness in a more holistic manner. I can give you a couple of specific examples from my courses to illustrate the interactions between these goals. One of our courses centered on advertisements and their role in our society. Throughout the course we examined the messages the advertisements were attempting to convey by analyzing symbolism, exploring graphic design elements, looking at common emotions advertisements attempt to harness, and even creating our own ads. Examples of how communication

skills were incorporated included the writing of analysis papers exploring specific ad examples and giving an informative speech on some aspect of advertising (mine was on food stylists). We also discussed the ethical ramifications that can be associated with advertising, including truth, manipulation, and how far is too far to push our influence on others, as well as health issues, such as the romanticism of unhealthy behaviors and peer pressure.

One of our big projects was to work cooperatively in groups to create two original advertisements, one for heaven and one for hell, using symbolism to convey worldviews we had read about and discussed in class. The advertisements were then placed anonymously on tables and analyzed by our peers for symbolism and the most effective message. This project integrated a discussion of a fundamental tenet of faith (heaven and hell) with a culturally relevant topic and valuable graphic design and communication skills.

A second class example is the course on Human Disciplines. This course sought to explore how discipline is necessary in all areas of our lives. We explored academic discipline as we wrote a large research paper on a topic within our realm of study[; it] required planning to accomplish all the required tasks and incorporated discussions of academic integrity and original thought. Spiritual discipline was discussed as we read a book on the topic and each person had to lead a discussion of one topic and give a class devotion to start class one day. Discipline in our personal health was addressed through discussions of healthy habits, personal health journals we had to keep weekly, and a fitness lab requirement. Two times each week we had to attend a fitness lab for one hour where we did both cardio and weightlifting exercises. This semester was by far one of the most work intensive, and with my fitness activity lab scheduled directly after honors class, I ended up learning the benefit of healthy activity for stress release firsthand!

As far as whether I would define the spiritual aspect as religious, I think most people, including myself, would. Olivet Nazarene University is a Christian institution with a conservative, evangelical background. The majority of the people in my cohort held some kind of established religious beliefs. Therefore, any discussions we had about spiritual aspects would of necessity be approached through the lens of the worldviews held by people in the class. We covered topics such as the Apostle's Creed, heaven and hell, and personal devotions, and we often started class with a devotion. We also discussed more global topics such as worldview and ethics. The discussions attempted to look at how people beyond the Christian community view different spiritual issues, but only someone living through that worldview could really comment on our success. The general education course that it replaces, known as Spiritual Formation, generally focuses on the basics of faith, with emphasis on the beliefs held by the Nazarene Church with which the university is associated.

I would say that the courses stimulated how I see the intersection of intellectual, physical, and spiritual pursuits. I found it interesting that each of our four topics was relevant to learning about intellectual, physical, and spiritual topics. So many times college courses focus on one narrow field, which only touches on one of these subjects. Instead, we had the opportunity to see how one narrow topic really impacts every part of what it means to be human. The "holistic view of humankind" is the most effective way to live. If you do not grow in just one area, it inhibits growth as a whole. Just like a flower would not be able to thrive if it was missing its stem, its leaves, or its petals, as students we do not learn as much if we abandon our faith and our physical wellness in the pursuit of intellectual knowledge.

Physical activities are necessary for my scholarly work. I am a geologist, and as a geologist I have to do fieldwork

> that involves moving rock, hiking, and climbing. Normal physical activity also helps reduce stress although it is often difficult to incorporate faithfully into a busy schedule!
>
> My spiritual growth and development during college challenged some ideas that I grew up with and strengthened my overall understanding of my personal belief system. Without this growth, I feel that I would have a much weaker handle on where I intend to go in the future and would be lacking an important moral compass. (Eccles)

It is gratifying to see the words of a student who clearly "gets it" when it comes to a holistic honors education. Eccles understands the complementary links between intellectual, spiritual, and physical development, and she is able to express that understanding winningly.

* * *

Honors programs and honors colleges have served as stalking horses for their institution in the realm of education for the whole student, as in much else. Here, for example, are two more instances of honors programs involving physical activity: Marshall University and Trinity Christian College.

Dr. Mary Todd, Dean of the Honors College at Marshall University in West Virginia, offers this report:

> The Honors College is new, so the freshmen we welcomed in August comprise our inaugural class. Marshall held its first extended orientation (Week of Welcome) before classes started, two very full days. The Honors College session was the last event on the last day, and we decided the students needed no more talking heads at 3 o'clock on a Friday afternoon. So we told them we were going to offer them some stress relief as well as a strategy for relaxing: one thing we knew about honors students was that they tended to be somewhat intense and often put a good bit of pressure on themselves. We hired a yoga instructor who led them through 30 minutes of exercise—while we prepared her to

> do this with students in chairs, we ended up with 150 students on the floor!
>
> The feedback has been nothing but positive. A student stopped me later that day to tell me how much he loved the yoga session. My staff has decided to do it again during finals week. (Todd)

Another small college honors program, in this case at Trinity Christian College in Illinois, is making an overt effort to include cultivation of the physical for students of above-average academic achievement. Aron Reppman, then the faculty director of Trinity's Honors Program, writes:

> I have a couple of anecdotes to offer that I believe are good signs of healthy connections: This fall, as part of our program of Honors Program co-curricular events, we fielded a team for Trinity's annual "Troll Trot" 5K race during Homecoming. (Our college mascot is the Troll.) Fourteen of us, students and faculty, wore matching T-shirts specially designed for the event by three student volunteers. While there were some accomplished athletes in the group, there were also several (including myself) for whom the camaraderie of this "community of challenge and support" freed us to participate when we likely would not have done so on our own
>
> In this semester's Honors Philosophy course (a GenEd replacement course primarily for sophomores), two varsity women's soccer team members have been writing perceptively on the connections they are finding between their embodied knowledge of the game and philosopher Michael Polanyi's concept of "personal knowledge." (Reppmann)

Why have honors programs and colleges embraced fitness activities enthusiastically? I believe that at least part of the reason has to do with the traditional image of honors students and honors programs within colleges and universities. Although not a shred of evidence to support such a notion exists, on many campuses honors is perceived as a haven for couch-potato geeks, students who bury themselves in the library or the honors center and never come out to play. Honors directors, deans, faculty members, and students wisely realize that including fitness activities within the structure of honors work may go some way towards dispelling this unattractive and inaccurate myth.

ORAL ROBERTS UNIVERSITY HONORS PROGRAM

Oral Roberts University (ORU) in Tulsa, Oklahoma, offers undergraduate majors in 65 subjects, 14 master's degrees, and the PhD in two areas, both of which are ministerial degrees. All students on campus are required to attend twice-weekly chapel services. ORU focuses vigorously on what it calls "whole person education"—mind, spirit, body. Thus the catalog description of general education has three sections: "For the Spirit . . . a continuing process of spiritual awareness and Bible study" that requires 9 credit hours of work; "For the Mind . . . a continuing process of developing skills, acquiring knowledge, and formulating a Christian world vision" (9 hours); and "For the Body . . . study and active participation in activities conducive to good health" (4.5–5 hours) (Oral Roberts University E-Portfolio 32–33).

In the physical education category, students are required to complete (a) two courses in "Health Fitness," (b) a swimming test, and (c) an activity course each semester they are enrolled as on-campus, full-time students. Moreover,

> a personal fitness program must be part of the student's lifestyle at ORU. Emphasis is placed on individual personal responsibility for health and upon recognition that lifestyle has a significant relationship to the quality and length of life. Students are also urged to participate daily in aerobic activity that is provided through individual programs and intramural sports throughout their college programs. (Oral Roberts University Catalog)

A key element in this whole-person focus is a very detailed, precise assessment mechanism that each student completes through an e-portfolio. This includes a lifestyle assessment with sections on personal health care, such as avoiding tobacco or getting enough sleep; drugs and alcohol, such as using only prescribed medicinal drugs, abstaining from alcohol consumption; and five items on physical fitness:

1. I do some light stretching before exercising and gradually increase my intensity during the workout.
2. I perform a variety of resistance exercises to help keep my body strong, a minimum of 2 days per week.
3. I drink plenty of water (or sports drink) before, during, and after a workout.
4. I exercise aerobically (continuous jogging, walking, cycling, etc.) for a minimum of 20 minutes, 6 to 7 days per week.
5. I stretch to improve/maintain my flexibility a minimum of 3 days per week. (Oral Roberts University E-Portfolio)

Moreover, faculty members at ORU are expected to pay attention to personal wellness and fitness. The current faculty handbook, for example, prescribes in the section on professional responsibilities: "All full-time faculty members shall engage in a healthy lifestyle which includes an aerobics exercise program" (Oral Roberts University Faculty Handbook 39).

An honors faculty member, Dr. John Korstad, explains his support for ORU's whole-person philosophy by noting a number of passages from scripture, including these:

> Do you not know that your bodies are temples of the Holy Spirit, who is in you, whom you have received from God? You are not your own; you were bought at a price. Therefore honor God with your bodies. (I Cor. 6:19–20)

> In him the whole building is joined together and rises to become a holy temple in the Lord. And in him you too are

> being built together to become a dwelling in which God lives by his Spirit. (Eph. 2:21–22)

> Whatever you do, work at it with all your heart, as working for the Lord, not for men. . . (Col. 3:2)

Students from the ORU Honors Program report that they participate enthusiastically in both the service and the wellness activities of the university. Two students sent comments to me through Korstad. One reports on an honors service program based in the honors residence:

> Girls from my floor, which is also one of the honors floors, participated in something called 'Illuminate' this spring where they wore the same shirt from this certain organization to raise money for a good cause. . . . The one [who] organized this and rallied everyone together was Vanessa Sweet, a fellow from the honors program who lives on the honors floor. (qtd. in Korstad)

Another student reports on physical activities, also in honors residences:

> I know that a group of honors kids from the honors floors would play basketball or some other sport for three hours almost every Friday to have some fun. (qtd. in Korstad)

UNIVERSITY OF MINNESOTA MORRIS

The University of Minnesota's Morris campus (UMM) is one of five campuses of the University of Minnesota. UMM is a public liberal arts college of about 1,800 undergraduates. This college has a larger-than-average responsibility to tend to all aspects of students' lives since the resources of the surrounding community are somewhat limited. It has responded with several initiatives that speak to the physical and spiritual needs of the students whose intellectual stimulation is the responsibility of its liberal arts academic program.

In the 1990s, UMM had seriously outgrown its gymnasium and recreation facilities. Other than an indoor ice-skating facility, the town of Morris had no public fitness options and no private commercial ones either. The college's facilities manager and the Morris City Manager conceived the idea of a new, shared wellness center. The creative concept of a campus/community fitness facility met with both support and skepticism, both on campus and in the community. The supporters prevailed: the completed building is called the Regional Fitness Center (RFC). It is open most days from 5:30 a.m. to 11:00 p.m. At any given time, individuals from both campus and community can be found using the center, but it turned out that the peak hours for college students and for community residents do not usually coincide. Operations are funded by memberships, with the campus administration subsidizing memberships for faculty and staff and the student body assessing a universal and thus modest fitness center fee. It is governed by a campus/community "joint powers board." The website states:

> The RFC supports many local community group and business needs; provides community services through 'worksite wellness', community garden, and healthy activity maps grants; and hosts community events such as the 'Health Fair.' Currently, the RFC has over 1,300 community member users and approximately 1,500 UMM student members. Facility uses total almost 100,000 entries per year and our programs serve over 10,000 community users each year including year round fitness classes, swim lessons, and summer programs for youth. (*University of Minnesota Morris Regional Fitness Center*)

This shared fitness center proved so successful and popular that the campus and community subsequently decided to build a new football stadium, to be shared by the high school and college teams, the former playing its games on Friday evenings, the latter on Saturday afternoons, as well some soccer matches. Again, pooled resources enabled the construction of a far better facility than either entity could have managed by itself.

In addition to an innovative approach to helping students keep their bodies physically fit, UMM's interest in wellness has also extended to what they put into those bodies: campus food. Usually, of course, campus food service is, along with parking, a prime source of student dissatisfaction. After a survey in a sociology class showed strong student interest in local and organic foods, the college founded a "Pride of the Prairie" local foods initiative. When the college put its food service out for bids in 2001, it made the use of locally produced foods an important part of the request for proposals. Now, according to Dr. Sandra K. Olson-Loy, the responsible campus administrator, "most of our meals are sourced within 150 miles of the campus rather than the 1,500–2,000 miles food travels to reach the average U. S. dinner plate" (Olson-Loy). Each fall and spring, there are special Pride of the Prairie meals, attended not only by students but by campus faculty and staff and local farmers and food producers. In several cases, this gastronomic venture has blended into academic work. So, for example, one studio art major did a senior capstone project telling the story of the wild rice harvest of the White Earth Band of Ojibwe of Northern Minnesota. Not surprisingly, like the campus/community fitness center, this venture has brought the college and its regional neighbors closer together.

The two enterprises described briefly above have moved closer together: a community garden space has been opened at the Regional Fitness Center, coordinated through the Morris Healthy Eating Initiative, and a principal occupant is the UMM Organic Gardening Club.

Another venture on the Morris campus, according to Shannon Hodges, has provided spiritual sustenance. In the 1990s the Office of the Chancellor and the Office of Student Counseling cooperated to create what was called "The Spiritual Pathways Series" (Hodges 25). Each event in this series featured a speaker from within the campus community who practiced a faith tradition outside the mainline Christian heritage. Speakers included Muslims, Jews, Wiccans, Native Americans, a member of a Gay Protestant group, Hindus, and Buddhists. Speakers were asked to outline some of the core beliefs and practices of their faith; to describe how they sought to practice that religion in an isolated, non-diverse environment; and then to participate in an open discussion session.

Although the Spiritual Pathways Series was successful, it atrophied after the individuals who created it left campus over a period of a few years. Soon thereafter, however, it was rekindled under the sponsorship of the Library and several other campus organizations as Asking the Big Questions (ATBQ). The ATBQ group meets six times a year for about 90 minutes. Although it has sometimes focused on religion and spirituality, the topics have ranged further afield than the predecessor Spiritual Pathways program to include sustainability and women's issues. Peter Bremer, the series coordinator has described it thus in a personal email conversation: "An annual campus and community-wide book discussion of some of the big questions facing our world. Each year thought-provoking readings are picked to read and then discuss. Guest speakers may occasionally drop by" (Bremer). Frequently the presentations and discussions have been directly linked to the campus' academic program. For example, some sessions on religion were co-sponsored by the Philosophy Department.

A relatively isolated, relatively small public liberal arts college in the rural upper Midwest, the University of Minnesota Morris has created a range of programs tied to its core academic mission that focus on physical wellness and spiritual inquiry and understanding.

TEXAS TECH UNIVERSITY HONORS COLLEGE AND THE UNIVERSITY OF ALBERTA AUGUSTANA: OUTDOOR LEARNING

One of the most productive curricular means of combining physical cultivation with cognitive development is outdoor education: students embarking on outdoor adventures that involve physical activity, even physical challenge, while simultaneously studying issues involving the regions through which they are traveling. Such site-based experiential programs offer opportunities to study the flora and fauna of the region, the impact of human development, the sociology and culture of the inhabitants, history, and literature. The NCHC-sponsored experiential programs of Honors Semesters and Partners in the Parks both are strongly site-specific, and both have sometimes involved physical challenges and spiritual opportunities. Here are two programs, one at an honors college, and the other at a public liberal arts institution in Canada.

The Honors College at Texas Tech University has created a major track entitled "Environment and the Humanities." This program was initiated by Dr. Gary Bell, the former dean. It combines field experiences involving a significant physical challenge with serious, honors-level cognitive study of environmental issues. The program has introduced students to canoe trips on the rivers of the Western U. S. The degree is described on the *Texas Tech University Honors College* website:

> The EVHM degree program is an interdisciplinary approach to the study of the environment and the human relationship to it. EVHM students learn from a variety of disciplines toward this end, including science, philosophy, literature, and the arts. Though it is focused on the natural world and our place in it, the degree can be customized to fit a student's future academic and occupational goals, such as nature or environmental writing, the study of law, pre-medicine, natural history interpretation, and photography. (Texas Tech University Environment and the Humanities)

Here is a description of a capstone experience for this program:

> *Leadership and Landscape—Seminar*
>
> The outdoors is our classroom in this field experience course. Students will spend two weeks traveling in canoes on a Montana river, while honing skills in leadership and group dynamics, creative writing, critical reading, and primitive camping. Students will take on leadership roles, and be offered peer feedback on judgment and decision making. In addition, we'll attend to experiences in solitude

> and in community in nature, and make a point of exploring the flora, fauna, geology, weather, archaeology, and history of the river canyon. (Texas Tech University Environment and the Humanities)

Bell describes his vision of a "perfect honors curriculum":

> some combination of and integration of the intellectual and physical elements in a young person's development—with a heavy emphasis on the out-of-doors element of education. This could include a curriculum of organized sports activities, in my judgment, with courses analyzing the role of the physical in one's intellectual development. (64)

* * *

The University of Alberta's Augustana Campus is located in Camrose, Alberta, Canada, about 60 miles southeast of Edmonton. It is a small branch of the large University of Alberta, in Edmonton. The Augustana Campus is a member of the Consortium of Public Liberal Arts Colleges (COPLAC). Its website describes the rather varied history of the campus as follows:

> Established in 1910 by Norwegian settlers, under the name Camrose Lutheran College, Augustana is still inspired by convictions that are part of its pioneer legacy: that personal wholeness emerges from a liberal education, that the proper end of leadership is service to others, and that the spirit of cooperation so crucial to rural life invigorates human endeavor. (*University of Alberta Augustana*)

Dr. Roger Epp, the former Dean of the Augustana Campus, observes that the outdoor/wilderness programs of the college are the signature ventures of their experiential-learning emphasis: "Safe to say that this is one place where academic, physical, and spiritual come together for students. One of the highlights of this program is an alternate-year summer canoe expedition on a selected Arctic river to the Arctic Ocean" (Epp). The college offers, in alternate years, an Arctic canoe expedition and a two-and-a half-week dogsledding excursion. The Arctic canoe trip takes place in late spring, in connection with course work in geography ("Geography of the Canadian North") and the physical education department. Past trips have gone down such rivers as the Hood, Kuujjua, Thelon, and Horton, and most expeditions have ended at the Arctic Ocean. Among the wildlife students see are caribou, grizzly bears, musk oxen, wolves, wolverines, and gyrefalcons. The students and their leaders travel through a largely treeless landscape, but one colored by wildflowers at this time of year. The dogsledding expedition takes place in the dead of winter. According to its description, "Students can expect an authentic northern experience marked by retrieving water from the Great Slave Lake, collecting firewood, ice-fishing, and, of course, dogsledding. Each student handles their own team of dogs . . . on the arctic tundra" (*University of Alberta Augustana Outdoor Programs*). In addition to camping, they spend time studying at and learning about a remote homestead. They read narratives of the Northland and study Canadian cultural identity and heritage.

These expeditions are designed to be physically challenging and spiritually stimulating as well as intellectually demanding. The lead professor for the Augustana Campus' expeditions is Associate Professor of Physical Education Morten Asfeldt. In regards to the physical challenges of the arctic expedition, he states:

> For example, in June, Glen [Hvenegaard] and I led a group on an expedition that included pulling our canoes over the ice of Artillery Lake; Artillery Lake is 95 km long. This took us four days and I think all students would agree that it was a physically demanding task that resulted in tired legs and backs each day. This was followed by portaging our canoes and gear from Artillery Lake to Great Slave Lake over Pike's Portage, which is a 36 km series of lakes and portages (about 12 km of portaging and 24 km of paddling). The last portage is 5 km long and we all carried 3 loads over these 5 km in one day—a total of 25 kms of walking, 15 of those with heavy loads. This was a significant accomplishment for us

> all, and we all felt a great sense of satisfaction on completing this stage of our journey.
>
> The physically demanding element is important for a number of reasons. First of all, for most of us, our lives do not require physical engagement in order to live. We no longer have to haul water in a bucket to drink or shovel coal or chop wood to heat our homes and to travel; most often we hop in a car or on a bus to get where we need to go. Rarely do we walk, ride a bike, or paddle a canoe to get from A to B except for self-chosen recreation. Therefore, the process of self-propelled wilderness travel is an important contrast to our daily lives that provides an opportunity to increase our physical fitness levels, to feel the satisfaction of a hard day's travel when our bodies feel tired—perhaps exhausted—yet alive with sensation and goodness, and to inspire and give students confidence to live a more physically engaged life. (Asfeldt)

This expedition seems to me an exceptionally well thought-out program taking advantage of the natural setting of this small university.

Asfeldt explains how these challenging expeditions become spiritually enlightening as well as physically challenging:

> What we intend to do is provide students the opportunity to experience and consider the "numinous". . . . By the "numinous," we mean that which is above and beyond the religious notion of goodness or holy. However, for some students, the numinous is rooted in the Christian idea of good and holy; and this is fine but we don't want to limit spiritual exploration to the narrow confines of the western notion of Christianity.
>
> Similar to our thoughts regarding the physically demanding aspects of these expeditions, the everyday life of our students is often aspiritual or strongly influenced—both negatively and positively—by their experiences with

> western ideas of Christianity. What we strive to do is to provide experiences where students might open themselves to experiencing and considering spiritual, or numinous, ideas, feelings, thoughts, and insights. Again, part of this motivation is driven by the fast-paced technologically overburdened lives that students live that rarely leave space for considering the spiritual. We often think of the insights that people such as Thoreau, Muir, Annie Dillard and others have come to by intentionally immersing themselves in the natural world. (Asfeldt)

With colleagues Glen Hvenegaard and Ingrid Urberg, Asfeldt has written at length on the theory and practice of these ventures. One essay, published as a book chapter, is entitled "Expeditions and Liberal Arts University Education." Here, the authors argue that educational expeditions recognize and partially correct some of the shortcomings of institutionalized education, and "are an attempt to return to a more intuitive, organic, and natural form of learning" (67). Such ventures offer faculty an opportunity to "engage students in a holistic manner that is difficult in the classroom" (67). Of particular note in this study, Asfeldt, Hvenegaard, and Urberg describe the goals of educational expeditions as "personal growth, leadership development, disciplinary-specific skill development and knowledge acquisition, . . . cultural awareness, community development, environmental sustainability, and spiritual exploration" (68). In addition, they make clear their strong belief that for expeditions to be truly worthwhile, they need to be "physically demanding" (69). Asfeldt, Hvenegaard, and Urberg cite research suggesting that wilderness travel provides "opportunities for solitude, challenge, reflection, and interaction with God" (70). They argue that such a holistic, dramatically interdisciplinary approach belongs in a liberal arts setting, and they link it to Augustana's efforts to educate the whole person. They conclude that adventures such as the Arctic canoe trip and the dogsledding expedition facilitate "student learning in their preparation for a life well-lived" (75).

In another scholarly discussion of their philosophy of challenging wilderness expeditions, Asfeldt, Urberg, and Bob Henderson of McMaster University focus upon the values of place-based teaching.[72] In this piece, they discuss the dogsledding expedition described above, including the visit to the northern Canada wilderness homestead, where they spend eight days of the two-week journey. The goal of the course is "to create 'landfullness' in our students by re-establishing a vital relationship to the world so that they may play a responsible role in their local and global landscapes" (34). The experience, according to Asfeldt, Urberg, and Hvenegaard, is physically adventurous and challenging, providing "authentic full-body sensory experiences" (39). Students are not spared some of the gritty aspects of life in the wilderness, aspects of life that seem in some ways to contradict the outdoors ethic of Leave No Trace. These experiences include hunting and fishing, trapping, even skinning wolves. As a direct consequence of the physical challenges, intellectual exercise, and spiritual reflection of these expeditions, they conclude:

> We see that our students begin to re-establish a vital relationship to nature, that they start to imagine a more direct means of living, and that personal narratives combined with the full-body sensory experience of the homestead and trail experiences are central to their development of place-consciousness. (10–11)

I was able to ask student participants about their reactions to one of the Augustana Campus expeditions. Here are some of my questions to one student, Erika Heiberg, and her responses:

1. *What were the expeditions on which you participated?*

   Dogsledding—February 2010 and Arctic Canoeing—June 2011

2. *Would you describe these experiences as physically demanding?*

   Yes, I would consider them to be physically demanding. I will answer separately for both courses:

   Dogsledding—the homestead stay has morning chores

that can be physically taxing—chopping wood, hauling fresh water from the lake. We also spend some of the time trekking through the snow, which can be physically taxing [because] there was much more snow than I am used to.

Arctic Canoeing—this was a very physically demanding course. Pulling canoes across the ice for 6 hours+/day, which included scouting across questionable ice patches, having to be ready to jump into a boat before the ice fell apart below you, as well as pulling across the pressure ridges and fresh snow, which proved to be harder than just ice. Portaging was very physically demanding. Especially in the beginning of our portage, the trail was unmarked and we had to wayfind while carrying substantial loads through thick brush, uphill, or across boggy areas. Canoeing in strong winds was also taxing at times, as well as breaking through ice in order to pull our canoes through proved to be very physically taxing.

For the most part, I found that both courses were also mentally taxing because they forced me to push myself forward when I did not think I could any more, or to do things that I did not think I would be physically capable of.

3. *Did you find that the physical challenges contributed to your intellectual growth? Did you learn?*

I would consider some of my learning to be scholarly. As a physical education major, I have taken physiology, biomechanics, and other exercise science courses. These physically demanding courses allowed me to see much of the theory that I had learned previously in practice, as well as employ some of those ideas in order to make my own actions more efficient and effective, such as what we eat and why we eat it, as well as distribution of loads while carrying them and the pressure or stress that it can put on one's body.

I also find that these physically demanding trips often allow me to reflect on things much more, allowing me to come to conclusions that I otherwise would not have. For example, what a necessary level of comfort is for living—do we need to have running water, electricity, gas heating, etc., or can we be just as satisfied, if not more, without it?

I also learn about the surroundings and what/how I can use them. For example, what different types of ice are and what is safe to travel on or easy to break apart, different plants and their uses (eating, antibiotic, etc), animal tracks and droppings—allow us to see what lives in the area, but can also help to distinguish a safe path of travel/ common path of travel.

I also consider it important to discuss the influences of nature on us as people and vice versa. It is amazing how much the environment can help or hinder someone while travelling. It can make things physically (and mentally) much easier or much harder. For example, the wind blowing all of the ice of Great Slave Lake into our direction and path of travel, forcing us to slow down and break it apart to get through, moving only 5 km in a day, while the wind can also clear our path allowing us to go 30+ km in a day with ease.

These physically demanding trips also allow me to think and learn about the historical significance and value of such activities. For example, without a portage route and canoeing, the fur trade, hunting, and diamond industries of Canada would have been stunted in growth, people may have starved and Northern Canada would be even less developed and populated than it is now. At the same time, it raises questions of the humanity of exploiting these natural resources for personal gain, such as diamonds, and the benefits vs. the losses of disturbing a fragile habitat and environment.

I have found these expeditions to be very beneficial to my spiritual growth. They have allowed me to be more at peace with the situations I find myself in, and rather than worrying or regretting what I could have done or could have had, I learned to focus on what I have and what I can do with that, rather than focusing on what I do not have.

These courses have helped me learn to distinguish [. . .] questions that can be answered quickly from those that need lots of time and deliberation and that it is okay to spend time and effort on some, rather than always feeling like I need to have an answer to everything.

I also think these experiences have helped to reinforce my spiritual beliefs because there are many things that I do not believe I could do on my own, and also there are experiences in nature that can help us and teach us so much that I do not think would happen if there was not some form of higher spiritual power.

4. *Did the expedition change the direction of your life in any way? If so, what way(s)? What exactly happened on the trip that led to those changes?*

Probably. I find that spending time with people such as the professors, fellow students, and people I have met along the way has really helped me to get where I am now. Many of my close friends are those who went on the trip with me, or had gone on them before/after me because I find that there are things that only they can relate to and understand, such as in trying to describe my Arctic Canoeing experience. It cannot be summed up in one or two words, such as "good," because there was so much that made that trip the way it was. It had its ups and downs, challenges and celebrations, but unless someone has experienced something similar, I do not think they can really comprehend its significance, or describe it. (Heiberg)

Clearly, an important lesson Heiberg learned through the University of Alberta Augustana outdoor programs was to understand how expeditions such as she describes have shaped her educational career and her philosophy of life.

Because of its relatively isolated location, it is particularly important that the college offers students the opportunity to explore different cultures. One such global education program focuses specifically on spiritual issues. Every other year Augustana offers a three-week summer study tour of India that concentrates on the intersection of religion and development. Visits are made to Indian universities and to a number of development sites animated out of the contexts of the Hindu, Christian, and Sikh traditions, among others. Following an on-campus introductory prerequisite class during the winter term, this three-credit summer course in either religion or economics provides an avenue for students to explore a majority-world country in a manner that makes them feel safe and secure. Firsthand experiences with Indian people and organizations give students an in-depth understanding of India, its cultural and religious diversity, and the challenges it faces in the twenty-first century (*University of Alberta Augustana International Programs*).

The Augustana Campus of the University of Alberta proclaims that it seeks to cultivate its students as whole persons, especially through the use of experiential pedagogies. The wilderness expeditions are an especially adventurous emblem of this institutional mission. By leaving the comforts of the campus, these teachers and students are showing new ways to combine scholarly activity with physical challenge and spiritual reflection. Winter dogsledders and Arctic canoeists are going to get cold and wet and despondent; they are also going to be tired and proud and ecstatic. And, surely, in doing so they learn things about themselves and their world that take them beyond the classroom.

SAINT FRANCIS UNIVERSITY HONORS PROGRAM

Saint Francis University is located in Loretto, PA, not far from Altoona. About 2,600 students are enrolled there; 1,800 are undergraduates. It is one of the oldest Catholic colleges in America, and it is the oldest Franciscan university in the country. The modest, service-oriented piety of the Saint for whom the university is named is a recurrent theme in its written, electronic, and personal communications. It is unusual to spend a half-hour speaking to someone from Saint Francis or reading any of their publications without encountering the story of Saint Francis meeting the leper and seeing in his countenance the face of Jesus. These Franciscan values are evident in the university's statement of its mission and in the shape of the education offered there, especially in the honors program. Professor Dan Fredricks, who teaches in the honors first-year course reflects: "I believe that students in our honors program are subtly but inescapably encouraged to remain open to the experiences that will come in the still, quiet, reflective, and even passive moments" (Fredricks). Saint Francis University's mission statement certainly emphasizes a higher-education experience aimed at the whole student, not just at developing her or his intellectual skills:

> A Mind for Excellence: Saint Francis University offers higher education in an environment guided by Catholic values and teachings, and inspired by the example of our patron, Saint Francis of Assisi.
>
> A Spirit for Peace and Justice: University programs and activities foster such Franciscan values as a humble and generous attitude toward learning, respect for diversity and the uniqueness of individual persons, understanding of ethical issues, and reverence for all life.
>
> A Heart for Service: We seek to inspire in all members of the University community a love of lifelong learning and a commitment to share their gifts and skills generously with others in a rapidly changing world. (Saint Francis University Statement)

According to Dr. Donna Menis, Director of the Saint Francis University Honors Program, "Our honors program provided a bit of the impetus for the now university-wide focus on spiritual wellness" (Menis). In 1984, when the honors program was inaugurated, it created a "semester of service" requirement for all its students, which was the beginning of formal service within the curriculum of Saint Francis (Menis). The service requirement was adopted ten years later in the all-college general education program, at which point the honors program incorporated service into its sophomore seminars. Currently students living at the Bach Family Honors House complete a group service project each year.

In an impressive and creative step, the Saint Francis Honors Program has each honors professor list the ethical dimensions of each particular course on the class syllabus. One faculty member notes "the kind of questions and discussions that students encounter in the honors classroom help them develop a sense of social and political awareness" (qtd. in Menis).

The university as a whole recently undertook a revision of its core curricular requirements. According to Dr. Don Walkovich, Associate Dean of Saint Francis University, the revised core has 14 Objectives and number 14 deals with "wellness" (Walkovich):

> Objective 14: Develop an understanding of key elements of personal health and wellness, major health care issues, and the well-being of communities. (Saint Francis University Goals)

It is noteworthy that this general education objective pertains both to physical fitness and to spiritual well-being. Saint Francis established a Wellness Task Force that articulated seven "dimensions of wellness," displayed below. That these dimensions of mental, physical, and spiritual wellness are carefully linked to the University's overarching statement of the "goals of Franciscan higher education" is impressive.

Operational Definitions

Wellness is an evolving, multi-dimensional state of being in which mind, body, and spirit are purposefully integrated in an active process designed to help individuals and communities become more aware of and make choices toward an optimal quality of life.

Dimensions of Wellness

Mind

Psychological Wellness is the process of recognizing that each individual person is a unique combination of God-given abilities. The individual is called to develop the skill to identify, assess and manage emotions and behaviors, while maintaining a balance between self-reliance and seeking help from others. Psychological wellness includes being motivated to engage in creative pursuits and effective problem solving, ultimately encouraging growth in oneself and others.

Relationship to the Franciscan Goals of Higher Education

- Respect for the Uniqueness of Individual Persons
- A Spirit of Simplicity and Joy

Financial Wellness is the process of developing stewardship over one's personal finances where income and expenditures are managed through a budget providing for self-sufficiency, peace of mind, and compassion to those in need, especially the poor and disenfranchised.

Relationship to the Franciscan Goals of Higher Education

- Service to the Poor and Needy
- A Franciscan Presence

Body

Physical Wellness is the process of making healthy choices related to exercise, nutrition, rest and sleep, intentional and responsible sexual choices, stress management, management of injury and illness, and the responsible use of alcohol and other drugs.

Relationship to the Franciscan Goals of Higher Education

- Respect for the Uniqueness of Individual Persons
- Reverence for All Life

Environmental Wellness is the process of appreciating our natural surroundings and understanding the role of individuals and groups in sustaining and protecting our environment. Our Franciscan heritage calls us to make responsible choices regarding the use of resources such as air, water, land and energy, which contribute to our wellness and the preservation of Mother Earth for future generations.

Relationship to the Franciscan Goals of Higher Education

- Reverence for All Life and for the Goodness of All Humanity
- A Global Vision

Occupational Wellness is the process of making a positive contribution to the workplace and striving for personal fulfillment from a career while maintaining balance in our lives. A commitment to lifelong learning gives us a sense of direction, goals, and skills to effectively collaborate with co-workers and those we serve.

Relationship to the Franciscan Goals of Higher Education

- A Global Vision
- A Humble and Generous Attitude Toward Learning

Spirit

Spiritual Wellness is the process of discovering meaning and purpose in life, and demonstrating values through behaviors. Spiritual wellness includes acceptance of the concepts of wholeness, unity, diversity, individual uniqueness, and the need for community as well as personal responsibility to oneself and that community.

Relationship to the Franciscan Goals of Higher Education

- A Community of Faith and Prayer
- A Franciscan Presence

Social Wellness is the process of creating, embracing, and maintaining healthy relationships through the choices we make at home, at work and in our communities. We are called to compassionately serve others, especially the poor and disenfranchised, and to empower future generations to peacefully work together in a spirit of mutual respect and cooperation.

Relationship to the Franciscan Goals of Higher Education

- A Spirit of Simplicity and Joy
- A Humble and Generous Attitude Toward Learning

(Saint Francis University Goals)

To meet these ambitious wellness goals, the university devised four core wellness courses. These courses are sequential, moving from the individual student out into the larger issues of global well-being. The syllabus of each of these courses reiterates the overall wellness policies and aspirations of Saint Francis University, then details how that specific course will fulfill particular goals, missions, and objectives.

In addition to the curricular effort to integrate mental, physical, and spiritual wellness, Saint Francis University maintains a vigorous program of service to its surrounding community, which provides numerous opportunities for service and volunteerism for its students. These programs are centered in the Dorothy Day Center, named for twentieth-century progressive activist Dorothy Day, the founder of the Catholic Worker movement and the newspaper of the same name.

Indeed, Saint Francis University's program of student volunteerism is sufficiently energetic that the responsible administrator, Fr. Daniel Sinisi, Vice President for Mission Effectiveness and

Integration, issued a 17-page "Service Leadership Report," covering the 2009–10 period and cataloging a dramatic range of service projects undertaken by the students (Sinisi). Here are several examples: the students in the honors program collected books to be sent to areas of the world that need them; the athletics department sponsored a "Sports 4 Kids" day for local youngsters; and students maintain a clothing pantry for families in need.

One recent addition to the campus is a rather unusual enterprise named the DiSepio Institute for Rural Health and Wellness; it opened early in 2010. This institute integrates a number of disparate health services under one roof, and its Executive Director is the Dean of the School of Health Sciences (DiSepio).

- The DiSepio Institute is linked to a continuing program of research in rural health issues, that the University has operated under the rubric of CERMUSA, an acronym for Center of Excellence for Remote and Medically Under-Served Areas.
- The Institute houses a complete rehabilitation center, serving the region, including physical therapy and cardiac rehabilitation programs.
- It is also the home of the campus fitness center, with a 3,500-square-foot gym and a 1,000-square-foot group exercise room. This facility serves students, faculty, and staff of the university, but is also open to community membership.
- The facility includes a conference center.
- The mission of the Institute also includes spiritual wellness, so the facility includes an outdoor meditation garden and labyrinth and an indoor ecumenical meditation center. The Institute intends to undertake programming in the "theology of wellness."
- Two travel study scholarships to undertake clinical work in foreign countries are funded by the Institute every year, benefiting students in the health sciences areas.

- Health and wellness programs for students, employees, and the community are sponsored by the Institute.
- There are two residencies in the area of Physical Therapy, one in Orthopedic Therapy, one in Sports Therapy.
- This facility is the home of the University Student Health Service.
- Finally, the DiSepio Institute sponsors a symposium series, for example a recent symposium focusing on Current Concepts in Mild Traumatic Brain Injury/Concussion Examination and management. (DiSepio)

Saint Francis University may be relatively small and it may advocate the humble modesty of its namesake, but its range of programs knitting together the intellectual, spiritual, and physical lives of its students, faculty, staff, and community is substantial and ambitious.

MINOT STATE UNIVERSITY HONORS PROGRAM

Minot State University (MSU) in North Dakota has an eightfold wellness program, which is primarily under the aegis of student support services. Located in Minot, whose population is 40,000, MSU is home to about 3,850 students, mostly undergraduates, but with several master's-level programs. This enrollment may seem relatively small, and indeed, compared to many public universities, it is, but MSU is the third-largest public university in the eleven-campus North Dakota state system. That system, as a whole, enrolls about 48,000 students, with North Dakota State University and the University of North Dakota each at a bit over 14,000. Thus MSU has some 8% of the students attending public four-year institutions in North Dakota.[73]

MSU defines "wellness" broadly: as a way of life that emphasizes the whole person through a positive approach to healthy living. It approaches wellness from eight different aspects: emotional, physical, occupational, intellectual, social, spiritual, environmental, and multicultural. Each area offers a definition of that aspect of wellness and a set of characteristics that would be a sign of wellness within that realm. Here are the descriptions from the university website of intellectual, spiritual, and physical wellness that MSU promulgates:

> **Intellectual Wellness**
>
> Involves lifelong learning through formal education and informal life experiences. It refers to active participation in scholastic, cultural, and community activities. Being intellectually healthy is having openness to new ideas and maintaining a sense of humor, creativity and curiosity.
>
> **Physical Wellness**
>
> Involves respecting your body's own uniqueness and diversity, and engaging in practices that move you towards a higher level of health. Developing healthy habits such as getting enough sleep, eating a balanced diet, exercising, abstaining from alcohol and drugs, learning about diseases and the symptoms that accompany them, getting regular medical checkups, and protecting yourself from injury can add years to life and help you remain focused on the balance of body-mind-spirit. The physical benefits of looking good and feeling terrific most often lead to the psychological benefits of enhanced self-esteem, self-control, determination and a sense of direction.
>
> **Spiritual Wellness**
>
> Integrating your beliefs and values with your actions. Having a sense of purpose, direction, and awareness and realizing that values, rights, and responsibilities take some thought and discussion. The capacities for love, forgiveness, compassion, joy, and peace are hallmarks of a spiritual wellness. To be spiritually well is to be in harmony with oneself and others. (Minot State University Wellness)

MSU has constructed a new $15 million Health and Wellness Center "designed to incorporate all aspects of a campus devoted to fostering education on health-related majors and healthy lifestyles in modern state-of-the-art facilities. It will do this by bringing together related programs into a new facility that will promote a synergistic sharing of ideas" (Minot State University Wellness).

Another wellness initiative, sponsored by the campus Lutheran group and focusing upon spirituality, was the creation of a series entitled "Spiritual Wellness," which was described at its launch:

> **Wellness Works**
>
> *Spiritual Wellness Series*
>
> Lutheran Campus Ministry is excited to announce a new lunchtime series, the Spiritual Wellness series, for the Minot State University community. When we think of health and wellness, we tend to aim our focus toward the well-being of our body and mind. A focus toward the well-being of our spirit seems to be a bit more limited. Yes, our levels of physical and mental health are key contributors to a life of meaning, contentment, and satisfaction. However, when we make an effort to nurture the well-being of our spirit at, or above, the levels that we nurture the well-being of our body and mind, we enable ourselves to optimize the levels of meaning, contentment, and satisfaction in our lives. Simply stated, a strong spirit makes life better. The Spiritual Wellness series is for everyone, and the Lutheran Campus Ministries facilitates the series. Regardless of your spiritual or religious background or experience, we invite you to join us as we strive to promote spiritual wellness throughout the campus and the community. The Spiritual Wellness series consists of discussions, presentations and other meaningful initiatives aimed at promoting spiritual health and wellness. (Minot State University Spiritual Wellness)

The residential life program at Minot State University has initiated wellness floors in a women's and a men's residence hall. These two areas invite students to develop a comprehensive health-oriented lifestyle, one that includes abstinence from all drugs and alcohol, on and off campus, and focuses upon the eight dimensions of wellness cited earlier.

The MSU Honors Program continues this emphasis on holistic higher learning. Its curriculum has a heavy emphasis on ethical issues: "course work emphasizes the complex relationship between individuals and their communities (local, regional, national and global). . ." (Minot State University Honors Program Mission). Among the seminars offered are the following:

HON 351H Integrity & the Examined Life

HON 391H Community Problem-Solving

HON 395H Global Citizenship & Service

(Minot State University Honors Program Coursework)

Overall, it is impressive that a relatively small public university can devise and implement a coordinated, multi-faceted wellness program that integrates physical, spiritual, and intellectual fitness.

PROMISING PRACTICES

I outlined at some length the work of the Spirituality in Higher Education project at the Higher Education Research Institute of UCLA. Jennifer Lindholm, one of the co-authors of that project's final report (*Cultivating the Spirit: How College Can Enhance Students' Inner Lives)*, has joined with three colleagues to compile *A Guidebook of Promising Practices: Facilitating College Students' Spiritual Development.* It begins with a "Foreword" by Alexander and Helen Astin, reaffirming their belief "that assisting more students to grow spiritually will help to create a new generation of young adults who are more caring, more globally aware, and more committed to social justice than previous generations" (*Guidebook* v). Lindholm et al. then review the Spirituality in Higher Education Project, its measures and methods, and the results of its exhaustive survey and interview processes. (See Chapter 3 above.) The remainder of the book is a broad survey of actual practices in the realm of spirituality, based on responses from 407 institutions, including doctoral research universities, other public universities, non-sectarian private colleges, and private faith-based or historically religious colleges. The text briefly describes the practices in several sentences although some are only listed, and the authors make no effort to judge the institutional reports.

The practices collected by Lindholm, Millora, Schwartz, and Spinosa are divided into three large groups, each with multiple subsections: curricular initiatives and teaching strategies, largely the responsibility of the faculty; co-curricular programs and services, primarily the responsibility of those in student affairs; and campus-wide efforts, that most often fall to the administration. Throughout, the authors also pay attention to the roles students, especially student leaders, can play in cultivating spirituality on various campuses. Below are a few representative illustrations from each area:

Curricular Initiatives and Teaching Strategies

- Academic degree programs—"George Mason University: 16 credit academic minor that includes courses in mindfulness, consciousness, and meaning, based in the Center for Consciousness and Transformation." (Lindholm et al. 26)

Co-Curricular Programs and Services

- Spiritual mentoring—"Monmouth College began a monthly series called 'Why Am I Here? The Unfolding of Life,' where faculty and staff talk about their personal lives and tell stories that help students understand that life does not always go in the direction one might expect." (Lindholm et al. 36)
- General wellness—"Purchase College State University of New York has a Wellness Center and a campus-wide Wellness Committee. One of the sub-committees is a Spiritual

Wellness Alliance. They also offer yoga every day of the week and meditation twice a week." (Lindholm et al. 52)

- Student leadership training and governance—"Kenyon College has developed a Spiritual Advisors Program that encourages students to reexamine the moral, religious, and spiritual values they have held all their lives. Spiritual Advisors aim to provide an ear and feedback to students struggling with spiritual questions of meaning and purpose. Advisors come from a diversity of faith backgrounds; some define themselves as seekers with no particular faith and are trained in listening skills, religious diversity, and active avoidance of anything that could be interpreted as proselytizing." (Lindholm et al. 53)

Campus-Wide Efforts

- Leadership and strategic planning—"Western Connecticut State University's strategic plan focuses on student engagement. One of the sub-goals stresses the importance of spiritual development as part of overall 'wellness.' The University has also established a wellness initiative that will include elements of spirituality in all of its dimensions." (Lindholm et al. 58)
- Campus centers and organizational units—"Oberlin College and Conservatory of Music's Office of Religious and Spiritual Life is involved in a variety of programming, including: offering courses to encourage students' exploration of life's big questions; promoting global worldview and awareness weeks; prioritizing caring and compassion through justice projects; hosting a Friendship Day Festival that draws upon Islamic concepts of friendship and global peacemaking; offering lectures on atheism and the apocalypse; and hosting a variety of other events like Multi-faith Awareness Week." (Lindholm et al. 60)
- University-wide initiatives—"Wilberforce University hosts an annual campus colloquium called "People of the Book," a

dialogue [involving] Judaism, Christianity and Islam. Other campus events include Men's Spiritual Empowerment Week; Women's Spiritual Empowerment Week; Bible studies, Meet the Chaplain Days; and Prayer Vigils." (Lindholm et al. 64)

- Designated physical spaces—*Promising Practices* lists several dozen institutions that have spaces inside and outside, chapels, prayer rooms, sanctuaries, gardens, labyrinths, and prayer circles. (Lindholm et al. 70–71)

Lindholm, Millora, Schwartz, and Spinosa conclude the book with a brief collection of institutional considerations, such as collegiate mission, physical space, and institutional culture, that will influence the support and encouragement of spirituality on any particular campus. The authors offer an outline of an individual "spirituality action plan" (88); they raise questions that help to formulate this plan: "Who else is engaged and involved in this work on your campus?" (80). They append a series of "Considerations for Campus Groups," each of which includes questions to ask and practices to consider (78–79). For example, administrators can ask themselves: "How do the values of your institution's mission align with the spiritual qualities in this guidebook?" (86). Faculty might consider practices such as "Employing self-reflection, journaling, meditation, and other reflective practices in your work with students" (87). Students can ask, "How do your peers define spirituality?" (87).

A Guidebook of Promising Practices: Facilitating College Students' Spiritual Development is a stimulating and helpful tool for individuals, groups, and institutions seeking concrete ideas on cultivating student spirituality.[74] The *Guidebook's* near-encyclopedic collection of actual programs and policies should provide a useful starting place for almost anyone or any instructor looking to move forward in this direction. Of course, many other institutions are engaged in interesting and worthwhile endeavors in the arena of holistic higher learning that are also promising. Just as one example: private, non-sectarian Prescott College has created a signature orientation program, including rigorous physical challenges, that focuses its students on the large issues that undergird the entire college: the complex issues and keen challenges of environmental sustainability in the twenty-first century (Prescott College Orientation).

* * *

The snapshots from the *Guidebook* are, I believe, an album of optimism, an anthology of hope. There are as many ways of enriching the spiritual and physical lives of college students as there are colleges and honors programs. Just as each college or university is, ultimately, a unique culture composed of its history, goals, people, and place, each needs to consider for itself how it can best serve the entire panoply of human needs of its populations.

None of these efforts is, of course, perfect: no human enterprise is. All probably have flaws that could be reduced or eliminated, opportunities to go further that could be exploited. None of the colleges and honors programs offer a model to be adopted *in toto* by anyone else; all offer some lessons from which virtually any college or university could learn. More impressively, they all offer concrete testimony to the range of ways in which contemporary colleges, universities, and honors programs and honors colleges can respond and are responding to the challenge of cultivating the whole humanity of students.

INTERVIEW FOUR

Dr. Diana Chapman Walsh

From 1993 to 2007, Dr. Diana Chapman Walsh served as the twelfth President of Wellesley College, her alma mater. Celebrating its 125th anniversary during her tenure, the college successfully completed a comprehensive fundraising campaign in 2005, raising over $472 million. Before coming to Wellesley, Walsh chaired the Department of Health and Social Behavior at Harvard University, where she held a named professorship. In addition to her undergraduate career at Wellesley, where she was an English major, she has an MS degree in journalism and her PhD in health policy from Boston University, and she has also been awarded several honorary doctorates. She has written extensively on issues of health and society. Walsh is a member of Phi Beta Kappa and the American Academy of Arts and Sciences. I asked Walsh to reflect on the role she has played in revitalizing the place of spirituality in American higher learning and about how she herself has been able to maintain her own personal balance and integration throughout her illustrious career.

I grew up in a suburb of Philadelphia, Chestnut Hill, and went to an independent girls' school and from there to Wellesley. I was active in a number of team sports in school but not so much in college, where I enjoyed individual sports and did become a "student leader." I married my husband [Dr. Christopher Walsh, Hamilton Kuhn Professor at Harvard University], now of 45 years, two weeks after graduation. My mother's family was Quaker, and we attended meeting sporadically while growing up; it was the religion I claimed when asked, but it was not central to my identity. My husband's family was Catholic and, on religious grounds, disapproved our marrying so we viewed organized religion as an impediment, not a support to our relationship.

I was drawn into spirituality much later, during a three-year fellowship sponsored by the W. K. Kellogg Foundation for leaders in mid-career. From the outset, some of the fellows were organizing discussions of "spirituality," but I was drawn instead to those in the group I thought were more like me at the time, a scholar with an interest in the conceptual intricacies of national health policy. I was not at all clear what these other people really meant when they said they were going off to talk about "spirituality" or to "be in community," words that triggered suspicions in me of fuzzy "new age" thinking. But, over time, I heard enough about these experiences from fellows I was learning to respect that they encouraged me to let down my guard, step by step, and I did. Parker Palmer was an important part of that story, and a week-long retreat with him in Taos, New Mexico, was a turning point in my life.

Something about the setting, the poetry Parker had us reading, the company, and the unsettling questions Parker was posing called forth from me at that retreat a completely unexpected outpouring of poems that kept coming to me, and—so it felt—through me, day and night that whole week. All of us were astonished as I emerged every morning with new poems that Parker encouraged me to read to the group. I left Taos with a sheaf of original poems, and, with them, new questions about the creative process and what, exactly, had overtaken me. I continued writing poetry after that, but never again with the abandon that had possessed me there in Taos, stimulated by the strong connection I had felt to Parker as a kindred soul with whom I shared roots in Quakerism and sociology, but, more than that, as a playful and wily spirit who had drawn me out of myself, in spite of myself. The poetry became an extension of journals I sporadically kept, a doorway to an inner voice I knew I could trust. Parker became a lifelong friend.

Victor Kazanjian deserves the credit for both the "Education as Transformation" and "Beyond Tolerance" programs. [See the discussion of these programs and Kazanjian in Chapter 4 above.] He had been selected as dean of religious and spiritual life the year before I arrived. His charge was to build and lead a new multi-faith program at Wellesley that a committee had spent the previous year designing. Peter Gomes, the legendary head of Harvard's Memorial Church, was a Wellesley trustee and participated in that discussion, with others. My predecessor, Nannerl Keohane, whose father was a minister, also deserves much of the credit for the creation of this path-breaking program.

What I did was support it, enthusiastically, because I was deeply impressed by the work Victor and the students on his multi-faith council were doing, bridging their differences in a way that enabled them to deepen their own faith commitments. This struck me as the key to the challenge of making differences a true resource for learning. In my second year, Victor organized a conference to celebrate the 125th birth anniversary of Mohandas Gandhi, a moving international gathering of leading advocates of nonviolence. Soon after that he and I began discussing his dream of convening representatives of colleges and universities to come to our campus and explore the challenges and possibilities for meeting students' religious and spiritual needs in the new context of diversity, pluralism, and globalization. That conference became a milestone on the road to a whole new way of thinking, nationally and even globally, about the role of religious and spiritual life in the context of higher education.

There were certainly people—students, faculty, alums, trustees—who were uneasy about what struck them as a threat to the centrality of Protestantism on the campus. The multifaith services took some getting used to—and their format took some refining—before they were fully accepted as they are now. And—a different and equally challenging concern—faculty members occasionally expressed discomfort with the idea that programs in religion and spirituality were part of a complete education, a responsibility of the institution to its students rather than simply a matter of personal choice to be exercised privately. Freedom of religion on campus translated, in the minds of some, to freedom from religion.

I am a great admirer of the Astins and their work. They have done the field a tremendous service by gathering reliable data on the evolution of students' religious and spiritual beliefs and practices during the college years, and ways in which institutions can be effective in supporting students' healthy development of spiritual qualities that enhance other positive outcomes during college, including academic performance, psychological well-being, leadership skills, and overall satisfaction. The hope is that these qualities will continue to ground graduates through their lives, bringing them purpose, meaning, and hope through good times and bad. One of the Astins' key findings was that students report a slight decline in religious engagement during their college years and yet substantial increases in their spirituality, that "they become more tolerant, more connected with others, and more actively involved in a spiritual quest." As Sharon Daloz Parks has laid out in her eloquent book, *Big Questions, Worthy Dreams,* the task of the "twenty-something years," or "early adulthood," increasingly being understood as a distinct phase of human development, is to find a place and purpose in a changing world. Whether we call this a spiritual quest or something else, it lays the foundation for a meaningful life.

As we have seen, the Astins' data do support the proposition that spiritual and intellectual growth are interrelated. Sharon Parks makes a strong case that critical thinking—one of the signal goals of a liberal education—requires stepping outside of and reflecting on one's own narrow perspective, experience, and assumptions. I saw firsthand at Wellesley the power of the interactions between students of various faith traditions as they explored the similarities and differences in belief structures they had brought to college and learned to move beyond tolerance to true appreciation of that which is other and alien. Surely this movement is the essence of critical thought.

Arthur Zajonc, a professor of physics at Amherst College, has been a leader, with colleagues, in the effort to open the academy to contemplative practices of various kinds. He and others founded the Association for Contemplative Mind in Higher Education, which supports ever-increasing numbers of faculty in developing courses and curricula drawing on contemplative pedagogy, methodology, and epistemology. Brown University has inaugurated new programs in this area, and a multidisciplinary group at Harvard University has come together to explore the frontiers of what seems to me to be emerging as a social movement in higher education. Stay tuned.

I asked Dr. Walsh if she sees any links between spiritual development and physical exercise.

I do. Throughout my presidency I ran the three miles around Lake Waban virtually every morning to clear my head and start my day. In every kind of weather, it was serene and beautiful early in the morning, with my dog at my side. For me this was a spiritual practice nearly as calming and grounding as meditation is. I am still a regular exerciser and expect always to be, within whatever limitations the aging process inflicts on me.

What a disciplined meditation practice offers, though, that goes beyond the endorphin high of aerobic exercise, is the mindfulness of bodily, emotional, and mental states that, over time and with practice, enhances one's sense of balance, clarity, ease, gratitude, and joy. For my part, exercise makes me feel alive, alert, energetic, and also calm, while mindfulness practice opens me up to the beauty of the world around me and in the people I encounter. The two disciplines are complementary, but produce, I think, somewhat different states of well-being.

CHAPTER 6

Concluding Thoughts

Only in fiction are there true beginnings and endings; in the real world, beginnings all have antecedents and the ending is always followed by the next chapter. American higher education starts with the foundation of Harvard University in 1636, but that institution had its roots in European learning reaching back through the Renaissance to the Middle Ages. And Medieval scholarship, in turn, was nourished by the curiosity and reason of antiquity, often through the transmission of Islamic culture. Similarly, today's American colleges and universities and their honors programs are certainly not in their final and highest flowering but are, rather, a perennial work in progress. The thesis of this monograph has been that that work should focus on students, and particularly on honors students, as whole persons, with minds, bodies, and spirits.

As I noted in my introductory pages, most of these observations and suggestions could apply to any and all colleges and universities in America, not just honors programs and colleges. Of course, the same might well be said of most of the practices that characterize honors education: interdisciplinary options, discussion classes, experiential learning, undergraduate research, and independent study. Just as honors has been a leader in American higher education in these areas, honors educators have the chance to show the way in restoring a holistic balance to the undergraduate experience today. I also believe that honors has, even more than most contemporary post-secondary education, too often focused exclusively on the development of students' minds and paid too little regard to the cultivation of their bodies and spirits.

As Chapter 2 demonstrates, American higher education had no qualms about making spiritual and physical demands on students until about the middle of the twentieth century, when most schools reduced, then frequently dropped, attention to the inner lives of their populations and relegated fitness to the outer darkness of the extracurriculum. The required gym classes and chapel attendance that were once nearly universal have now largely disappeared from schools in the public sector and those private colleges and universities with a non-sectarian character. As a college student myself in the early 1960s, I was happy to see them go and do not now lament their passing. In the well-intentioned efforts to rid college culture of these often antiquated elements, however, too often educators forgot that they served a real and important purpose, and so they failed to substitute anything for them. This failure has seemed especially true in the honors community, which has often been zealous in defining itself in wholly intellectual terms. Thus, educators have been left, I believe, with a fragmentary view of higher education, or, more accurately, a system of higher education that fragments the personhood of students and declares that it will address only part of their complex, intertwined natures.

THE PHYSICAL

Researchers at the exciting edge of contemporary brain science are discovering that vigorous physical exercise demonstrably contributes to intellectual vitality. Fitness activities lead to the growth of new brain cells that enhance memory and learning. Exploratory programs, such as that in the Naperville, IL, high school, have established a direct correlation between exercise and academic performance. Exercise at the collegiate level, of course, can mean anything from the solitary morning walker striding by the cornfields of central Iowa to the NCAA Division I quarterback calling plays in front of a live audience of tens of thousands, a broadcast attendance of millions. Grave dangers are inherent in intercollegiate sports, especially at the highest levels of competition in the most popular sports, but college athletes can also learn important values.

Far more gentle than competitive football, basketball, or volleyball are the integrative or contemplative physical disciplines, such as yoga and tai chi, that are offered and practiced often in colleges around the country. Several colleges, as this study shows, have integrated work programs into the core of their experience, and some researchers are looking carefully at the cognitive aspects of seemingly simple physical labor. Moreover, colleges, universities, and honors programs, as the Snapshots section demonstrates, are building physical challenges into their orientation or expedition programs, challenges that they believe speak to student learning and to spiritual growth at the same time. In fact, institutions are integrating wellness into their core missions. Finally, the myriad voices of honors student athletes, coaches, physical educators, and fitness administrators have testified to the varied ways in which they believe that cultivating the body can be an important part of the college experience.

THE SPIRITUAL

The Spirituality in Higher Education project of the Higher Education Research Institute at UCLA has uncovered and promulgated important information about the spiritual lives and aspirations of today's college students and teachers. It turns out that a significant majority of students across the spectrum of American higher education see themselves as spiritual people and spiritual seekers. They come to college looking for answers to the big questions about the meaning and purpose of life. Although students grow and develop in college, often they do not find the kind of spiritual sustenance that they expected and wanted. Meanwhile, their professors similarly define themselves as spiritual persons, but, except in the faith-based schools, they often believe that spiritual matters do not belong in their classrooms. Interest in various contemplative and meditative practices, however, in a wide variety of institutions, large and small, public and private, faith-based and secular, has grown. This growth has been reflected as well in honors programs and colleges. Some well-regarded thinkers such as Parker Palmer have affirmed the value of recognizing the ways in which spiritual matters intersect instructional ones, the ways in which faculty members cannot and should not seek to remove their own inner lives from their teaching and their students' learning. Some promising initiatives, such as "Beyond Tolerance" and "Education as Transformation" have brought together college and university personnel—faculty, students, staff, and administrators—to probe ways in which today's institutions can deepen the impact of higher education on students as whole human beings.

In a kind of parallel development, institutions are paying significant attention to moral education, which is sometimes seen as spiritual, sometimes as religious, and sometimes as wholly secular. Critics of moral learning have been acerbic about its appropriateness at contemporary colleges and universities; its defenders have been equally vigorous. Particular institutions, ranging from a public liberal arts college in rural Minnesota through the catalog of "promising practices" compiled by the HERI researchers, all have sought ways to nourish the spirits of their students (Lindholm et al.). A campus chaplain has spoken eloquently of the evolution of the campus ministry from sectarian celebrant to pastor for all students, faithful, questioning, and faithless alike. Religious colleges and universities are putting new emphasis on service as well as piety. Finally, students have offered their own stories of how they have found spiritual sustenance everywhere from the campus athletic facilities to a campfire in the arctic wilderness to honors courses.

* * *

Honors administrators, professors, and students, as well as scholars, coaches, chaplains, institutions, and organizations, are exploring the deep interconnections of intellectual growth, physical wellness, and spiritual reflection. The contemporary American higher education community is rediscovering the importance of understanding college students as complex, whole people, a variegated mix of mind, body, and soul. The final purposes of universities and colleges are surely to help students become more thoughtful members of society; to help them learn to lead fulfilling and healthy lives; to seek their answers to life's big questions; and to embrace virtue, shun vice, and to act accordingly. This vision is as old as civilization and as compelling today as it has ever been. For honors programs and honors colleges to lead American higher education towards that vision is a realistic and noble calling.

Notes

Chapter 1

[1]The following material on student spirituality is all from Astin, Astin, and Lindholm, *Cultivating the Spirit.*

[2]See Robert J. Nash and Michele C. Murray, *passim.*

[3]See Beth Potier's "College Students Face Obesity, High Blood Pressure, Metabolic Syndrome." There was some coverage of this issue on Fox TV news.

[4]A recent study at Oregon State University by Bradley J. Cardinal, Spencer D. Sorensen, and Marita K. Cardinal found that only 39% of contemporary colleges require physical education, down from two-thirds in the 1980s and 97% in the 1920s.

[5]Who am I to undertake such a wide-ranging and daunting compositional task? Since my childhood, I have been engaged in one form or another of competitive athletics. For many decades I have been a fitness fanatic: a marathon runner, triathlete, bicycle rider, swimmer, and gym rat. Very early in my life, I thought I might like to be a gym teacher when I grew up. Later, in high school, religion and religious activities became very important to me, and, when I matriculated at Grinnell College in 1960, my intention was to prepare for a career as a clergyperson. Later the fascination of scholarship and the lures of the academic life led me into a professorial career as a teacher of literature. Finally, I evolved (or devolved, depending upon one's perspective) into an administrative role, serving as an honors director, then a chief academic officer, and finally as the chancellor of two public liberal arts colleges. Nearly two decades as a college chief executive gave me the opportunity to gaze upon the collegiate enterprise as a whole and to cultivate and refine my sense that colleges and universities were places that should attend to students as whole women and men.

Recently, I found myself engaged in two seemingly unconnected investigations in the field of American higher education. A presentation I had made at an annual meeting of the AAC&U with a group from the College Sports Project morphed into a lead article in the *Journal of the National Collegiate Honors Council.* That journal was doing a special forum on "Honors and Athletics," and my contribution suggested some of the ways in which I thought participation in competitive athletics might enhance the learning of honors students. Simultaneously, I was finishing a book (*Seeing the Light: Religious Colleges in Twenty-First Century America*), which explored, among other topics, the yearning of college students for exploring and deepening their understandings of spiritual matters. It struck me that my investigation of college athletics, my book on college student spirituality and religious colleges, and my work as a teacher and scholar of literature were not unconnected. In fact, I realized that my sense of what happens to students in college and what colleges and universities were (to some extent) and should be (to a greater extent) cultivating in students reflected a growing holistic perspective. Sports, athletics, fitness, the physical self were important. The search for life's meanings and the development of values were important. The cultivation of intellectual skills and knowledge were important. And each of these important areas depended upon and nourished the others.

[6]Surely not everyone would agree that contemporary colleges and universities do a good job of cultivating students' intellectual capacities, but, in the overall sweep of things, that remains my conclusion.

[7]I possess a T-shirt created by the students of one of America's best honors programs that suggests, positively, that those students are a "nerd herd."

[8]See also important studies by James Tunstead Burtchaell, George Marsden, and Julie Reuben. A much fuller discussion is in my *Seeing the Light* (287–292).

[9]Astin is the author of over 20 books and 400 other publications; he is the founding director of the Higher Education Research

Institute (HERI) at UCLA, and he has won awards from over a dozen national educational associations. A poll of readers of *Change* magazine found Astin the scholar "most admired for creative, insightful thinking" in higher education, and the *Journal of Higher Education* found him the most frequently cited author in the field.

[10]The definitions and statistics in this and the following paragraph are from Astin, Astin, and Lindholm, *Cultivating*. Some students of spirituality in higher education are less enthusiastic than I about this study, especially his very broad definition of "spirituality," but the project's contribution to this discussion remains seminal.

[11]Another valuable study of student spiritual seeking is by Nash and Murray, who carefully define "meaning" and "purpose" and focus on the often-cited big questions. Nash and Murray also offer concrete, pragmatic suggestions on helping college students in their search for a meaningful life; for example, they urge teachers and student affairs professionals to "tell stories" (179–202).

[12]See also Ernest Pascarella and Patrick Ternzini's *How College Affects Students* and George D. Kuh's et al. *What Matters to Student Success.*

[13]The Spring/Summer 2011 edition of the *Journal of the National Collegiate Honors Council* included a "Forum" on Honors Study Abroad, featuring six essays; Vol. 9 of *Honors in Practice* (2013) featured two articles on honors study abroad; and a forthcoming monograph from the NCHC Monograph Series will focus on the same subject (*Preparing Tomorrow's Global Leaders: Honors International Education*).

[14]This illustrative information about study abroad, service learning, and interdisciplinary courses comes from the websites of the College of New Rochelle, Wayne State University, Keene State University, and the University of Mississippi.

[15]I detail some of these studies in *Seeing the Light*, 300–302. In addition to Astin, cited above, see for example, Pascarella and Terenzini (36–41); Mahoney, Schmalzbauer, and Youniss; Redden; and Denton-Borhaug.

[16]See, for example, Riley ("Not all Colleges" and *God on the Quad*) who praises what she calls the "missionary generation" of students who snub the spiritual but not religious attitude. (Her work is subtitled *How Religious Colleges and the Missionary Generation Are Changing America.*) Recently I took an informal and non-scientific survey of several dozen students at a selective public liberal arts college, asking them to classify themselves as one of the following: 1) spiritual but not religious; 2) spiritual and religious; 3) neither spiritual nor religious. Those who saw themselves in category #1 exceeded those in categories #2 and #3 put together. Interestingly, one student classified himself as "religious, but not spiritual."

[17]See Chapter 4 for a discussion of the intellectual, physical, and spiritual dimensions of service learning, intergenerational projects, and religious dialog.

[18]For good historical summaries, see Lee, Mechikoff, and Turner and Hurley.

Chapter 2

[19]See, for example, the historical surveys of A. Cohen, S. Cohen, and Thelin.

[20]The very first Catholic schools (not colleges) in America predate Harvard: Spanish Franciscans created a school (the name of which I cannot locate) in St. Augustine, Florida, in 1606.

[21]When I attended Grinnell College in the 1960s, the institution had a universal "religion" requirement. One could fulfill that requirement by taking a course in Old Testament or New Testament or History of Christianity, or the like.

[22]The material on Colonial Colleges is from A. Cohen, S. Cohen, and the current websites of the nine institutions. See also Schuman, *Old Main,* especially Chapter 2.

[23]Several historians of physical education, such as Lee and Mechikoff, contrast the Greek belief in active, amateur sporting endeavors with the Roman passion for spectator sports, especially

gladiatorial contests. The Greek philosopher of anatomy Herophilos, according to Galen, said: "To lose one's health renders science null, art inglorious, strength unavailing, wealth useless and eloquence powerless" (qtd. in *Herophilos*). This motto would add a certain classical cachet if engraved over the entrance to a college gym!

[24]Ringenberg notes that many of the earlier state universities had religious practices and assumptions that would seem out of place today at public institutions.

[25]See, for example, Lee 35ff.

[26]The famed quotation is splendid, but it is probably important to note that no actual, direct record of its having been uttered in any form exists.

[27]The Harvard "Red Book" is discussed by Levine in his study of the undergraduate curriculum.

[28]Since I was one of "them," perhaps I should say "us."

[29]Burtchaell's history of Davidson College, for example, chronicles successful student and faculty anti-Presbyterian activism in *The Dying of the Light*.

[30]When I was a student at Grinnell College, an outpost of student freedom and liberalism, there remained both a gym requirement and a swimming test into the 1960s.

CHAPTER 3

[31]This section borrows from an earlier article of mine: Schuman, "Jogging the Scholarly Mind."

[32]At Guilford College, Greensboro, NC, in the mid 1980s. The explanation of how this strange transmutation came about is rather mundane. Throughout my years in academic administration, I have tried to teach at least one class per semester. And, I have tried to vary those classes from introductory writing courses to graduate seminars, from literature courses to interdisciplinary ones. Knowing

that I was seeking a multiplicity of pedagogical challenges, the politically acute Department of Sports Studies asked if I might be willing to teach an "activity class," a two-credit participation-style course entitled "Jogging for Fitness." An avid runner at the time, I leaped at the bait. And for reasons I would not have guessed, I was glad I did.

[33]This experiment is discussed by A. F. Kramer et al. in an article in *Nature*.

[34]For example, physical education is ignored in the AAC&U's project LEAP (Liberal Education and America's Promise), which in its *Principles of Excellence* makes no mention whatsoever of fitness or wellness. See AAC&U's "Core Commitment to Educate Students for Personal and Civic Responsibility."

[35]See my essay entitled "Colleges Sports, Honors, Five Liberal Lessons, and Milo of Crotona."

[36]I compare the percentages of student athletes at the University of Minnesota Morris (with 1,800 students) with that at the University of Minnesota, Twin Cities (52,000 students), or those at the University of North Carolina Asheville with the percentage at the University of North Carolina, Chapel Hill.

[37]During my conversation with Steve McNamara, Director, Fellowship of Christian Athletes, Western North Carolina, he stated that part of the "Creed" of the FCA affirms: "My body is the temple of Jesus Christ. . . . My sweat is an offering to my master. My soreness is a sacrifice to my Savior."

[38]Among the critiques of collegiate sports are those of Sperber, Thelin, and Shulman and Bowen.

[39]The Honors College of the University of New Mexico has recently created a position specifically to work with varsity athletes who are honors students.

[40]I discuss meditation in the next chapter.

[41]See <http://www.pe.cornell.edu/physed>.

[42]A 2011 revival of Arnold Wesker's *The Kitchen* at London's National Theatre makes dramatically visible the demands of the food-service workplace.

[43]For a related social-psychological look at one dimension of the work of a waitress, see Zweigenhaft and Stephen.

[44]I was, at one point in my youth, an apprentice pipe fitter.

[45]The websites of Berea and Blackburn detail the historical origins of the labor programs at those institutions.

[46]Deep Springs' Board of Trustees voted to move to coeducation, but that issue remains (Summer 2013) tied up in litigation because some alumni have sued to block that step.

[47]Dr. David Schuman, my brother, from whom, with his wife Dr. Sharon Johnson, I first learned about Deep Springs College.

Chapter 4

[48]For much more of this perspective and some equally pointed rejoinders, see the "Essay on Sources" in my *Seeing the Light*, 281–318.

[49]This assumption, of course, is not true. See the discussion later in this chapter.

[50]I find this measure a bit troubling because a student (or anyone else) could be a devout Unitarian or Reform Jew and still be extremely liberal, socially and religiously.

[51]This finding is consistent with the research I did for *Seeing the Light*. I found that at most faith-based colleges there is a strong faculty desire to wean students from unthinking acceptance of parental religious perspectives, to make them think through spiritual issues for themselves. This engagement, obviously, would result in increased religious struggle. The colleges, though, believe that from such a struggle emerges a stronger, more thoughtful, mature faith.

[52]For a discussion of how spiritual traits enhance the lives and academic performance of college students, see Supiano.

[53]I am grateful to Cornell's Chaplain Catherine Quehl-Engel for sharing this resource with me.

[54]This study features a particularly useful bibliography of works on race and spirituality.

[55]The results of another major research study on college professors and religion by Neil Gross of the University of British Columbia and Solon Simmons of George Mason University were published in 2009 in the journal *The Sociology of Religion.*

[56]I found this statistic surprising. A colleague who taught at a Catholic college for a decade did not.

[57]Private correspondence to me. The writer, for obvious reasons, wishes not to be identified.

[58]See also the companion book by Rachel C. Livsey.

[59]Patterson is commenting upon Jyl Lynn Felman's ideas concerning performance art and teaching.

[60]See Chapter 3 above for a related discussion of the physical aspects of such "integrative disciplines" as tai chi and yoga.

[61]Sharts-Hopko's essay is reprinted from Holistic Nurse Practitioner 21.1 (2007): 3–9.

[62]Thurman, the father of actress Uma Thurman, teaches at Columbia University. *The New York Times* called him "The Dalai Lama's Man in America."

[63]The reference of course is to Martin Buber's 1923 work *I and Thou*, which distinguishes between two modes of addressing existence, of relationships, and of communication: "I—thou" and "I—it."

[64]This camping trip is similar to the experiences of honors students in the NCHC "Partners in the Parks" program. See Digby.

[65]See the interview with Walsh below.

[66]It is worth pausing to remember that "honors programs" are called "honors" programs! Implicit in the nomenclature, it seems to

me, is the idea that there is something "honorable" about academic excellence.

[67]Stanley Hauerwas amusingly comments that "no one makes the case more clearly than Fish that the purpose and justification of the university is quite simply to support Stanley Fish's work as a literary critic" (93).

[68]Ruth W. Grant is also skeptical that humanizing education actually produces humanizing results.

INTERVIEW THREE—REV. CATHERINE QUEHL-ENGEL

[69]See, for example, his work entitled *Sex, Ecology, Spirituality*, for a discussion of what Wilber calls "holons."

[70]The Association for Contemplative Mind in Higher Education is part of the Center for Contemplative Mind in Society, a multidisciplinary professional organization located in Northampton MA.

CHAPTER 5

[71]Except where otherwise noted, the material in this chapter comes from personal communications with faculty, students and administrators at the institutions depicted and from their websites.

[72]See also the chapter "Embracing Friluftsliv's Joys: Teaching the Canadian North Through the Canadian Wilderness Travel Experience" by Glen Hvenegaard and Morten Asfeldt, which discusses Canadian versions of a Scandinavian effort to build closer links between people and nature.

[73]Minot calls itself "The Magic City" or, sometimes, "The Magic City of the North." Given its location in Northwestern North Dakota, less than 60 miles south of the Canadian border, it is certainly in the "North," whether or not it is "magic" is debatable: in January, the average daily high temperature is 3.2 degrees.

[74]Another recent effort to suggest actual, real-world tactics to cultivate college student spirituality is a collection of essays entitled *Spirituality in College Students' Lives: Translating Research into Practice,* edited by Alyssa Bryant Rockenbach and Matthew J. Mayhew.

Works Cited

Asfeldt, Morten. "Re: University of Alberta Augustana outdoor programs." Message to the author. 8 Aug. 2011. Email.

Asfeldt, Morten, Glen Hvenegaard, and Ingrid Urberg. "Expeditions and Liberal Arts University Education." *Understanding Educational Expeditions*. Ed. S. K. Beams. Rotterdam, The Netherlands: Sense Publishers, 2009. 67–78. Print.

Asfeldt, Morten, Ingrid Urberg, and Bob Henderson. "Wolves, Ptarmigan and Lake Trout: Critical Elements of a Northern Canadian Place-Conscious Pedagogy." *Canadian Journal of Environmental Education* 2009. 33–41. Print.

Association for Contemplative Mind in Higher Education. Web. 14 July 2013. <http://www.contemplativemind.org/programs/acmhe>.

Association of American Colleges and Universities (AAC&U). "Core Commitment to Educate Students for Personal and Civic Responsibility." Association of American Colleges and Universities. 2006. Web. 30 June 2013. <http://aacu.org/core_commitments>.

Astin, Alexander W. "Why Spirituality Deserves a Central Place in Liberal Education." *Liberal Education* 90.2 (2004): 34–41. Print.

Astin, Alexander W., and Helen S. Astin. Foreword. *Encouraging Authenticity and Spirituality in Higher Education*. By Arthur W. Chickering, Jon C. Dalton, and Liesa Stamm. San Francisco: Jossey-Bass, 2006. vii-xii. Print.

—. Foreword. *A Guidebook of Promising Practices: Facilitating College Students' Spiritual Development*. By Jennifer A. Lindholm,

Melissa L. Millora, Leslie M Schwartz, and Hanna Song Spinosa. Create Space (An Amazon Company): 2011. 3–26. Print.

Astin, Alexander W., Helen S. Astin, and Jennifer A. Lindholm. *Cultivating the Spirit: How College Can Enhance Students' Inner Lives.* San Francisco: Jossey-Bass, 2011. Print.

—. "Spirituality and the Professoriate." Higher Education Research Institute, the Graduate School of Education and Information studies, UCLA (2006). Web. 9 July 2013. <http://www.spirituality.ucla.edu/docs/results/faculty/spirit_professoriate.pdf>.

Awbrey, Susan M. et al., eds. *Integrative Learning and Action: A Call to Wholeness.* New York: Peter Lang, 2006. Print.

Baddeley, Alan. *Working Memory.* Oxford: Oxford UP, 1984. Print.

Baker, George A. *A Handbook on the Community College in America.* Westport, CT: Greenwood P, 1994. Print.

Banerji, Shilpa. "Accelerating Hispanic Progress in Higher Education." *Diverse Issues in Higher Education.* 20 Mar. 2007. Web. 9 July 2013. <http://www.diverseeducation.com>.

Baurecht, William C. "Appearance of a Successor: The National Collegiate Honors Council." *National Honors Report* 11.3 (Fall 1990): 1–4. Print.

Beauchemin, James, Tiffany L. Hutchins, and Fiona Patterson. "Mindfulness Meditation May Lessen Anxiety, Promote Social Skills, and Improve Academic Performance Among Adolescents with Learning Disabilities." *Journal of Evidence-based Complementary and Alternative Medicine* 13.1 (2008): 34–45. Print.

Bell, Gary. "Honors and Intercollegiate Athletics." *Journal of the National Collegiate Honors Council* 11.1 (2010): 61–65. Print.

Bennett, Douglas C. "Quaker to the Core, Welcoming All." Kazanjian and Laurence 187–93. Print.

Berea College. *Berea College.* Web. 2 July 2013. <http://www.berea.edu>.

Berrett, Dan. "Exercising Only Their Minds." 9 May 2011. Web. 4 Apr. 2012. <http://www.insidehighered.com/news/2011.05/09>.

"Beyond Tolerance." *Wellesley College*. Web. 3 July 2013. <http://www.wellesley.edu/rellilfe/beyondtolerance>.

"Beyond Tolerance." *Juniata College*. Web. 3 July 2013. <http://www.juniata.edu/services/diversity/BeyondToleranceSeries.html>.

Bhatia, V. N., and Kathleen M. Painter. "Honors Programs: An Historical Perspective." *Forum for Honors* 10.2 (1980): 1–6. Print.

The Holy Bible. Revised Standard Version. New York: Thomas Nelson and Sons, 1952. Print.

Blackburn College. *Blackburn College*. Web. 9 July 2013. <http://www.blackburn.edu>.

Bloomsburg University. *Bloomsburg University*. Web. 10 July 2013. <http://www.bloomu.edu>.

Blum, Lawrence. "Multiculturalism and Moral Education." Kiss and Euben 140–61. Print.

Boorstein, Sylvia. *Don't Just Do Something, Sit There*. San Francisco: Harper, 1996. Print.

Boston Women's Health Book Collective. *Our Bodies, Ourselves.* Boston: New England Free P, 1971. Print.

Bowen, William G. and Sarah A. Levin. R*eclaiming the Game: College Sports and Educational Values*. Princeton: Princeton UP, 2005.

Boyd, George A. "The Role of Meditation in Learning and Study." 2003. *The Mudrashram Institute of Spiritual Studies*. Web. 3 July 2013. <http://www.mudrashram.com/meditationandlearning1.html>.

Boynton Health Service, The University of Minnesota. *2010 College Student Health Survey Report: Health and Health-Related Behaviors—Minnesota Postsecondary Students*. Pamphlet. Minneapolis: U of Minnesota, 2011. Print.

Boyte, Harry, and Elizabeth Hollander. "The Wingspread Declaration." *Campus Compacts*. Web. 18 July 2013. <http://www.compact.org/initiatives>.

Bremer, Peter. Messages to the author. June 2011. Email.

Breneman, David. *Liberal Arts Colleges: Thriving, Surviving, or Endangered*. Washington, D.C.: Brookings Institution, 1994. Print.

Buber, Martin. *I and Thou*. 1923, Eng. 1937. Eastford, CT: Martino Fine Books, 2010. Print.

Burtchaell, James Tunstead. *The Dying of the Light: The Disengagement of Colleges and Universities from Their Christian Churches*. Grand Rapids, MI: Eerdmans, 1998. Print.

Bush, Mirabi. "Compassionate Practices in Higher Education." Bush and Zajonc 77–82. Print.

—. Introduction. *Contemplative Practices in Higher Education: A Handbook of Classroom Practrices*. Mirabi Bush and Arthur Zajonc, eds. TS. Northampton, MA: Center for Contemplative Mind in Society, 2008. 5–8. Print.

Bush, Mirabi, and Arthur Zajonc, eds. *Contemplative Practices in Higher Education: A Handbook of Classroom Practices*. TS. Northampton, MA: Center for Contemplative Mind in Society, 2008.

—. "Contemplative Practices and Their Applications in the Classroom." Bush and Zajonc 13-43. Print.

Bushrui, Suheil Badi, and James Malarkey. "Education as Transformation: A Bahá'í Model of Education for Unity." Kazanjian and Laurence 91–102.

Campus Compact. "Presidents' Declaration on the Civic Responsibility of Higher Education." *Campus Compact*. Web. 4 July 2012. <http://www.compact.org/initiatives>.

Cardinal, Bradley J., Spencer D. Sorensen, and Marita K. Cardinal. "Historical Perspectives and the Current State of the Physical Education Requirement on American 4-Year Colleges and Universities." *Research Quarterly for Exercise and Sport* 83.4 (2012): 503–12. Print.

Carmichael, Mary. "Stronger, Faster, Smarter." *Newsweek*. 25 Mar. 2007. Web. 18 July 2013. <http://www.thedailybeast.com/newsweek/2007/03/25/stronger-faster-smarter.html>.

Carnegie Foundation. Carnegie Classification 2000. *Carnegie Foundation*. Web. 9 July 2013. <http://classifications.carnegiefoundation.org>.

Center for Contemplative Mind in Society. *Center for Contemplative Mind in Society*. Web. 4 July 2013. <http://www.contemplativemind.org>.

Chaucer, Geoffrey. *The Canterbury Tales*. Ed. E. Talbot Donaldson. New York: John Wiley, 1975. Print.

Chaves, Mark. *American Religion: Contemporary Trends*. Princeton: Princeton UP, 2011. Print.

Chickering, Arthur W., Jon C. Dalton, and Liesa Stamm. *Encouraging Authenticity and Spirituality in Higher Education*. San Francisco: Jossey-Bass, 2006. Print.

Clark, Burton R. *The Distinctive College: Antioch, Reed, and Swarthmore*. Chicago: Aldine, 1970. Print.

Cobb, Peter W., ed. *Gateways to Spirituality: Preschool through Grade 12*. New York: Peter Lang, 2005. Print.

Cohen, Arthur M. *The Shaping of American Higher Education*. San Francisco: Jossey-Bass, 1998. Print.

Cohen, Sheldon S. *A History of Colonial Education, 1607–1776*. New York: John Wiley, 1974. Print.

Colcombe, Stanley J. et al. "Aerobic Fitness Reduces Brain Tissue Loss in Aging Humans." *Journals of Gerontology* 58 (2003): 176–180. Print.

College of New Rochelle. *College of New Rochelle*. College of New Rochelle. Date. Web. Date. <http://www.cnr.edu>.

College Sports Project. *College Sports Project*. Web. 18 July 2013. <http://www.collegesportsproject.org> and <http://www. middlebury.edu/newsroom/archive/2010/node/266828>.

Cornell College's Office of Institutional Research and Assessment. "Pathways: A Study of Spirituality and Vocation at Cornell College." Mt. Vernon, IA: Cornell College, n.d. Print.

Cornell University. "PE Reinvented as Kinesiology." *Cornell Report* 33.2 (2010): 22–27. Print.

—. *Physical Education*. Web. (4 July 2013.) <http://www.pe.cornell.edu/physed>.

Cremin, Lawrence A. *American Education: The Metropolitan Experience, 1876–1980*. New York: Harper and Row, 1988. Print.

Dalke, Anne, and Barbara Dixson, eds. *Minding the Light: Essays in Friendly Pedagogy*. New York: Peter Lang, 2004. Print.

Dalke, Anne French. *Teaching to Learn, Learning to Teach: Meditations on the Classroom*. New York: Peter Lang, 2002. Print.

Deep Springs College. *Deep Springs College*. Web. 8 July 2013. <http://www.deepsprings.edu/home>.

Deep Springs College Board of Trustees. "The Constitution of Deep Springs/Deed of Trust." *Deep Springs College* 1950. Web. 4 July 2013. <http://www.deepsprings.edu>.

Deep Springs College Brochures. Deep Springs College. Deep Springs, CA: n.d. Print.

Deep Springs College Forum. *Deep Springs College*. Web. 7 July 13. <http://deepsprings.edu/forum>.

Deep Springs College Letters. *Deep Springs College*. Web. 12 June 2012. Web. 8 July 2012. <http://www.deepsprings.edu/downloads/DStrust 12 June 2012>.

DeGioia, John. "Intercollegiate Athletics: Two Compelling, Competing Logics of Excellence." 55–58. Web. 4 July 2013. <http://net.educause.edu/it/library/pdf/ffp0513s.pdf>.

de la Durantaye, Leland. *Style is Matter: The Moral Art of Vladimir Nabokov*. Ithaca: Cornell UP, 2007. Print.

Denton, Diana, and Will Ashton, eds. *Spirituality, Action, and Pedagogy: Teaching from the Heart*. New York: Peter Lang, 2004. Print.

Denton-Borhaug, Kelly. "The Complex and Rich Landscape of Student Spirituality: Findings from the Goucher College Study." *Religion and Education* 31.2. 2004. Web. 4 July 2013. <http://www.uni.edu/coe/jrae/Fall2004>.

Digby, Joan. *Partners in the Parks: Field Guide to an Experiential Program in the National Parks*. Lincoln: National Collegiate Honors Council, 2010. NCHC Monograph Series. Print.

DiSepio Institute for Rural Health and Wellness. *Saint Francis University*. Saint Francis University 14 July 2013. Web. <http://www.Francis.edu/disepio>.

Eccles, Katie. "Re: Olivet Nazarine College Honors Program." Message to the author. 26 Aug. 2011. Email.

Eck, Diana. *Encountering God: A Spiritual Journey from Bozeman to Banaras*. Boston: Beacon P, 1993. Print.

Education and Spirituality Network. *Education and Spirituality Network*. Web. 4 July 2013. <http://www.Interspirit.net/east met.cfm>.

"Education as Transformation." *Education as Transformation*. Wellesley College. Web. 9 July 2013. <http://www.wellesley.edu/rellife/transformation>.

Eliot, T.S. *The Wasteland.* New York: Horace Liveright, 1922. Print

Elkins, Becki, and Stephanie Preschel. *Pathways: A Study of Spirituality and Vocation at Cornell College.* Mt. Vernon, IA: Cornell College, Spring, 2010. Print.

Epp, Roger. "Re: Augustana Campus of the University of Alberta." Message to the author. 27 Sept. 2010. Email.

Epstein, Jennifer. "A Different Kind of Test." *Inside Higher Ed.* 20 Nov. 2009. Web. <http://www.insidehighered.com/news/2009/11/20/lincoln>.

Euben, J. Peter, and Elizabeth Kiss, eds. *Debating Moral Education: Rethinking the Role of the Modern University.* Durham: Duke UP, 2010. Print.

Felman, Jyl Lynn. *Never a Dull Moment: Teaching and the Art of Performance.* New York: Routledge, 2001. Print.

Ferrara, Cynthia M. "The College Experience: Physical Activity, Nutrition, and Implications for Intervention and Future Research." *Journal of Exercise Physiology* 12.1 2009 Web. 6 July 2013. <http://www.asep.org/journals/jeponline>.

Fish, Stanley. "Aim Low." *Chronicle of Higher Education.* 16 May 2003. Web. 6 July 2013. <http://chronicle.com>.

—. "I Know It When I See It." Kiss and Euben 76–91. Print.

—. *Professional Correctness: Literary Studies and Political Change.* Oxford: Clarendon P, 1995. Print.

—. "Save the World on your Own Time." *Chronicle of Higher Education* 23 Jan. 2003. Web. 18 July 2013. <http://www.chronicle.com>.

—. "Why We Built The Ivory Tower." *New York Times.* 21 May 2004. Web. 6 July 2013. <http://www.nytimes.com/2004/05/21/why-we-built-the-ivory-tower.html>.

Fredricks, Dan. "Re: The honors program at St. Francis University." Message to the author. 13 Aug. 2011. Email.

Gage. Fred H. "Brain, Repair Yourself." *The HD Lighthouse*. 2006. Web. 9 July 2013. <http://www.hdlightouse.org/research/brain/updates/0059neurogenesis.php>.

Gillespie, Michael Allen. "Players and Spectators: Sports and Ethical Training in the American University." Kiss and Euben 296–316. Print.

Gleason, Phillip. *Contending with Modernity: Catholic Higher Education in the Twentieth Century*. New York: Oxford UP, 1995. Print.

Gollnick, James. *Religion and Spirituality in the Life Cycle*. New York: Peter Lang, 2005. Print.

Grant, Ruth W. "Is Humanistic Education Humanizing?" Kiss and Euben 281–95. Print.

Grasgreen, Alan. "Making Their Frosh Fit." *Inside Higher Ed*. 10 Aug. 2011. Web. 10 Aug. 2011. <http://www.InsideHighered.com/news/2011/08/10>.

Green, Arthur. "Judaism, Religious Diversity, and the American Academy." Kazanjian and Laurence 113–123. Print.

Gross, Neil, and Solon Simmons. "The Religiosity of American College and University Professors." *The Sociology of Religion* 70:2 (2009): 101–129. Print.

—. "The Politics of the American Professoriate." 2 Feb. 2006. Web. 9 July 2013. <http://www.Religion.sscc.org/reforum/gross-simmons.pdf>.

Grossman, Cathy Lynn. "Study by Philip Schwadel." *USA Today*. 3 August 2011. Web. 8 Aug. 2011. <http://www.usatoday.com/news/religion/2011-08-03-education-religion_n.htm?csp=34news>.

Hart, Tobin. "The Inner Liberal Arts." *The Garrison Institute Newsletter*. Spring 2011. Web. 8 July 2013. <http://www.garrisoninstitute.org>.

Hauerwas, Stanley. "The Pathos of the University: The Case of Stanley Fish." Kiss and Euben 92–110. Print.

Heiberg, Erika. "Re: University of Alberta, Augustana outdoor program." Message to the author. 29 Aug. 2011. Email.

Herophilos: The Art of Medicine in Early Alexandria. Ed. and trans. H. von Staden, Cambridge: Cambridge UP, 1989. Print.

Higher Education Research Institute, University of California Los Angeles. Spirituality in Higher Education project. "Strong Majority of College and University Faculty Identify Themselves as Spiritual." 28 Feb. 2006 Web. 1 July 2011. <http://www.spirituality.ucla.edu >.

Hill, Cindy. "Re: National Collegiate Honors Council." Message to the author. Email.

Hillman, Charles H., et al. "The Effect of Acute Treadmill Walking on Cognitive Control and Academic Achievement in Preadolescent Children." *National Institutes of Health*. Web. 9 July 2013. <http://www.ncbin.nim.nih.gov/pmc/articles/PMC 2667807>.

Hodges, Shannon. "Making Room for Religious Diversity on Campus: The Spiritual Pathways Series at the University of Minnesota-Morris." *About Campus* 4.1 (March–April 1999): 25–27. Print.

Hoekema, David A. "Is there an Ethicist in the House? How Can We Tell?" Kiss and Euben 249–266. Print.

Hofstadter, Richard, and Wilson Smith. *American Higher Education: A Documentary History*. Chicago: U of Chicago P, 1961. Print.

Hoover, Eric. "Lincoln U. Requires Its Students to Step on the Scale." *Chronicle of Higher Education*. 19 Nov. 2009. Web. 9 July 2013. <http://chronicle.com/article/Lincoln-U-Requires-Its/49223>.

Hope College. Course Description. *Hope College*. Web. 9 July 2013. <http://www.hope.edu/student/life/yoga>.

Horowitz, Helen Lefkowitz. *Alma Mater: Design and Experience in the Women's Colleges from Their Nineteenth-Century Origins to the 1930s*. New York: Knopf, 1985. Print.

—. *Campus Life: Undergraduate Cultures from the End of the Eighteenth Century to the Present*. New York: A. Knopf, 1987. Print.

Hunt, Virginia. "Governance of Women's Intercollegiate Athletics: An Historical Perspective." Diss. U of North Carolina–Greensboro, 1978. Microfilm. Ann Arbor, MI: University Microfilms (1977).

Hvenegaard, Glen, and Morten Asfeldt. "Embracing Friluftsliv's Joys: Teaching the Canadian North Through the Canadian Wilderness Travel Experience." *Nature First: The Outdoor Life and the Friluftsliv Way*. Ed. Nils Vikander and Bob Henderson. Toronto: Dundurn P, 2007. 168–76.

Illinois State University. *Illinois State University*. Web. 8 July 2013. <http://www.ilstu.edu>.

Jencks, Christopher, and David Riesman. *The Academic Revolution*. Garden City, NY: Doubleday, 1968. Print.

Kazanjian, Victor H., Jr., and Peter L. Laurence, eds. *Education as Transformation: Religious Pluralism, Spirituality and a New Vision for Higher Education in America*. New York: Peter Lang, 2000. Print.

Kazanjian, Victor, and the Students of the Wellesley Multi-faith Council, "Beyond Tolerance: From Mono-religious to Multi-religious Life at Wellesley College." Kazanjian and Laurence 213–30. Print.

Keene State University Honors Program. *Keene State University*. Web. 1 March 2011. <http://www.keene.edu/academics/honors>.

Keeva, Stephen. "On Being a Human at Law." Awbrey 173–86. Print.

Khalsa Gurucharan, Singh. "Pluralism, Awareness, and Mastery of the Mind: A Sikh Imperative for Education." Kazanjian and Laurence 143–58. Print.

Kirk, Megan A., and Ryan E. Rhodes. "Performance Pressure." *Academic Matters*. May 2011. Web. 9 July 2013. <http://www.academicmatters.ca>.

Kiss, Elizabeth, and J. Peter Euben, eds. *Debating Moral Education*. Durham: Duke UP, 2012. Print.

—. Introduction. *Debating Moral Education*. Ed. Elizabeth Kiss and J. Peter Euben. Durham: Duke UP, 2012. 3-26. Print.

Korstad, John. "Re: Oral Roberts University." Messages to the author. Nov. 2012. Email.

Kramer, A. F., et al. "Aging Fitness and Neurocognitive Function." *Nature* 400 (1999): 418–19. Print.

Kuh, George D., and Robert M. Gonyea. "Spirituality, Liberal Learning and College Student Engagement." *Liberal Education* (2006). Web. 9 July 2013. <http://www.aacu.org/liberaleducationb/le-wi06/le-wi06_perspectives1.cfm>.

Kuh, George D., Jillian Kenzie, Jennifer Buckley, Brian Bridges, and John C. Hayek. *What Matters to Student Success: A Review of the Literature. National Postsecondary Education Cooperative,* 2006. Web. 9 July 2013. <http://www.nces.ed.gov/npec.pdf.kuh_team_report.pdf>.

Lama, Dalai. *Ethics for the New Millenium*. New York: Riverhead Books, 1999. Print.

Lawson, Tiana Y. "Opinion." *The Lincolnian*. 18 Nov. 2009: 1. Print.

Lee, Mabel. *A History of Physical Education and Sport in the U.S.A.* New York: John Wiley and Sons, 1983. Print.

Levine, Arthur. *Handbook on Undergraduate Curriculum*. San Francisco: Jossey-Bass, 1978. Print.

Library of Congress Archive. *Library of Congress*. Web. 18 July 2013. <http://www.memory.loc.gov>.

"Lincoln University Blog." Comment. Lincoln University. 27 Nov. 2009. Web. 14 July 2013. <http://thechoice.blogs.nytimes.com>.

Lindholm, Jennifer A., Melissa L. Millora, Leslie M. Schwartz, and Hanna Song Spinosa. *A Guidebook of Promising Practices: Facilitating College Students' Spiritual Development*. N.p. CreateSpace, an Amazon Company, 2011. Print.

Livsey Rachel C., with Parker J. Palmer. *The Courage to Teach: A Guide for Reflection and Renewal*. San Francisco: Jossey-Bass, 1999. Print.

Longfield, Bradley, "From Evangelism to Liberalism: Public Midwestern Universities in Nineteenth-Century America." Marsden and Longfield 46–73. Print.

Loras College. *Loras College*. Web. 10 July 2013. <http://www.loras.edu>.

Lucas, Christopher J. *American Higher Education: A History*. New York: St. Martin's P, 1994. Print.

Mahoney, Kathleen A., John Schmalzbauer, and James Youniss. "Religion: A Comeback on Campus." *Liberal Education* 87.4 (2001): 36–41. Print.

Marsden, George. *The Soul of the American University: From Protestant Establishment to Established Nonbelief*. New York: Oxford UP, 1994. Print.

Marsden, George, and Bradley J. Longfield, eds. *The Secularization of the Academy*. New York: Oxford UP, 1992. Print.

Mastermeditation. *Mastermeditation*. Web. 9 July 2013. <http://www.mastermeditation.com>.

McNamara, Steve. Personal interview. 15 Dec. 2010.

Mearsheimer, John. "The Aims of Education." *Philosophy and Literature* 22.1 (1998): 137–55. Print.

Mechikoff, Robert. *A History and Philosophy of Sport and Physical Education from Ancient Civilizations to the Modern World.* 5th ed. Boston: McGraw Hill, 2010. Print.

Medina, John. *Brain Rules: 12 Principles for Surviving and Thriving at Work, Home and School.* Seattle: Pear P, 2009. Print.

Meditation and learning website. Web. 18 July 2013. <http://www.mastermeditation.com/meditation-and-learning>.

Menis, Donna. "Re: Honors Program at Saint Francis University." Message to the author. Email.

"Middlebury College." *Encyclopedia Africana.* Web. 4 July 2013. <http://www.africana.com>.

Miller, Vachel W., and Merle M. Ryan, eds. *Transforming Campus Life: Reflections on Spirituality and Religious Pluralism.* New York: Peter Lang, 2001. Print.

Milton, John. *Paradise Lost.* Indianapolis: Hackett Publishing, 2005. Print.

Minot State University Honors Program Coursework. *Minot State University.* Minot State University. 15 July 2013. Web. <http://www.minotstateu.edu/honors/coursework.shtml>.

Minot State University Honors Program Mission. *Minot State University.* Minot State University. 15 July 2013. Web. <http://www.minotstateu.edu/honors/mission.shtml>.

Minot State University Spiritual Wellness Series. *Minot State University.* Minot State University. 14 July 2013. Web. <http://www.Minotstateu.edu/newsletter/archive.php?x=1146>.

Minot State University Wellness. *Minot State University.* Minot State University 15 July 2013. Web. <http://www.minotstateu.edu/wellness>.

Mount Union College. *Mount Union College.* Web. 10 July 2013. <http://www.mountunion.edu>.

Murphy, James Bernard. "Against Civic Education in Schools." Kiss and Euben 162–85. Print.

Nabokov, Vladimir. *Speak, Memory: An Autobiography Revisited.* New York: Vintage, 1989. Print.

Nagarantha, R. *Yoga. Health and Yoga.* 2010. Web. 18 July 2013. <http://www.healthandyoga.com/html/news/therapy/rtherapy73.asp>.

Nash, Robert J. *Religious Pluralism in the Academy: Opening the Dialog.* New York: Peter Lang, 2001. Print.

—. *Spirituality, Ethics, Religion and Teaching: A Professor's Journey.* New York: Peter Lang, 2002. Print.

Nash, Robert J., and Michele C. Murray. *Helping College Students Find Purpose: The Campus Guide to Meaning-Making.* San Francisco: Jossey-Bass, 2010. Print.

National Center for Educational Statistics. *NCES.* National Center for Educational Statistics. Web. 18 July 2013. <http://www.nces.ed.gov>.

National Hispanic University. "History of the University and Higher Education." *National Hispanic University.* Web. 18 July 2013. <http://www.nhu.edu>.

National Organization of Women. *NOW.* National Organization of Women. Web. 18 July 2013. <http://www.now.org/issues/title_ix/index.html>.

Nino, Andres G. "Spiritual Quest Among Young Adults." Kazanjian and Laurence 43–57. Print.

Oakley, Francis. *Community of Learning.* New York: Oxford UP, 1992. Print.

Oberlin College. *Oberlin College.* Web. 3 July 2013. <http://new.oberlin.edu/about/index.dot>.

Ohio State University. "Global Climate and Environmental Change." *Ohio State University*. Web. 18 July 2013. <http://www.geography.osu.edu/faculty/emt.H410/description.pdf>.

Olson-Loy, Sandra K. "Re: University of Minnesota Morris Regional Fitness Center." Message to the author. Email

Oral Roberts University Catalog 2011–12. *Oral Roberts University*. Oral Roberts University. Web. 14 July 2013. Web. <http://www.oru.edu/academics/catalog>.

Oral Roberts University E-Portfolio. *Oral Roberts University*. Oral Roberts University, 14 July 2013. Web. <http://www.oru.edu/current_students/my_academics/resources/whole_person_assessment>.

Oral Roberts University Faculty Handbook. *Oral Roberts University*. Oral Roberts University. Web. 15 July 2013. <http://portal3.oru.edu/dynmgr/dynelmt.getDoc?_docid=1179>.

Owens Community College. *Owens Community College*. Web. 10 July 2013. <https://www.owens.edu>.

Palmer, Parker. *The Courage to Teach: Exploring the Inner Landscape of a Teacher's Life*. San Francisco: Jossey-Bass, 1998. Print.

—. "A Vision of Education as Transformation." Kazanjian and Laurence 17–22. Print.

Paredes-Collins, Kristin, and Christopher S. Collins, "The Intersection of Race and Spirituality: Underrepresented Students' Spiritual Development at Predominantly White Evangelical Colleges." *Journal of Research on Christian Education* 20 (2011): 73–100. Print.

Parks, Sharon Daloz. *Big Questions, Worthy Dreams: Mentoring Emerging Adults in Their Search for Meaning, Purpose, and Faith*. Rev. Ed. San Francisco: Jossey-Bass, 2011. Print.

Pascarella, Ernest, and Patrick Terenzini. *How College Affects Students: A Third Decade of Research*. San Francisco: Jossey-Bass, 2005. Print.

Patterson, Laura Sloan. "Fashion, Out of the Closet." *Chronicle of Higher Education* 17 June 2011: B20. Print.

Pennsylvania State University, *Schreyer Honors College*. Pennsylvania State University. Web. 10 July 2013. <http://www.shc.psu.edu>.

Pereira, Ana C., et al. "An In Vivo Correlate of Exercise-Induced Neurogenesis in the Adult Dentate Gyrus." *Publications of the National Academy of Sciences* 104.13 (Mar. 2007) 5638–43. Print.

Potier, Beth. "College Students Face Obesity, High Blood Pressure, Metabolic Syndrome." *Medical News Today* 19 (June 2007): n. pag. Print.

Preparing Tomorrow's Global Leaders: Honors International Education. Ed. Mary Kay Mulvaney and Kim Klein. Lincoln: National Collegiate Honors Council, 2013. NCHC Monograph Series. Print.

Prescott College Orientation. *Prescott College*. Prescott College. 15 July 2013. Web. <http://www.prescott.edu/learn/on-campus-undergraduate/orientation/index.html>.

Pulliam, John D. *History of Education in America*. 4th ed. Columbus: Merrill, 1987. Print.

Ratey, John R. *Spark: The Revolutionary New Science of Exercise and the Brain*. New York: Little Brown, 2008. Print.

Redden, Elizabeth. "Adding Spirituality." *Inside Higher Education* (8 May 2007). Web. <http://www.insidehighered.com/news/2007/05/08/spirituality>.

Reppman, Aron. "Re: Trinity Christian College Honors Program." Message to the author. Email.

Reuben, Julie. *The Making of the Modern University: Intellectual Transformation and the Marginalization of Morality*. Chicago: U of Chicago P, 1996. Print.

Reynolds, Gretchen. "Lobes of Steel." *New York Times*. "Play Magazine." 19 Aug. 2007. Web. 12 May 2011. <http://www.nytimes.com/2007-08/19/sports/playmagazine/0819play>.

Riley, Naomi Schaefer. *God on the Quad: How Religious Colleges and the Missionary Generation Are Changing America.* New York: St. Martin's P, 2005. Print.

—. "Not all Colleges are the Same." *National Review Online.* 11 Jan. 2005. Web. 18 July 2013. <http://www.nationalreview.com/interrogatory>.

Ringenberg, William C. "The Old-Time College, 1800–1865." *Making Higher Education Christian: The History and Mission of Evangelical Colleges in America.* Ed. Joel A. Carpenter and Kenneth W. Shipps. Grand Rapids: Christian UP, 1987. 77–97. Print.

Roberts, Jon H., and James Turner. *The Sacred and the Secular University.* Princeton: Princeton UP, 2000. Print.

Rockefeller, Steven C. "Meditation, Social Change, and Undergraduate Education." Bush and Zajonc 55–64. Print.

Rockenbach, Alyssa Bryant, and Matthew J. Mayhew, eds. *Spirituality in College Students' Lives: Translating Research into Practice.* London: Routledge/Taylor and Francis, 2011. Print.

Rose, Mike. "The Working Life of a Waitress." *Mind, Culture and Activity* 8.1 (2001): 3–27. Web. 9 July 2013. <http://www.epnet.com>.

—. *Speaking of Faith*. Natl. Public Radio. 7 Jan. 2010. Radio.

Saint Francis University Goals of General Education. *Saint Francis University*. Saint Francis University. Web. 14 July 2013. <http://www.Francis.edu/preview_program.php>.

Saint Francis University Statement of Mission and Values. *Saint Francis University*. Saint Francis University. Web. 14 July 2013. <http://www. Francis.edu/mission_and_Values>.

Sax. L. J., et al. *Findings from the 2002 Administration of "Your First College Year" National Aggregates.* Los Angeles: U of California Higher Education Research Institute, 2002. Print.

Schmalzbauer, John. *People of Faith: Religious Conviction in American Journalism and Higher Education.* Ithaca: Cornell UP, 2003. Print.

Schuman, David. "Education and Solipsism." *The CoEvolution Quarterly* Spring 1981: 132–139. Print.

—. "Re: Deep Springs College." Message to the author. 12 May 2013. Email

Schuman, Samuel. "College Sports, Honors, Five Liberal Lessons, and Milo of Crotona." *Journal of the National Collegiate Honors Council* 11.1 (2010): 15–19. Print.

—. "Jogging the Scholarly Mind." *Educational Record* 66.3 (Summer, 1985): 53–5. Rpt. in *Jogging*. Ed. David Corbin. Glenview, IL: Scott, Foresman, 1988: 148–51. Print.

—. *Old Main: Small Colleges in Twenty-First Century America.* Baltimore: Johns Hopkins UP, 2005. Print.

—. *Seeing the Light: Religious Colleges in Twenty-First-Century America*. Baltimore: Johns Hopkins UP, 2010. Print.

Schwartz, Madeleine. "The Most Important Course? Do Harvard Undergraduates Ponder the Meaning of Life." *Harvard Magazine*. Web. 14 July 2013. <http://harvardmagazine.com/2011/05/most-important-course>.

Seaton, Jacqueline, and Nicole Lockley. "University Decides to Scrap BMI Requirement." *The Lincolnian* 5 Dec. 2009. Web. 14 July 2013. <http://www.thelincolnianonline.com/media/storage>.

Shakespeare, William. *Hamlet. The Complete Signet Classic Shakespeare.* Ed. Sylvia Barnet. New York: Harcourt, 1972. 910–61. Print.

—. *King Lear. The Complete Signet Classic Shakespeare*. Ed. Sylvia Barnet. New York: Harcourt, 1972. 1174–1226. Print.

Sharts-Hopko, Nancy C. "Personal and Professional Impact of a Course on Contemplative Practices in Health and Illness." Bush and Zajonc 91–100. Print.

Shulman, James L., and William. G. Bowen, "The Game of Life: Taking Stock." *Sport, Power and Society: Institutions and Practices.* Eds. Robert E. Washington and David Karen. Boulder CO: Westview P, 2010. 158–75. Print.

Sidman, Cara "Re: Honors College of the University of North Carolina Wilmington." Message to the author. 2012. Email

Sinisi, Daniel. "Service Leadership Report." Saint Francis University, internal document. Loretta, PA: Saint Francis U, 2011. Print.

Sloan, Douglas. *Faith and Knowledge: Mainline Protestantism and American Higher Education.* Louisville: Westminster John Knox, 1994. Print.

Smith, Page. *Killing the Spirit: Higher Education in America.* New York: Viking, 1990.

Somerville, C. John. "The Exhaustion of Secularism." *Chronicle of Higher Education.* 9 June 2006. Web. 18 July 2013. B6–B7.

Southern Methodist University's Perkins School of Theology. *Southern Methodist University.* Southern Methodist University. Web. 10 July 2013. <http://www.smu.edu/newsinfo>.

Spelman, Elizabeth V. "On the Distribution of Moral Badges: A Few Worries." Kiss and Euben 109–21. Print.

Spenser, Edmund. *The Faerie Queene.* London: Penguin Classics, 1979. Print.

Sperber, Murray. *Beer and Circus: How Big-Time College Sports Has Crippled Undergraduate Education.* New York: Henry Holt, 2000. Print.

Stock, Brian. "The Contemplative Life and the Teaching of the Humanities." Bush and Zajonc 65–68. Print.

Strauch, Barbara. *The Secret Life of the Grown-up Brain*. New York: Viking, 2010. Print.

Supiano, Beckie. "How Spiritual Traits Enhance Students' Lives—and Maybe Their Grades." *Chronicle of Higher Education*. 16 Nov. 2010. Web. 9 July 2013. <http://chronicle.com/article/How-Spiritual-Traits-Enhance/125408>.

Tewksbury, Donald G. *The Founding of American Colleges and Universities Before the Civil War*. New York: Teachers College P, 1932. Print.

Texas Tech University Environment and the Humanities Program. *Texas Tech University Honors College*. Texas Tech University. Web. 14 July 2013. <http://www.depts.ttu.edu.honors.evhm/course.php>.

Thelin, John R. *Games Colleges Play: Scandal and Reform in Intercollegiate Athletics*. Baltimore: Johns Hopkins UP, 1994. Print.

—. *A History of American Higher Education*. Baltimore: Johns Hopkins UP, 2004. Print.

Thurman, Robert A. F. "Meditation and Education: India, Tibet, and Modern America." Bush and Zajonc 69–76. Print.

Todd, Mary. "Re: Honors College at Marshall University." Message to the author. 20 July 2011. Email.

Turner, H. Spencer, and Janet L. Hurley, eds. *The History and Practice of College Health*. Lexington: UP of Kentucky, 2002. Print.

United States. Dept. of Agriculture. *Dept. of Agriculture*. Web. 3 July 2013. <http://www.csrees.usda.gov>.

University of Alberta Augustana. University of Alberta Augustana. Web. 14 July 2013. <http://www.augustana.ualberta.ca>.

University of Alberta Augustana International Programs. University of Alberta Augustana. Web. 14 July 2013. <http://www.Augustana.ualberta.ca/programs/lab/international/india>.

University of Alberta Augustana Outdoor Programs. University of Alberta Augustana. Web. 14 July 2013. <http://www.augustana.ualberta.ca/programs/lab/outdoor>.

University of Colorado. University of Colorado, Boulder. Web. 10 July 2013. <http://www.colorado.edu>.

University of Indianapolis. "Description of Healthy Diploma." *University of Indianapolis*. University of Indianapolis. Web. 5 July 2013. <http://www.uindy.edu/education/kinesiology/healthy-diploma>.

University of Maryland. "Class Description." *University of Maryland* University of Maryland. Web. 14 July 2013. <http://www.compmed.umm.edu/pathways>.

University of Minnesota Morris Regional Fitness Center. University of Minnesota Morris. Web. 14 July 2013. <http://www.regionalfitnesscenter.com>.

University of Mississippi. *Sally McDonald Barksdale Honors College*. University of Mississippi. Web. 30 Aug. 2013. <http://www.honors.olemiss.edu/about-the-college/benefits>.

University of Vermont. "An Ecological Approach to Living Well in Place." Web. 14 July 2013. <http://www.uvm.edu/~honcoll/syllabus/S12-HCOL186F_Poleman.pdf>.

Van Dalin, Deobold D., and Bruce L. Bennett. *A World History of Physical Education*. Englewood Cliffs, NJ: Prentice Hall, 1971. Print.

Van Praag, Henriette, et al. "Running Enhances Neurogenesis, Learning and Long-Term Potentiation in Mice." *Publications of the National Academy of Science* (9 Nov. 1999): 13427–31 Web. 14 July 2013. <http://www.pnas.org/content/96/23/13427>.

—. "Running Increases Cell Proliferation and Neurogenesis in the Adult Mouse Dentate Gyrus." *Nature Neuroscience* 2.3 (March 1991): 266–70. Print.

Walkovich, Don. St. Francis University Objectives. *Saint Francis University*. Saint Francis University. Web. 18 July 2013. <http://www.faculty.francis.edu/senate/minutes/content/96/23/o31202.htm>.

Walsh, Diana Chapman. "The Search for Meaning and Uncommon Values." Awbrey 117–28. Print.

—. "Transforming Education: An Overview." Kazanjian and Lawrence 1–14. Print.

Warren Wilson College, Warren Wilson College. Web. 26 Sept. 2011. <http://warren-wilson.edu>.

Webb, L. Dean, Arlene Metha, and K. Fordis Jordan. *Foundations of American Education*. New York: Merrill, 1992. Print.

Wilber, Ken. *Sex, Ecology, Spirituality: The Spirit of Evolution*. 2nd Rev. Ed. Boston: Shambhala Publications, 2001. Print

Williams, Sue E. "Re: Honors Program at Olivet Nazarine University." Message to the author. 26 Sept. 2012. Email.

Wolterstorff, Nicholas. *Reason within the Bounds of Religion*. Grand Rapids: Eerdmanns, 1984. Print.

Wright, David, and Hanna Siegel. 14 Apr. 2010. Web. 18 July 2013. <http://www.abcnews.go.com/wh/exercise-school-leads-learning/story?id=10371315>.

YouTube of Naperville High School. Web. 18 July 2013. <http://www.youtube.com/watch?v=ULciZ8jSgHa>.

Zajonc, Arthur. "What is Contemplative Pedagogy?" Bush and Zajonc 9. Print.

Zimmer, Christine G. "Health Promotion in Higher Education." Turner and Hurley 311–27. Print.

Zweigenhaft, Richard L., and Renee Stephen. "The Effect on Tipping of a Waitress Touching Male and Female Customers." *Journal of Social Psychology* 126.1 (1985): 141–42. Print.

About the Author

Dr. Samuel Schuman created the "Beginning in Honors" workshop of the National Collegiate Honors Council in 1984 and served as its first director. His work in honors and academic administration has included service as Chair of the Honors Committee at Cornell College, Mt. Vernon, Iowa; Director of the Honors Program at the University of Maine; Vice President for Academic Affairs and Dean at Guilford College in Greensboro, NC; Chancellor, Dean of the Faculty, and Professor of English at the University of North Carolina Asheville; Chancellor and Professor of English at the University of Minnesota Morris; and the Garrey Carruthers Distinguished Visiting Professor in Honors at the University of New Mexico.

Schuman has been a member of the Executive Committee of the National Collegiate Honors Council, and he served as well on its Honors Semesters Committee, Publications Board, and Portz Grant Committee. His contributions to NCHC also include being Chair of the Committee on Small Colleges, the Beginning in Honors Committee, and the Conference Planning Committee. He became President of NCHC in 1992.

Additional service to honors education included directing the Maine Coast Honors Semester, being the editor of the *Northeast Region NCHC Newsletter*, helping to create the North Carolina Honors Association and serving as its first President, and co-hosting the first National Honors Forum. He has been a consultant on honors at over two dozen colleges and universities.

Schuman has written for the *National Honors Report* (*NHR*), *Forum for Honors*, and the *Journal of the National Collegiate Honors Council* (*JNCHC*). NCHC has also published two other monographs by Schuman: *Beginning in Honors* (now in its 4th Ed.) and *Honors Programs in Smaller Colleges* (now in its 2nd Ed.).

In addition to his honors work, Schuman is the author of six books, most recently *Old Main: Small Colleges in Twenty-First-Century America* (Johns Hopkins University Press, 2005) and *Seeing the Light: Religious Colleges in Twenty-First Century America* (Johns Hopkins University Press, 2010), as well as numerous scholarly articles, mostly on non-Shakespearean English Renaissance Drama and modern literature, especially Vladimir Nabokov. (He has served as President of the Vladimir Nabokov Society.) Schuman's book on Vladimir Nabokov and William Shakespeare is scheduled for publication by Bloomsbury Publishers in 2014.

NCHC Monographs & Journals

Assessing and Evaluating Honors Programs and Honors Colleges: A Practical Handbook by Rosalie Otero and Robert Spurrier (2005, 98pp). This monograph includes an overview of assessment and evaluation practices and strategies. It explores the process for conducting self-studies and discusses the differences between using consultants and external reviewers. It provides a guide to conducting external reviews along with information about how to become an NCHC-Recommended Site Visitor. A dozen appendices provide examples of "best practices."

Beginning in Honors: A Handbook by Samuel Schuman (Fourth Edition, 2006, 80pp). Advice on starting a new honors program. Covers budgets, recruiting students and faculty, physical plant, administrative concerns, curriculum design, and descriptions of some model programs.

Fundrai$ing for Honor$: A Handbook by Larry R. Andrews (2009, 160pp). Offers information and advice on raising money for honors, beginning with easy first steps and progressing to more sophisticated and ambitious fundraising activities.

A Handbook for Honors Administrators by Ada Long (1995, 117pp). Everything an honors administrator needs to know, including a description of some models of honors administration.

A Handbook for Honors Programs at Two-Year Colleges by Theresa James (2006, 136pp). A useful handbook for two-year schools contemplating beginning or redesigning their honors program and for four-year schools doing likewise or wanting to increase awareness about two-year programs and articulation agreements. Contains extensive appendices about honors contracts and a comprehensive bibliography on honors education.

The Honors College Phenomenon edited by Peter C. Sederberg (2008, 172pp). This monograph examines the growth of honors colleges since 1990: historical and descriptive characterizations of the trend, alternative models that include determining whether becoming a college is appropriate, and stories of creation and recreation. Leaders whose institutions are contemplating or taking this step as well as those directing established colleges should find these essays valuable.

Honors Composition: Historical Perspectives and Contemporary Practices by Annmarie Guzy (2003, 182pp). Parallel historical developments in honors and composition studies; contemporary honors writing projects ranging from admission essays to theses as reported by over 300 NCHC members.

Honors Programs at Smaller Colleges by Samuel Schuman (Third Edition, 2011, 80pp). Practical and comprehensive advice on creating and managing honors programs with particular emphasis on colleges with fewer than 4,000 students.

If Honors Students Were People: Holistic Honors Higher Education by Samuel Schuman (2013, 256pp). What if Honors students were people? What if they were not disembodied intellects but whole persons with physical bodies and questing spirits. Of course...they are. This monograph examines the spiritual yearnings of college students and the relationship between exercise and learning.

Inspiring Exemplary Teaching and Learning: Perspectives on Teaching Academically Talented College Students edited by Larry Clark and John Zubizarreta (2008, 216pp). This rich collection of essays offers valuable insights into innovative teaching and significant learning in the context of academically challenging classrooms and programs. The volume provides theoretical, descriptive, and practical resources, including models of effective instructional practices, examples of successful courses designed for enhanced learning, and a list of online links to teaching and learning centers and educational databases worldwide.

NCHC Monographs & Journals

The Other Culture: Science and Mathematics Education in Honors edited by Ellen B. Buckner and Keith Garbutt (2012, 296pp). A collection of essays about teaching science and math in an honors context: topics include science in society, strategies for science and non-science majors, the threat of pseudoscience, chemistry, interdisciplinary science, scientific literacy, philosophy of science, thesis development, calculus, and statistics.

Partners in the Parks: Field Guide to an Experiential Program in the National Parks by Joan Digby with reflective essays on theory and practice by student and faculty participants and National Park Service personnel (2010, 272pp). This monograph explores an experiential-learning program that fosters immersion in and stewardship of the national parks. The topics include program designs, group dynamics, philosophical and political issues, photography, wilderness exploration, and assessment.

Place as Text: Approaches to Active Learning edited by Bernice Braid and Ada Long (Second Edition, 2010, 128pp). Updated theory, information, and advice on experiential pedagogies developed within NCHC during the past 35 years, including Honors Semesters and City as Text™, along with suggested adaptations to multiple educational contexts.

Preparing Tomorrow's Global Leaders: Honors International Education edited by Mary Kay Mulvaney and Kim Klein (2013, 400pp). A valuable resource for initiating or expanding honors study abroad programs, these essays examine theoretical issues, curricular and faculty development, assessment, funding, and security. The monograph also provides models of successful programs that incorporate high-impact educational practices, including City as Text™ pedagogy, service learning, and undergraduate research.

Setting the Table for Diversity edited by Lisa L. Coleman and Jonathan D. Kotinek (2010, 288pp). This collection of essays provides definitions of diversity in honors, explores the challenges and opportunities diversity brings to honors education, and depicts the transformative nature of diversity when coupled with equity and inclusion. These essays discuss African American, Latina/o, international, and first-generation students as well as students with disabilities. Other issues include experiential and service learning, the politics of diversity, and the psychological resistance to it. Appendices relating to NCHC member institutions contain diversity statements and a structural diversity survey.

Shatter the Glassy Stare: Implementing Experiential Learning in Higher Education edited by Peter A. Machonis (2008, 160pp). A companion piece to *Place as Text*, focusing on recent, innovative applications of City as Text™ teaching strategies. Chapters on campus as text, local neighborhoods, study abroad, science courses, writing exercises, and philosophical considerations, with practical materials for instituting this pedagogy.

Teaching and Learning in Honors edited by Cheryl L. Fuiks and Larry Clark (2000, 128pp). Presents a variety of perspectives on teaching and learning useful to anyone developing new or renovating established honors curricula.

Journal of the National Collegiate Honors Council (JNCHC) is a semi-annual periodical featuring scholarly articles on honors education. Articles may include analyses of trends in teaching methodology, articles on interdisciplinary efforts, discussions of problems common to honors programs, items on the national higher education agenda, and presentations of emergent issues relevant to honors education.

Honors in Practice (HIP) is an annual journal that accommodates the need and desire for articles about nuts-and-bolts practices by featuring practical and descriptive essays on topics such as successful honors courses, suggestions for out-of-class experiences, administrative issues, and other topics of interest to honors administrators, faculty, and students.

NCHC Publication Order Form

Purchases may be made by calling (402) 472-9150, emailing nchc@unl.edu, visiting our website <http://www.nchchonors.org>, or mailing a check or money order payable to: NCHC • University of Nebraska–Lincoln • 1100 Neihardt Residence Center • 540 N. 16th Street • Lincoln, NE 68588-0627. FEIN 52–1188042

	Member	Non-Member	No. of Copies	Amount This Item
Monographs:				
Assessing and Evaluating Honors Programs and Honors Colleges: A Practical Handbook*	$25.00	$45.00		
Beginning in Honors: A Handbook (4th Ed.)	$25.00	$45.00		
Fundrai$ing for Honor$: A Handbook*	$25.00	$45.00		
A Handbook for Honors Administrators	$25.00	$45.00		
A Handbook for Honors Programs at Two-Year Colleges*	$25.00	$45.00		
The Honors College Phenomenon	$25.00	$45.00		
Honors Composition: Historical Perspectives and Contemporary Practices	$25.00	$45.00		
Honors Programs at Smaller Colleges (3rd Ed.)*	$25.00	$45.00		
If Honors Students Were People: Holistic Honors Higher Education	$25.00	$45.00		
Inspiring Exemplary Teaching and Learning: Perspectives on Teaching Academically Talented College Students*	$25.00	$45.00		
The Other Culture: Science and Mathematics Education in Honors	$25.00	$45.00		
Partners in the Parks: Field Guide to an Experiential Program in the National Parks	$25.00	$45.00		
Place as Text: Approaches to Active Learning (2nd Ed.)	$25.00	$45.00		
Preparing Tomorrow's Global Leaders: Honors International Education	$25.00	$45.00		
Setting the Table for Diversity	$25.00	$45.00		
Shatter the Glassy Stare: Implementing Experiential Learning in Higher Education	$25.00	$45.00		
Teaching and Learning in Honors*	$25.00	$45.00		
Journals:				
Journal of the National Collegiate Honors Council (JNCHC) Specify Vol/Issue ____/____	$25.00	$45.00		
Honors in Practice (HIP) Specify Vol ____	$25.00	$45.00		
Total Copies Ordered and Total Amount Paid:				$

Name ______________________ Institution ______________________

Address ______________________

City, State, Zip ______________________

Phone ______________ Fax ______________ Email ______________

*Print-on-Demand publications—will be delivered in 4-6 weeks.

Shipping costs will be calculated on the number of items purchased.

Apply a 20% discount if 10+ copies are purchased.